ESCAPE
FROM
SADDAM

ESCAPE FROM SADDAM

LEWIS ALSAMARI

The Incredible True Story of One
Man's Journey to Freedom

CROWN PUBLISHERS NEW YORK

Originally published in slightly different form in Great Britain as *Out of Iraq* by Bantam
Press, an imprint of Transworld Publishers, a division of The Random House Group
Ltd., London, in 2007. This edition published by arrangement with Bantam Press, an
imprint of Transworld Publishers, a division of The Random House Group Ltd.

Library of Congress Cataloging-in-Publication Data
Alsamari, Lewis.
  Escape from Saddam : the incredible true story of one man's
journey to freedom / Lewis Alsamari.—1st ed.
    1. Alsamari, Lewis. 2. Iraqis—Biography. 3. Refugees—
Iraq—Biography. I. Title.
  CT1919.I78A47   2008
  956.7044092—dc22
  [B]   2007032660

ISBN 978-0-307-39401-9

Printed in the United States of America

DESIGN BY BARBARA STURMAN

10 9 8 7 6 5 4 3 2 1

First American Edition

For my family

AUTHOR'S NOTE

Throughout my life I have been helped and hindered in equal measure by many people. Some of these people operated within the law; others didn't. As a result, I have changed certain names to protect both the innocent and the guilty.

When I arrived in England, I took the name Lewis. My Arabic name is Sarmed, which is how I refer to myself throughout much of the book.

CONTENTS

We set forth these parables to men
that they may reflect.

—KORAN 59:21

ESCAPE
FROM
SADDAM

PROLOGUE

August 1994. The Iraqi desert,
somewhere near the Jordanian border,
several hours before daybreak

I stood perfectly still and tried to accustom myself to the solitude and the silence.

It took me some minutes to compose myself, but eventually I started to make my way toward the road. Now I was alone, and my senses became more heightened as I strained my eyes and my ears to judge if any unknown danger was close by. Occasionally I looked back and thought that I caught a glimpse of the patrol cars' headlights; but if I did, they were distant—the patrol officers would not be able to see me from so far away. I could just make out the road from where I was, and there were no patrols ahead. I would be very unlucky to meet anybody now, but all seemed reasonably silent around me. Unless I was forced to fire the Beretta, I was determined not to do so.

I soon realized, however, that sounds in the desert could be deceptive. More than once I stopped still because I thought I heard a

noise alarmingly close, but I told myself over and over again that it was a faraway sound carried to me by the fickle night breeze. I kept the pace as fast as my wounded leg would allow, keeping my eyes fixed on the occasional light from the road ahead. I realized that it was not only sounds that could be deceiving, but distances also. Although I had no conception of time, the road did not appear to be getting any closer, and the longer I hurried through that dark expanse, the more unnerving my solitude became. As I walked, I could feel the swab around my bullet wound become wet—clearly the stitches had opened slightly from the movement.

Then, out of the darkness, I heard a sound that immediately stopped me dead. It was not new to my ears—it was unmistakably the same howling that I had heard earlier that evening—but it was shockingly close. I stood perfectly still for some moments, aware only of the trembling whisper of my own heavy breath, before hearing another howl that made the blood stop in my veins. It was as loud as the first and no less desperate. But it was not its closeness that filled me with a sickening sense of horror; it was the direction from which it came. The first wolf was somewhere to my right, the second to my left.

I have never known fear like it. A cold wave of dread crashed over me; I felt nauseous and all the strength seemed to sap from my body. I know I should have fired my gun in the air, but in that minute some other impulse took over, an impulse that forced any faculty of reason from my head and replaced it with blind panic. Foolishly, I ran.

I could never have outrun them. They were lean, desperate, and hungry; this was their territory. I was limping and terrified. The more noise I made, the more I attracted their attention. I became aware of other animals around me—I don't know how many—but it was clear they were hunting as a pack and I was their quarry. Blinded by my tears, I stumbled, and their baying became more frenzied.

Then, as if by some prearranged signal, the pack fell silent . . .

PART ONE

THE ESCAPE

THE INTERROGATION

Baghdad. Nine months earlier

Baghdad military training center lay by a main road on the out-skirts of the city. It was large and utilitarian, and I felt dwarfed by it as I approached the main entrance. The sun was burning, and the cars in the busy street had all their windows wound down, their drivers crumpled and oppressed by the midday heat. I wiped a trickle of sweat from my own forehead and looked around up at the high walls of the building: a huge picture of Saddam Hussein returned my gaze. It was a familiar sight, one that had been commonplace in my life for as long as I could remember. The gates of Al-Zahawi primary school, which I had attended as a child, were colorful, painted with a huge yellow bumble bee to welcome the children; but on the walls on either side of the bumble bee were paintings of Saddam. His Excellency smiled down benevolently upon us, and around his head flew birds painted in the colors of the national flag. Inside the walls, high up, were more pictures of Saddam, and the slogans of the Ba'ath party were written large—"One Arab nation with an everlasting message," "Unity, Freedom, and Communism"—as well as one of Saddam's favorite sayings: "Always look your enemy in the eye."

Today, however, the images seemed more imposing and threatening than ever—the very embodiment of everything from which I had been trying to break free.

"I don't want to be in the army," I had told my Uncle Saad petulantly when it had become apparent that there was no other option open to me.

"You haven't got any choice. You've been called up, and if you don't go they will consider you to be a deserter. When they catch up with you—which they will if you are still in the country . . ." He made a deft flicking sign by his right ear to indicate its removal—the standard punishment for anyone who went AWOL. "I've seen people selling these ears on the black market so that deserters can have them sewn back on. Trust me, they are not a pretty sight."

For a moment I thought he was joking, but one look at his face told me that he wasn't. "Will you keep looking for someone to help us?"

Saad looked around nervously, checking that no passersby—no matter how innocent they looked—could overhear our conversation. Idle talk had a tendency to find its way back to military intelligence, and the consequences could be severe. "I don't know, Sarmed. The stakes are higher now. Not attending university is one thing, but running away from the army is quite another. If any of my colleagues were caught deserting during the Iran-Iraq war, they were shot in front of their relatives and the families had to pay for the ammunition. They were told it was their fault their sons were being executed, because they had allowed their children to grow up into opponents of the regime."

"I know," I insisted quietly. "That's why I want to leave. I don't want to be part of it. Please, keep looking for me."

I handed my call-up papers to the guard at the entrance. He did not speak as he looked through them. "Go to reception," he said finally and opened the heavy gates.

Inside the center everything was painted an austere military green. Huge metal structures around the edge of the main parade ground housed the various quarters, and nowhere was there any sign of ornament—apart, of course, from the ubiquitous pictures of Saddam in military uniform. In some pictures his military decorations were on display; others showed him firing an RPG-launcher or an AK-47. I was handed my military ID and given my provisions—uniform, boots, beret, and belt—before being shown to my quarters. I was in a huge dormitory with bunk beds neatly arranged along its length. A thin strip of window along the top of the wall let in only a small amount of light. Once I had stowed my few belongings under my bed, I was taken off to have my head shaved. There was no time after that to get settled in: my training began that very day.

The first month at the center was an extension of the national education program I had undergone at school. We were taught all about the army: how it was split into divisions and what the responsibilities of each division were. We were told about the facilities of the compound, and it was explained to us that we would be expected to undergo a very tough regime of physical and military training to ensure that we were fit enough in three months to join our unit—wherever that might be. We were taught how to salute superior officers, how we should store and look after our weapons once they were issued—all the little nuggets of knowledge that would start to make this mismatched bunch of citizens look a bit more like soldiers.

The officers could not have cared less about our mental education; it was our physical education with which they were most concerned. We were rudely woken at first light one morning—about six o'clock—and told to present ourselves immediately in the training area of the parade ground. Five minutes later, a group of sleepy recruits did their best to form an orderly line by a bed of evil-looking barbed wire. Two *arifs*—not officers, exactly, but the men in

charge of our training—stood stony-faced, AK-47s at the ready. We stood silently as they examined each and every one of us, checking our fingernails and our hair and making sure our uniforms were spotless. Then they spoke. "You each have sixty seconds to crawl under the barbed wire and come out unscathed at the other end," one of them barked. I looked at the barbed wire more carefully. It was spindly and knotted and raised little more than a foot from the ground. To crawl underneath it without getting scratched horribly, you would need to take it slowly. "You," the *arif* shouted at the first recruit in line. "Go!"

The recruit crouched down on all fours, then flattened himself on his belly. As he crawled gingerly under the barbed wire, the two *arifs* started firing their Kalashnikovs into the ground. The guns were clearly shooting blanks, but the poor recruit did not know this. As the first shot was fired, he jumped almost out of his skin. A piece of barbed wire tore into his trousers, and the rough cloth was quickly stained red. He started scurrying more quickly and sustained a few more wounds to his flesh, but he made it out the other side in the allotted time and was packed off to tend to his injuries.

I was next. Reluctantly I crouched down in front of the barbed wire with my gun in my hand. Trying to ignore the explosions of the nearby AK-47s, I gently wove my way to the other side, managing to emerge unscathed. As I stood up, the first *arif* looked at his watch. "Sixty-eight seconds," he told me with menace in his voice. "Come with me."

He grabbed me by the shoulder, pushed me in front of him, and kicked me hard from behind. I fell to my knees. "Over there," bellowed the second *arif.*

About twenty meters from the barbed wire was a muddy pit, perhaps four meters in diameter and a couple of meters deep. The two *arifs* pushed me toward it while my comrades looked on. Once

we were by its side, one of them struck a blow to the pit of my stomach with the butt of his Kalashnikov. Winded, I collapsed to the ground once more. Gasping to catch my breath, I felt a heavy boot kick into my ribcage as the two proceeded to beat me with their hands and feet until my body was bruised and bloodied. At no point, however, did they touch my face. I later found out why: I was expected to look presentable when I was on display, and bruises or cuts to the face were not acceptable. But any parts of my body that could be covered by a uniform were fair game.

The beating felt as though it lasted an hour—it probably lasted only a minute—and when the *arifs* finished making an example of me, I was pushed roughly over the side of the pit. I fell heavily into a pool of cool mud at the bottom and felt it seeping through the coarse material of my uniform.

"Stand up!" one of the *arifs* shouted at me. Painfully I pushed myself up off the ground. "Now," he shouted. "Climb out of there, and next time I tell you to do something in sixty seconds, do it in sixty seconds. Understood?"

That was my first encounter with the pit, but it was not to be my last. Whenever one of us failed to achieve a task that had been set—maybe we had not climbed over a wall as quickly as we had been instructed to, or not let ourselves remain suspended at the top of an obstacle course for long enough—we were beaten and thrown over its sides. The beatings varied in their intensity, according either to the gravity of our misdemeanor or to the whim of the *arif* in charge, but they were always brutal enough to persuade us to pay very close attention to what we were told to do, and to carry it out to the letter. We soon learned to make every attempt to land on our feet when we were thrown over the side of the pit: if our uniforms became too muddy, we were likely to be forcefully hosed down and left to complete our exercises in sopping wet clothes. The soaked

material chaffed unpleasantly against our torn skin, and if the hosing-down happened to take place in the heat of the day, the wet uniform turned boiling hot and scorched our skin before the water evaporated and the cloth dried.

Nobody was spared these beatings, even those who performed well. The *arif* wanted all of us to know exactly what sort of brutality we could expect if we stepped out of line. Gradually as our skill at the various tasks increased, the beatings became less frequent. But when they did occur, they were inflicted with even greater vigor and with a larger dose of humiliation, for the *arifs* knew it would reflect poorly on them if they delivered substandard recruits to the unit bases at the end of the three-month training period.

At the other end of the parade ground we could see the more recent recruits receiving the same treatment that had been meted out to us only weeks earlier. Some members of our group laughed when they saw this. It was only natural, I suppose, that having been treated like animals, some of them would turn into animals themselves. The rest of us just looked on grimly as we did our best to get on with the job at hand.

Once a week, a graduation ceremony was held at the training compound, and those recruits who had completed their training were assigned to the unit that would be their home for the next three years. The ceremony was held on the parade ground: we saluted the flag, and then the names of all departing soldiers were read out, along with their destinations. On the morning of my ceremony, I awoke with a dreadful feeling of foreboding. I had endured the hardships of the training compound with the vague hope in the back of my mind that I would be able to get out of Iraq, away from the brutality and the torment, before being assigned to my unit, and

was comforted by the knowledge that my family was only a few miles away. How would I cope if I were sent to one of the distant reaches of the country, where my family and my hopes of freedom would seem even more remote?

We lined up in front of the whole population of recruits and saluted the flag. Then, one by one, our names were called out. When I heard mine, I stepped forward to be told my fate. "The brave and courageous soldier Sarmed Alsamari will be leaving to join our glorious regiment in Al-Amarah!"

My heart sank. Al-Amarah was a good four hundred kilometers from Baghdad, more than halfway to the southern city of Basra and close to the Iranian border. The road there was slow, and getting back to see my family on leave would be difficult. But I did not let these thoughts appear on my face as I received my honor. The camp officers were eyeing us all carefully, and a look of disappointment would have been insubordination if they were of a mind to make it so. The news had bruised me enough as it was; I felt no desire to add physical pain to my mental turmoil.

I couldn't believe it. I had never been to the south before, and now I was being packed off to a military unit miles from anywhere for three years. I called Uncle Saad to see if there was anything he could do, any favors he could call in or bribes he could pay to keep me at least in Baghdad. But there was nothing he could do, and when the day came, I prepared to be transported to my unit.

We piled into the green-painted Russian-built trucks covered with thick green canvas that were waiting outside the compound. There were perhaps twenty other recruits who were going to Al-Amarah with me, but we would be dropping other soldiers off at various units along the way. The front seats were already taken up by the *arif* and some of the more thuggish recruits. As the rest of us

walked on, they eyed us threateningly as if daring us to complain about the seating arrangements.

As we left Baghdad, I felt as though I was leaving civilization behind. The roads became less well cared for, and the villages we passed seemed to become more ragged the farther south we went. Villagers stopped and stared at the convoy of Mercedes vans as they passed through, making me feel like a curiosity. I had become used to acting around soldiers with a care born of suspicion; now, I suddenly realized, I would be treated with suspicion by others. At each checkpoint we were stopped and thoroughly searched by the Red Berets, but as we headed farther south, our number dwindled as the soldiers were dropped off at their respective units. By the time I alighted at Al-Amarah, only the few poor souls who had been stationed at Basra remained.

The unit building was practically identical to the military training compound, both inside and out. Observation posts covered with scrambled barbed wire stood at each corner, and a heavy military presence was on display guarding the entrance. On the front wall was yet another massive picture of Saddam in military uniform. One of the *arifs* from the training camp lined us up inside the barracks and barked at us to stand quietly; we stood there waiting for the head of the unit to come and take charge of us. After perhaps half an hour he came out of his office and looked us up and down disdainfully. "I hope you have all come prepared," he called out in a teacherly tone of voice. "If any of you feel you have *not* come prepared, tell me now and I will arrange for you to be sent back to the training camp."

Not one of us moved a muscle. We didn't want to make any gesture that could be interpreted as a desire to go back to that godforsaken place.

"Good," continued the officer. "You are now under my command. Any action that brings shame upon this regiment or upon

our beloved leader, may God protect him and bless him, will be dealt with swiftly and severely. If you are called upon to fight for the great and glorious Iraqi army, it will be an honor. You will therefore keep yourselves in a state of utmost readiness. You will continue to train in the art and techniques of warfare, and I advise you to pay close attention at all times. You never know when our leader, may God protect him and bless him, will call upon you to make use of them to serve and protect our glorious country from our cowardly enemies."

He gave us a look of barely concealed contempt as the *arif* shouted, "Attention!" We saluted; the officer saluted back before turning on his heel and returning to the comforts of his office.

We were taken to our quarters. Again I had been allocated a bunk bed in a large dormitory that housed about sixty people; one white sheet had been supplied, and the rest of the bedding was a dirty army green. I stowed away my few personal belongings—a pen and some paper for writing home and a small portable cassette player with a few Western tapes. Western music, unlike the music of Israel or Iran, was allowed in Iraq, with a few exceptions. "By the Rivers of Babylon" by Boney M was one of those exceptions, though I remember that Saad and I had blasted it in his car when I was young—a small gesture of defiance. But in the army, Western music was banned, so those of us who wanted to bring it in were forced to use subterfuge. On one of my short periods of leave from the training camp, I had taken some tapes of the music I liked to listen to— Michael Jackson, Bon Jovi, Wet Wet Wet, A-Ha—and placed them in cassette boxes on which I had written the names of Middle Eastern singers so that they would not be confiscated.

I took a shower before changing into more-comfortable clothes. A number of people tried to phone home from one of the communal telephones. A stern-faced *arif* sat next to the telephone, listening intently to everyone's conversations and making a note of how long

each person spent on the phone so that everyone could be charged appropriately. The waiting lines for the telephone were long, however, and I was not in the mood to hear the playful laughs of my brother and sister in the background. So I decided to rest before the rigors of the next day.

The following morning we were each assigned a weapon—an Iraqi-made AK-47. Each gun had a piece of what resembled black surgical tape stuck on the side, on which was scrawled a number so that the quartermasters could keep track of who had been issued which weapon. I soon found out that, although our training period was at an end, there was much that we were still expected to learn. At the Baghdad training compound, we had been taught how to handle weapons at the most basic level; now our skills were to be honed and specialized. A special unit came in, for example, to teach us how to plant land mines. We were each given a box containing several heavy, defused land mines. As I slowly took one of the weapons from its packaging, I was very aware that this was the instrument that had almost killed my uncle during the Iran-Iraq war.

While stationed on the front line, on Iranian territory near Basra, Saad had been ordered to lead his men into a minefield. He was one of the lucky few to escape with his life. Debris from a nearby explosion detonated a cluster of mines, and he was knocked unconscious. He awoke to discover that he had been blown one way, his leg the other. His remaining leg had been cut deep enough to expose the bone of his knee, and his whole body was deeply splintered with sharp, angry pieces of hot shrapnel. How he survived is a mystery even to him.

The day I went with my family to visit Saad in the hospital is one of the most vivid memories of my youth. We all packed into his tiny hospital room, and had I not known it was Saad lying in the bed, I wouldn't have recognized him. His face and body were ban-

daged up. The outer layer of his skin had been burned and peeled away by the force of the blast; what remained was red and sore. The land mine had severed his leg below the knee, but the remainder of that limb was so riddled with shrapnel that it had been removed several inches above the knee. The other leg was little more than a patchwork of skin grafted from different parts of Saad's body. You could place a magnet on certain parts of him and it would stick because of all the shrapnel embedded beneath his skin. He was unconscious when we saw him, and my mother and grandmother wailed with tears at the sight of their beloved Saad in such a state. I remember my father standing emotionless in the corner of the room. "I told you this is what would happen if you ran off to war" the look on his face seemed to say. It was a stark introduction for a six-year-old to the realities of battle.

Now I was learning how to plant the same weapon so that it could mutilate some other foreign soldier or maybe an unsuspecting civilian unlucky enough to stumble across it. A thick circle of gray metal, perhaps two inches thick, the mine had a second, smaller circle protruding from the top. The mine was to be placed in the dirt, or underwater in the mud, so that it was not visible, and then a small pin was removed to arm it. The slightest movement above the mine would detonate it, and the results would be devastating. We were not taught how to defuse land mines. For that knowledge, we were told, we had to wait until our second year.

We were taught how to arm and fire heavy BKC machine guns that could hit targets over two kilometers in the distance. Two soldiers were needed to operate them—one to fire the weapon, the other to feed the long chain of ammunition into it. On the grounds of the unit was the shell of a Russian-style tank. We were not taught to drive tanks—that was a specialized job not suited to such low-ranking soldiers as ourselves. Instead we were taught how to fire the

machine gun perched at the top. In a battle situation the gunners would be on full display—cannon fodder for enemy troops, who could pick them off with the greatest of ease.

I remembered the maxim I was taught at school, a favorite saying of Saddam's that we were forced to commit to memory: "He who does not sweat to build his country will not bleed defending it." We had been trained since childhood to see weaponry as part of everyday life. Guns were commonplace, of course, but even when I was young I had come into contact with weapons of far greater destructive power. As a young boy I spent time living with my father in the northern city of Mosul, in the semirural surroundings of the College of Forestry and Agriculture. One day my friends and I decided to go hunting for the foxes that had been terrorizing my beloved chickens, which I kept in the yard, so we set off along the road that led into the forest.

After walking for an hour or so, we came across an area enclosed by barbed wire. We had all been into the forest before, but none of us had stumbled across this enclosure. Not far inside, we saw a huge mound covered with army camouflage material. Peeping out from under the camouflage were large, metal, pointed tips; they were clearly either Scud missiles or some other form of rocket-propelled weapon. A family of foxes were scurrying over the missiles or nestling peacefully under their tips. We stood in silence for a few moments, staring at our discovery, when suddenly we heard the sound of a car approaching. A red Chevrolet drove up slowly; not wanting to be caught here by a member of the security forces, we ran away as quickly as we could, vowing to return the next day.

Every time we went back to spy on our discovery, the red Chevrolet was always nearby. We never got close enough to find out who was in it, nor did we want to, for fear of being seen. Gradually, though, we began to work out the times that it disappeared—presumably so that the driver could get something to eat or go off

duty and swap with somebody else—and we started to formulate a plan. We took an old wheelbarrow to a section of the surrounding wall that either had crumbled naturally or had been destroyed by villagers trying to get in. We filled the wheelbarrow with small pieces of rubble and then took it to the weapons dump, waited for the Chevrolet to disappear, and rolled it close to the barbed wire. If we could throw the rubble at the missiles, we naively thought, and explode one of them, we could launch our first strike in the battle against the foxes. They would be painlessly dispatched, and we would be far enough away to avoid getting hurt.

Of course, the missiles were too deep inside the barbed-wired area for us to score many direct hits, and our aim was not that true in any case. Occasionally a small stone rebounded off the metal with a satisfying clunk, but when we saw the red Chevrolet approaching after about forty-five minutes, we scampered away, and the foxes lived to scavenge for chickens another day.

The next time I spoke to Uncle Saad on the phone, I casually told him about our exploits. He listened attentively before speaking very quietly but with the full weight of his authority: "Listen to me very carefully, Sarmed. You must *never* do that again. The chances of exploding one of those missiles with a piece of rubble are minuscule, but if you did manage it, you wouldn't just be wiping out your foxes—you'd be wiping out your home and probably the surrounding villages too."

I fell silent as the implications of our stupidity were spelled out to me.

"Promise me you'll never go back there, Sarmed," Saad continued, "even just to look. It's not the sort of place you want to be caught snooping around."

"I promise," I replied quietly.

Back at my unit, we learned how to use different types of grenades. Special honor was reserved for those soldiers who threw

grenades the farthest, and the day after a training session our arms were bruised from the effort of several hours of hurling these heavy weapons into the desert surrounding the camp. We also practiced disassembling and assembling AK-47s. As a child I had practiced using these weapons on the wasteland outskirts of Baghdad with my uncle, so I required no instruction in this part of my training. None of my superiors questioned me about my almost natural ability with the guns, and my sharpshooting skills went from good to excellent.

We were taught basic martial arts movements so that we could become proficient in hand-to-hand combat, and we learned how to fight with the bayonet attached to the end of a Kalashnikov. After only a few weeks of training I learned how to break a man's kneecap with one solid kick, and I mastered several methods of rendering an opponent helpless so that I could plunge my Kalashnikov bayonet deep into his throat. I learned how to approach a person from behind and kill him in one swift, simple move. Gradually, despite my reluctance, I was being carefully and proficiently instructed in the mechanics of killing. There was an unspoken acknowledgment that, as simple soldiers, we were the pawns in Saddam's bombastic shows of military bravado. Iraq was never far away from war, and everybody knew somebody who had been killed or horribly injured in one of the leader's campaigns. Should we find ourselves on the front line, our ability to kill other men would be the only thing with any chance of saving us from a similar fate.

A couple of months into my time at the unit, I looked at the notice board that listed everybody's duties and training sessions for a particular day. *"Al'Tadreeb ala Al-Istijwab"* announced one of the sheets, "Interrogation Training." My name was one of four on the list.

At the appointed time, I made my way to the prison cells. At the training center, misdemeanors had been punished by the pit; here the *arifs* simply hurled you into prison if you refused to toe the line, or into solitary confinement if you had been particularly wayward. Next to the cells were small, bare interrogation rooms. The room in which my resistance-to-torture training was to take place had nothing but a dull lamp, a metal table, and three metal chairs. Two *arifs* with clipboards and pencils sat at the table; the third chair had been placed in the middle of the room, directly under a fan that did not so much provide ventilation as simply move the stale air. I stood at attention against one of the walls while I waited for my colleagues to arrive.

Once we were all assembled, one of the *arifs* addressed us. "You," the *arif* pointed at one of our number, "sit down."

The man singled out was the burliest of the four of us and was from the south. Until now I had avoided him, as did most of the camp. Occasionally in the dining room I had noticed him spitting into the communal food to put people off from eating it. He fraternized only with the members of his own community who also found themselves at this unit—all of them also large and thickset and displaying arrogance bordering on contempt for anybody not in their clique. Despite his overpowering self-confidence, however, he could not hide his nervousness as he took a seat. His hands were bound tightly with rope behind the back of the chair.

"You have been captured," the *arif* continued. "Your regiment is moving north, and this is the information that your captors are trying to force you to reveal. They will use any means to get it, but you must reveal nothing." He turned to the three of us still standing against the wall. "Do what you must to find this information out," he told us, "with one exception: you are not to cut his face, and you are not to break his bones. He needs to be presentable for lineup. Anything else is acceptable."

The three of us remained silent; the only noises in the room were the regular whirr of the ceiling fan and the heavy breathing of the soldier tied to the chair. We looked at each other apprehensively, unwilling to attack our colleague but uncertain how to avoid it.

"You!" the *arif* pointed at me. "You start."

I stared into the eyes of the prisoner; he looked back defiantly. Slowly I approached him and then, with a brief look at the *arif*, struck him in the stomach. The blow was as gentle as I dared make it, although it was enough to make the prisoner cough sharply and catch his breath. As he did so, the *arif* raised his voice. "Harder!" he shouted.

I looked apologetically into the eyes of my victim and punched him more forcefully. His eyes bulged as he struggled to breathe. "Harder!" the *arif* shouted again. He grabbed a thick cane and hit me hard across the back of my legs.

I found myself shaking as I prepared to deliver another blow; my deep breath trembled in my lungs. Suddenly I heard scuffling behind me. I turned around in time to see one of my colleagues hurl himself at the chair, knocking the victim sideways to the ground. His head cracked as it hit the floor and he cried out; almost simultaneously my associate started to kick him violently in the stomach and the genitals, screaming as though he himself were being attacked. Each time the victim tried to say anything, he received another sharp blow that knocked the power of speech from him. After a minute and a half of severe beatings, the attacker stopped for breath. The victim took advantage of the pause to whimper, "North. My regiment is headed north."

Suddenly the two *arifs* were on their feet. Still carrying their clipboards, they placed themselves in front of the chair. "You," one of them pointed at the attacker who stood shaking with suppressed rage, "good." He looked down at the victim. He was still lying on his side, his hands were still bound, his tears of pain and humilia-

tion fell directly to the floor, and the chair clattered against the ground as his body occasionally convulsed. "The rest of you *niswan* [women]—unimpressive. I hope you will act in a manner more befitting your uniform at our next session." He looked directly at me. "Untie him."

I bent down and fumbled at the knot, managing finally to loosen it and free the battered body of my fellow soldier. Slowly he stood up. As he did so, he gave me a look of absolute venom, and without waiting to be dismissed by the *arif*, he stumbled from the room.

I was totally shocked by what had just happened: not so much by the fact that we were expected to do this to our fellow soldiers—when random brutality becomes the norm, you start to accept it almost without thinking—but rather by the effect the situation had had on my colleague who had gone on the attack with fire in his eyes. When I saw him around the base over the next few days, he walked with his head held high, and his arrogant bearing seemed to suggest that his actions had bolstered his own opinion of himself. I saw our victim too, although I tried to avoid him. He refused to speak to me, but every time we met, his eyes seemed to say "Just wait."

My time was to come quicker than I thought. A couple of weeks later, the four of us were called to the interrogation room once more. On this second occasion, the *arif* directed me to the chair. The rough rope dug into my skin as he tied my hands tightly; if I tried to move my wrists, they burned even more.

"This prisoner has recently been caught. He was wearing a white T-shirt under his coat with a picture of Saddam Hussein. He claims to be a civilian, but we know that he is a member of military intelligence. You need to make him admit this."

Sometimes the threat of violence is more terrifying than the violence itself. The air was tense with what was to come; even the *arif* sensed it. "When you undergo interrogation or torture at the hands

of the enemy," he told me quietly, "you must think of your family and your country. Remember, the pain will be transitory, but Iraq and her glorious armies will live forever. They will soon come and rescue you in repayment for your loyalty and your silence."

There was eagerness in the eyes of the soldier who had performed the terrible beating during our last session—he had clearly developed a taste for this part of our education—and in the eyes of the victim whose attack I had been forced to precipitate. As the latter man stood before me, waiting for the *arif*'s permission to start the questioning, he smirked vaguely. My body went weak with dread. Involuntarily I shook my head as I looked up at my two inquisitors, and those few moments seemed to last an age.

There were no shouts this time, neither from me nor from my attackers: they went about their business in ruthless silence. Having already witnessed one of these beatings, I was vaguely prepared for what was in store, so when my chair was pushed over onto its side, I had the foresight to tilt my head so that it did not slap against the ground. Nevertheless, my right arm was crushed between the back of the metal chair and the concrete floor. I tried to shuffle the weight away from my bruised arm, but before I could even move I felt the first kick to my ribs. The force of the strike seemed to thud through my whole body, and I barely had time to let out an involuntary grunt before I felt a blow to my genitals that sent a shriek of pain down my legs. Who did what in the melee that followed, I have no idea. I vaguely remembered trying to shout out the information that they wanted, but the blows were incessant and utterly debilitating. After a while I stopped feeling the pain—my body became numb as the kicks and punches merged into one brutal cocktail.

The last thing I remember seeing was the face of the *arif,* looking on approvingly. Then I blacked out.

THE SHADOW OF A TYRANT

In December of 1982—ten years before I was drafted into the Iraqi army—I had been taken as a child to England. My father had a government scholarship to study in England for a Ph.D., and my parents, my brother and sister, and I were to go with him. He attended the University of Manchester, so we lived around the Manchester area—Fallowfield and Moss Side—where my father became deeply involved in the Middle Eastern community centered around the local mosque. My mother, however, pined for Baghdad and the family that she had left behind. Her reluctance to throw herself into the increasingly religion-oriented world my father was making for himself led to terrible tensions between them, and our little family unit, so far from home, became volatile. Eventually my parents' relationship failed, and my mother, along with my brother and sister, returned to Iraq. My relationship with my father, even as a young boy, was not good; but I loved England, where I spent five of my formative years, so I was pleased to remain.

By 1987, the Iran-Iraq war was coming to an end. It had been devastating for both countries. It cost more than $250 billion in

total damages and, thanks to the fact that both armies had launched massive air strikes against each other's oil infrastructures, the economies of these two once-wealthy nations were damaged almost beyond recognition. But the human cost of the war was more shocking than any economic effects. More than 1.5 million people lost their lives, decimated by forms of warfare that horrified the civilized world. Chemical and biological weapons killed and mutilated soldiers and civilians on both sides. Almost every family had someone involved; practically no one remained untouched by the horrors of that conflict.

Saddam was faced with an unforeseen social and economic quandary: so many men had lost their lives in the war that Iraq suddenly found itself with a surfeit of widowed women. Their lives destroyed, and most having no means of supporting themselves after the deaths of their husbands, they became an intolerable burden on the already damaged economy. The government had to decide what to do with these burdensome widows who had no means of support other than welfare incentives.

Saddam's answer was novel: he decided to sell them off. Iraqi men were offered 10,000 Iraqi dinars—at the time about $33,000—to marry a war widow and thus shoulder the economic burden that the women presented to the government.

Word of this tempting offer reached my father's ears in England via his brother. Unbeknownst to me, a widow was found for my father, and he traveled back to Iraq to meet her, with me in tow. Ostensibly the trip was for a holiday; I had no idea at the time that I was returning to Baghdad for good. But my father's plans with his new wife back in England did not include me, and without warning I was left with my mother and her family in the middle of Baghdad. I was twelve years old, and the culture shock was massive.

My young friends in the West were cajoled into good behavior

by threats of an imaginary bogeyman. In Iraq, there was no need for invented horrors.

I was not yet a teenager and had been back in Iraq only a couple of months when, one day in 1988, I saw a cavalcade of black Mercedes with blacked-out windows sweep up the length of Al-Mansour Street. They had no license plates. Iraqis from all walks of life turned to stare, but not too hard: none of the spectators wanted to draw attention to themselves, especially not knowing whom these official cars were carrying. My friend Hakim and I, perhaps emboldened by our youth, stared more intently than the other pedestrians as the sleek, expensive vehicles pulled up, not outside one of the fashionable shops lining this desirable road in Baghdad, but in front of a fast-food restaurant. The restaurant's sign—a familiar golden M—gave an impression of the West, even if it was not McDonald's.

After school that day, Hakim and I had met at the beginning of 14th Ramadan Street, by Souk Al-Ghazi. Shopkeepers stood guard as passersby examined their goods: watermelons, baklava, fabric for *dishdash*—the same wares that could be found at any number of similar places across the Middle East, and items that were of no interest to my thirteen-year-old mind. The few coins in the pocket of my prized black jeans would be spent on something far more precious: Coca-Cola.

Chatting happily, we turned onto 14th Ramadan Street and entered a run-down kebab shop. Its rusting, corrugated-iron roof protected the owner from the fierce rays of the afternoon sun, but the large shop windows—plastered in garish Arabic letters—along with the grills that burned all day long and the chatter of people constantly congregated there meant that it was at least as hot inside as out. I caught the eye of the shopkeeper and he smiled. "Sarmed, my young friend," he called. "Falafel?"

"And a bottle of Coca-Cola," I nodded. "Put it on my tab," I added nonchalantly.

The owner raised his hand dramatically as we continued our little play, which we performed several times every week. "Are you trying to put me out of business?" he shouted in mock indignation. "The falafel I'll put on your tab. But you pay me next week— otherwise I shall be having words with my friends at Abu Ghraib." He winked at me. "The Coca-Cola, you pay for now."

I handed him a coin and watched him fill a piece of flat bread with a generous helping of falafel and the fiery sauce of which I was fond. Then he turned to the fridge behind the counter and removed an icy bottle with the famous logo written in red Arabic letters along its length. He turned to Hakim. "And for you, sir?"

Carrying our treats, we started to walk the length of 14th Ramadan Street, holding our bottles like status symbols, smiling at any girls who passed, and talking animatedly. As we walked, the shops became gradually more sophisticated, catering to the expensive tastes of the rich families who lived in the vicinity of nearby Princess Street. Computer shops, clothes shops, antiques shops: it would be another couple of years until the sanctions against Iraq made these small but expensive luxuries a thing of the past and the Coca-Cola that was one of the few remaining links I had with the West disappeared for good, to be replaced by a poor fizzy approximation made from dates.

When that happened, though, the lack of Coca-Cola became the least of our worries. During the first Gulf War, the water tanks were bombed, and water itself became scarce. Families had to make do with what they needed merely to survive. Hair-washing, for example, became a thing of the past. After a few months, however, children began to develop head lice. Gasoline was considerably cheaper than water—you could fill up your car for the equivalent of less than a few American cents—so gasoline was used to kill the

head lice. Scrupulous mothers then used rough washing powder to remove the gas from their children's hair. You could always tell who had received this type of shampoo—the strange cocktail flecked people's hair with a ruddy orange color when they went out into the sun.

For now, though, I could pretend: pretend that I lived a life that at least bore some small resemblance to the life I had enjoyed in England; pretend that hanging around the stalls where unscrupulous merchants made a living pirating cassettes of Western music to order was a good alternative to being able to turn on the radio at will and listen to Michael Jackson; pretend that I was not living in a country where, at every turn, I was told by a domineering regime what to do, what to say, and what to think.

Hakim and I did not expect that afternoon to be different from any other. Perhaps we would wander down Al-Mansour Street and I would visit the animals in the pet shops I loved so much, only to be chased out by the shopkeepers when they saw me: they knew that I seldom had any money to buy anything. Perhaps we would loiter around one of the pirate cassette shops hoping to hear some Western music. Occasionally I had enough money to buy a cassette, but not today.

If Hakim and I found ourselves in a residential area, we might watch men at the front of their houses cajoling their roosters to fight. Perhaps we would see a young woman being followed by a potential suitor. For a young man to approach a woman in the street would have been most unseemly—such was not the Arab way—but if his intentions were to be encouraged, the girl would nonchalantly drop to the ground a scrap of paper with her phone number scrawled on it. If the relationship thrived across the telephone wires, perhaps they might be permitted to meet in person. And if the sun was setting, we might see young Iraqi women sprinkling water on the front driveways—to cool down the house, certainly, but also to

make sure that they were on show, ready to attract the attention of any young men who were passing.

On this particular day we happened to be outside *Al Multakaa*—The Meeting, Baghdad's answer to McDonald's—when three black Mercedes stopped. The traffic slowed as the cars blocked an entire lane. The rear doors opened, and four men wearing the distinctive uniform of the Special Republican Guard and carrying AK-47s swiftly alighted and surrounded the front car. A fifth guard entered the fast-food restaurant and quickly came back carrying a milkshake. As the front passenger door of the first car opened, Hakim tugged on my sleeve. "L . . . Sarmed," he said conspiratorially with his characteristic stutter. "It's U . . . U . . . Uday."

I looked closely. The man in the front seat, perhaps in his late twenties, was tall and wore a close-cropped beard. His short hair shone and appeared expensively groomed. He wore a black suit with an open collar and sat with one foot inside the car and the other on the pavement. In his right hand he held a large cigar, in his left the milkshake that he had just been given. He surveyed the street with an arrogant look, clearly aware that people shuffling by were avoiding his gaze. Hakim was right: it was Uday Hussein, Saddam's son.

Uday's reputation was fearsome. He was known throughout Baghdad for his almost psychopathic contempt for ordinary Iraqis, and stories about his terrible deeds abounded. As a fifteen-year-old he had taken part in a massacre of cabinet ministers who opposed his father. It was rumored that he sometimes killed the girls who were brought to the presidential palace to entertain him. On one occasion he shot a civilian in the street, with no provocation and in full view of many witnesses. Nobody intervened or complained—doing so would have given Saddam's henchmen carte blanche to execute them on the spot—but word of the shootings soon spread and Saddam was forced to take action. It was announced that a punishment would be imposed upon Uday: he was to be exiled from his

beloved Iraq for a period of two months. Nobody was fooled, how-ever: this was in the days when the Hussein family could travel freely in the West, and Uday's "punishment" was little more than a vacation in the casinos of Geneva.

Back in Iraq, Uday took charge of the Iraqi soccer team, and under his supervision players were routinely beaten and tortured if they played poorly. His diversions became increasingly extreme. He kept lions as pets. Zoological experts later said that it seemed prob-able these lions were fed human meat and sometimes killed and ate human beings. Saddam's son was breeding man-eaters for his own amusement.

Several meters away, Hakim and I stood staring for some mo-ments, caught between apprehension and the excitement of seeing a famous—if notorious—face. Suddenly Uday's eyes met mine and, unsmilingly, he held my gaze. Whether through fear or not I can't say, but as I stood only a few meters away from one of the most dan-gerous men in Baghdad, my Coca-Cola bottle slipped from my fin-gers and smashed on the ground. I looked down to see the black liquid foaming over my shoes; when I looked up again, Uday had raised his hand and was gesturing at me and Hakim to approach him.

Slowly we walked up to the Mercedes. The pungent smell of the cigar was not strong enough to mask the sickly sweet aroma of the strawberry milkshake. A solid-silver Colt handgun with a glass handle rested on Uday's lap. He had a satisfied air, but who knows what twisted desires he had recently satiated.

"Why did you throw that bottle?" Uday asked, the quiet of his voice barely concealing its menace. He had a lisp, but Hakim and I were in no mood to mock.

"I didn't," I replied honestly. "I dropped it."

Uday dragged on his cigar, shrouding himself in smoke. The hubbub of the busy street seemed to disappear into the background as he eyed me, cobra-like. "Where do you live?"

"At the bottom of Princess Street," I lied.

"Really?" He looked unconvinced, and with good reason. I did not have the bearing of a well-to-do Iraqi, but even in this situation I was ashamed to admit that we lived in a poor house. Why I felt I could lie to this man, I cannot say—it was probably the recklessness, or stupidity, of youth. "What is your name?" he continued.

"Sarmed."

"Sarmed what?" he intoned wearily.

"Sarmed Alsamari."

"Alsamari?" His interest had been caught. The Alsamari tribe had a long-standing feud with the Hussein tribe, which dated back years before Saddam's coming to power. The dispute was over something fairly insignificant—the ownership of a stretch of the Tigris River, which divided their two villages; but old enmities run deep, and Uday was the sort of person who would use any pretext to spark his particular brand of unpleasantness. "From Samarra?"

I nodded. "Yes."

"But you live in Baghdad?" He continued his interrogation.

"With my grandparents. They are from Baghdad."

He stretched out in the front seat of the car, making himself more comfortable. He was clearly enjoying himself. "And what is your father's name?"

"Saadoon Alsamari."

"Where is he?"

"In London."

"What is he doing there?"

"Studying for a Ph.D."

Uday nodded his head slowly. "And is he there thanks to the government?"

"Yes," I nodded.

"Good." Suddenly Uday looked over my shoulder. I turned and saw that he was staring at a passerby who had dared to take an inter-

est in our conversation. Knowing what was good for him, the passerby hurried on under the threatening heat of Uday's glare. Then he turned his attention back to me. "How old are you?" he asked.

"Nearly thirteen."

"Right." For the first time he smiled, but there was no warmth in that smile. He exuded the confidence of a cat playing with a mouse. Leaving his cigar in his mouth, he leaned forward, took my chin between his thumb and forefinger, and lifted my head. "So we can have you married soon."

I didn't know what he meant, but as Uday surveyed my face through a cloud of smoke, he must have seen the fear in my eyes and it amused him. He chuckled to himself, and as he did so he resembled his father so closely that I was momentarily taken aback. I stood there awkwardly, not knowing what to say. Uday turned his attention to Hakim. "What about you? What is your name?"

Hakim opened his mouth to speak, but the tenseness of the situation accentuated his stutter. He attempted to say his name but found himself unable to spit it out. Uday had no time for this. "Shut up," he spat waspishly. "Go away." Hakim looked nervously to me, unsure what to do. Uday raised his voice and touched his Colt with his cigar hand. "I said go away!"

Hakim scurried away, leaving me there. Uday said nothing; he just sat looking at me with his dead eyes, taking deep drags on his cigar. I shifted my weight uncomfortably from one foot to the other. Finally he spoke. "You may go," he told me. For a few brief moments I stood there, somehow not comprehending that I had been dismissed. Then I became aware of two of the guards moving toward me, their hands firmly gripping their weapons. I turned and hurried away.

As the cars drove away—all other vehicles in the street having been diverted to allow their passage—Hakim and I were left with

our sense of fear. As that fear subsided, our encounter with Uday turned into a great adventure, and our exploits were recounted to our contemporaries with increasing elaboration. But as I grew older and became more aware of the reality of life around me, such events took on a more sinister meaning—less a cause for bravado, more a cause for despair. Many Iraqis were unwilling to go into detail about the horrors they experienced, but plenty of rumors reached my ears. That was how the regime worked. There would have been no point to the continuing brutality if ordinary Iraqis did not get to hear of it: how else would Saddam maintain his grip of fear?

Rumors were spread by word of mouth. Some of them were exaggerated in the telling, no doubt, but even the most grisly were not, I am sure, so very far from the truth. AIDS, we were told, was a Western disease, an epidemic confined to the relative promiscuity of the non-Arab world. I was walking down 14th Ramadan Street with Hakim one day, however, when we noticed a poster in a shop window. The names of four women were printed in large letters, and text below the names urged anyone who knew these women to report them to the authorities. They were HIV-positive, the poster informed us, and were part of a wicked Zionist plot to deliberately spread AIDS around our great nation.

Hakim and I did not know the women, of course, so we thought little more about them, although the posters continued to appear in shop windows across Baghdad. A few weeks later, however, word spread that the women had been apprehended. The authorities had made no effort to arrest them formally, and they certainly had not been given any opportunity to defend themselves through any legal process. Instead, they had been taken to Abu Ghraib prison, twenty miles west of Baghdad.

The notoriety of Abu Ghraib was enough to chill the fervor of even the most revolutionary citizens. It was said that thousands of men and women were crammed into tiny cells and that abuse, tor-

ture, and executions were daily occurrences. The regime tested chemical and biological weapons on the inmates, and some prisoners were given nothing but scraps of shredded plastic to eat. Chunks of flesh were torn from the bodies of some prisoners and then force-fed to others. Gruesome tortures involving power tools and hungry dogs were routine, and thousands of people who entered the doors of that fearsome place were never heard of again. It was known that mass graves existed around the country, and it was known in general terms where they were situated; but of course nobody dared to hunt out the final resting places of those poor men and women who had become victims of the enthusiastic guards at Abu Ghraib, for fear of becoming one of their number.

The four AIDS-stricken women were dealt with in a fashion brutal even by the standards of the prison. Stripped of their clothes, they were placed, alive and screaming, into an incinerator so that they and their "vile disease" could be utterly destroyed. In this way Saddam "delivered" our country from the horrific infections of the West and from the iniquities of the "evil Zionist state." I kept quiet about my maternal grandmother's Jewish heritage. She was one of only a handful of Jews who remained in Iraq during the great exodus of 1950. Before that time there were about 150,000 Jews living in Iraq; now there were fewer than a hundred, and it would have done me no favors if anybody suspected that I might embrace Zionism.

Other atrocities took place more openly. As living conditions became increasingly intolerable, many women were forced into prostitution in order to make enough money to feed themselves and their families. It was an occupation deemed unacceptable by the state, punishable by death. The swift hand of justice was left to officials of the Ba'ath party, who were given orders to seek and behead all those suspected of prostitution. The standard of proof required was low, but the enthusiasm with which these officials carried out

their work was high. Accompanied by two "witnesses" from the local community, they forced their way into the house of a suspect, then dragged her out into the street, where a specialist executioner was waiting with a sword. He sliced off the head of the screaming woman with one deft, well-practiced stroke. The head hung outside the woman's house for two days, and her front door was branded with the warning "*Hathihee Al-Qahba'a.*" "This Is the Whore."

I remember a parade down one of the main thoroughfares of Baghdad when I was a child. The road was closed to traffic, and thousands of people joined the march, which was intended to celebrate the glory of Saddam. As the day wore on, however, a small group of insurgents became vocal in their criticism of the regime and started to shout anti-Saddam slogans. There weren't very many—certainly only a small proportion of the crowd—but the Republican Guard was quick to react. A helicopter immediately flew overhead, and white paint was poured over the entire crowd—insurgents and noninsurgents alike. Heavily armed soldiers were then dispatched with orders to shoot anybody stained with white paint. The whole operation took less than an hour. A few lucky souls with paint only on their clothes managed to escape the crowd and change, but people with paint in their hair or on their bodies, where it was more difficult to remove, fared less well. The military scoured the area and shot dead anybody suspected of being part of the "uprising."

The town of Balad north of Baghdad had long been a place of neglect and oppression. Compared to Saddam's hometown of Tikrit, it suffered unbearable poverty and degradation. The people of Balad extended an official invitation to Saddam to come to the town to discuss matters. As a cultural mark of respect, the wife of one of the leading tribesmen arranged for Saddam's car to be marked with henna. Secretly, the tribesmen arranged for militia armed with RPG-launchers to be stationed on rooftops on the street where Sad-

dam's fleet would pass; their instructions were to destroy the henna-marked car on sight.

As arranged, the militia destroyed the marked car, along with nineteen other cars. They then came down to street level and destroyed all except three of the remaining vehicles, which retreated with great haste. A checkpoint guard who was collaborating with the tribe reported that Saddam was in one of those three cars. His head of security had been suspicious and arranged for him to be moved to an unmarked vehicle.

The entire town immediately fled to Mosul or Samarra: everyone knew retribution would be swift and uncompromising. Within hours, armed helicopters arrived and laid waste to Balad. Then bulldozers arrived to destroy whatever was left of the place. In twenty-four hours, a whole town was turned to rubble; any civilians unlucky enough to have remained in what was left of their homes were bulldozed or burned to death.

During my teenage years, I made no secret to my family of the fact that I wanted to leave all this. As I grew up, I witnessed more and more of my friends in Baghdad—many of whom were older than I—somehow managing to make it across the border. Some made the dangerous trip into Iran, others made it to Kurdistan. I even heard that some claimed asylum in Israel. I longed to do the same. "At least finish your schooling," my mother would beg me. "Then at least you will have some sort of grounding." So I persevered at school, but with a certain reluctance: I simply saw it as an obstacle to be got out of the way before I could make attempts to leave the country.

But there were other obstacles too. In 1990, when I was fourteen, my father—who was by now back from England—took me against my mother's will and my own to live with him at the College of Forestry and Agriculture near Mosul, where he was based. I didn't

want to be there, but my father had a hold on me, and there was little I could do.

From an early age it had been drummed into me that the best career path I could possibly follow would be medicine. Doctors would always be in demand, it was said, and medicine would be a noble calling. To gain a place at medical school, however, was not easy. Applications to university were accepted on the basis of your average mark for your final exams in high school. Unfortunately for me, academic merit was not the only factor to be taken into account when this final mark was calculated. If the father of a student was an active member of the Ba'ath party, for example, the student would receive an extra five points; if the father was an officer in the military, the student would be awarded another five. It was reasonably common for students to finish high school with an average mark of 110 out of 100.

My father had no military or political connections. I was not a bad student, but my final mark of 86 was always going to be insufficient for me to achieve what I wanted to. I applied for medical school, but I knew that I was unlikely to make the grade against people whose marks had been doctored as a result of their parents' connections. Sure enough, I was rejected.

I made other applications too. My father persuaded me to apply to the College of Forestry and Agriculture—he would be able to keep an eye on me, he said, and make sure my grades were good— and I was offered a place. But I had no desire to live with him any longer than I had to, so I also did some research into which colleges in Baghdad were likely to accept me, and I was offered two other places: one to study veterinary medicine, the other to study accounting and finance. I made the applications without much enthusiasm and chose to enroll in the latter course almost at random. I never expected to attend; I already had made other plans.

There was a period of two months between the end of high

school and starting at university. During that time, if the proper applications were made, the government allowed students to spend a brief time traveling outside Iraq. My dream had always been to return to England, but that would not be allowed. However, I reasoned, if I could at least make it to Jordan, where border control was less strict, I could apply for a student visa and make my way to the UK. My plans were hazy but bolstered by an inexorable desire to leave. Secretly I made contact with a college in England, and I was accepted for a basic medical course. My mother's brother, Faisal, was a doctor in England, and I was sure that my uncle would help me study to become a doctor myself. But first I had to get there.

In order to make my application for a visitor's visa, certain papers needed to be compiled. During my final few weeks at school, I applied for a certificate of nationality. When that came through, I had the most difficult hurdle to cross. I approached my father with a certain amount of trepidation. As part of the application, I needed his written permission, and I had no reason to believe that he would give it willingly. I fully expected to have to beg, cajole, and finally argue furiously with him.

My relationship with my father was an unhappy one. When I was a child, he had taken me from my mother in Baghdad and forced me to live in a place I hated, in the north: the compound of the College of Forestry and Agriculture, which was next to a village called Hamam Al-Aleel, near Mosul. Hamam Al-Aleel was something of a Sunni stronghold, a bastion of Saddam's supporters. The village was populated by people who were loyal to the regime, and a significant proportion of the Special Republican Guard was recruited from that area. The college itself was part of a massive compound that included not only living quarters for the lecturers and the students but also a vast expanse of forest. Surrounding it all was a high, concrete wall that made it resemble a prison. But the

fortifications were not to keep students in; they were to keep the vicious inhabitants of Hamam Al-Aleel out.

In places, the wall had crumbled and toppled, so the compound itself was never completely secure. Sometimes, groups of young men entered the college and attacked anyone they saw wearing good clothes—not because they needed or wanted clothing but simply because they could. Nobody was going to argue with these fearsome animals brandishing Kalashnikovs. On other occasions these marauding groups wandered around looking for girls—there were a good number of female students at the college—and broke into the female residence halls. Sometimes at night I lay in bed and heard the yelling. The police and other authorities, many related to the villagers, typically turned a blind eye. These people were loyal to Saddam, and an unspoken law gave them carte blanche to act more or less as they wished.

I occasionally spoke on the telephone to my family in Baghdad, but fear of my father kept me rooted in Mosul. Nevertheless, all the years I spent in that place were filled with a desire to leave. So it was that I carefully waited until he was in what passed for a good mood before I brought the matter up with him. "If I am to make an application for students' leave, I will need your permission," I told him.

"Indeed?" he replied with an uncharacteristic note of joviality. "Well then," he stretched his arms out in front of him, "you have my permission!"

I was so astonished I barely knew what to say. I looked hard at my father and could sense that beneath the veil of helpfulness something was not right. Over the past few years he had gone to all sorts of lengths to keep me close to him, ranging from bribery to abduction to physical and mental violence. Why was he now surrendering me without a fight?

"I need your permission in writing," I told him.

"Certainly," he said and accompanied me to my school to sign

the piece of paper that I hoped would be my ticket out of Iraq: "I, Saadoon Alsamari, give my permission for my son Sarmed to travel out of the country before returning to attend university."

I couldn't believe how readily he had granted his permission, but I still required permission from my school. It was not simply a matter of gaining a signature from the right person, however. I approached the registrar with gifts of baklava and bananas—which were scarce at the time because of the sanctions—and literally begged him to take the relevant document to the dean to be signed.

The next step was to take the three documents to military headquarters in Samarra, for that was where my paternal family was originally from, along with the application fee of 15,000 dinars—at that time worth about $300. "Sure," said my father, "I'll take you to Samarra."

"When can we go?"

My father shrugged. "Two weeks, maybe three."

"But it's already the middle of July," I told him. "They would expect me back in the country at the end of August—it won't give them enough time to process the application."

"Well, I'm sorry, Sarmed. I'm busy here—I can't just drop everything to take you to Samarra. You'll have to be patient." Suddenly his attitude seemed to be changing, as though he knew I was going to encounter these difficulties but was pleased that I would not be able to pin them precisely on him.

"Okay," I replied, "I'll take the coach to Baghdad and get Uncle Saad to take me."

My father turned stony-faced, as he always did when my uncle was mentioned. "Saad, eh? *Arrooj*. Peg-leg. Very well."

I had one more favor to ask. "I need the application fee," I told him. "Fifteen thousand dinars."

His eyes went flat. "I'm not going to give you that sort of money," he told me adamantly.

"Please," I begged him. "If you don't lend me the money, there's no way I can get out of the country—no way I can study to become a doctor. The only other way I can raise it is to sell all my stuff."

"What stuff?"

"My computer, my bike . . ."

"They're not yours to sell. They're mine—you only borrow them. Everything in this house belongs to me." He turned to leave the room. "If you need money," he said with a hint of sarcasm, "maybe *arrooj* can give it to you. But somehow, I doubt it."

My father left me to simmer on that thought for a while. The following day I called Saad. I told him about the conversation as he listened quietly. "Okay," he said when I had finished. "Get the coach to Baghdad and we'll sort it all out."

"What about the money?" I asked.

"Don't worry about that—I'll get the money."

"Where from?"

"I said don't worry about it. Just get here."

My father seemed uncharacteristically unconcerned when I informed him boldly that I was going to Baghdad. With any luck, I was to be departing Mosul for the last time before leaving Iraq, but he clearly did not think my chances of success were high. "I'll see you soon," he told me before I left. It was almost as though he knew something I did not.

The office in Samarra was deliciously cool, and the immaculately dressed military official who was to authorize my application made a stark contrast to Saad and me, rumpled and sweating from the torturous heat of the car journey from Baghdad. The room itself was bleak—a table, three chairs, and an old metal filing cabinet in the corner—but the official maintained an imperious bearing nevertheless. We needed this man's help, so we made every effort

to be scrupulously polite. "What is the boy's name?" he asked as he examined my papers. His voice was thick with the accent of Samarra.

"This is my nephew, Sarmed Alsamari. He wishes to make an application to travel outside the country."

"I'm sure he does." He eyed me with suspicion. "What is his status?"

"He has just finished high school, and will start university in Baghdad in September."

"Who is his father?"

"Saadoon Alsamari." A flicker of recognition crossed the officer's face. "You will see from the documents that he has given his permission for the application to be processed. He has asked me to accompany Sarmed today."

"Indeed?" questioned the officer skeptically. "He should be here himself. Why could he not come?"

"He is an important lecturer in Mosul," Saad replied smoothly. "A very busy man. I'm sure you understand."

The officer remained expressionless as he placed my documents into a folder and scribbled something on a piece of paper. "Here is a telephone number," he told Saad. "You can call it to check the status of your application. Good day."

"But we were under the impression that the application could be approved today."

"Then I am afraid, my friend, that you were under the incorrect impression. There are a number of checks I have to make."

"What sort of checks?"

"Just checks," he replied evasively. "Now, if you don't mind, I am extremely busy."

Saad looked pointedly at the empty desk. "So I see," he said and led me from the room. "Something's not right," he told me once the door was closed and we were out of earshot. "There's no reason why

he shouldn't have processed that application immediately. There's something he wasn't telling us."

We phoned the number every day for the next couple of weeks, but on each occasion the official made himself unavailable.

"We'll have to go there again and talk to him face to face," Saad decided. "If you're to get out before the end of August, time is short. Someone is leaning on this pen-pusher to delay the application, and I think I know who it is."

The military official was, if anything, even less welcoming this time. "Listen," he told us impatiently, "I told you that checks need to be made."

"Well, have you made them?" Saad put him on the spot.

"It's a very busy time of year." The official avoided the question. "The schools have all finished. There's a great deal to do."

Saad eyeballed him for a few moments before leaning back in his chair and breathing deeply. "Okay," he said quietly. "*Akhee* [brother], I am very well connected in Baghdad. People high in the military. It is only a matter of one phone call to military headquarters for me to find out what is going on. Now, are you sure you don't want to move a little more quickly?"

The official gazed back impassively. He had no way of knowing if Saad was bluffing—my uncle was not from Samarra, so no word of this pushy ex-officer with a false leg and a smooth tongue from Baghdad would have reached his ears—but he decided to take the risk. "You do what you have to do," he replied. "I know my job."

But Saad was not bluffing. As we drove back to Baghdad he seemed quietly confident that he could get things moving. "I have a favor to call in" was all he would say. Back at his compound in Baghdad, he elaborated. "I have a contact," he told me. "He sometimes comes to visit us here. He is very high up, a deputy minister, and I have his private number. I've never made any requests of him before now, and this will be a small matter for him. I'm sure he will help us."

That afternoon he made the call. "This is officer Saad from Al-Zaafaraniya compound. My nephew is having trouble with an official in Samarra who is being slow in processing his application to travel before he goes to university, and time is becoming short. Is there anything you can do to help things along?"

Approval from Samarra came through the very next day.

One final hurdle remained between me and the Jordanian border. The approval from Samarra had to be taken to the central military office in Baghdad for the final document to be stamped. Saad and I went there that day; I was buoyant with excitement at the prospect of being able to leave as soon as the final piece of this interminable jigsaw of bureaucracy was in place. Outside the huge, revolving glass doors a crowd of bearded Iraqis wearing *dishdash* sat at small portable tables, umbrellas protecting them from the sun. These were the statement-makers: anybody with a request to be made had to pay one of these statement-makers to draw the request up as an official document before it could be taken to one of the clerks inside the office. Some of them had old-style cameras on tripods with black hoods at the back, because all documents required an accompanying photograph. We paid several hundred dinars to one of these men to produce our written request, and he attached my papers to it using a needle before giving it to us to take inside.

A harassed-looking official took my papers and looked at them. After a few moments he shook his head. "Too late," he said.

"What do you mean, too late?" Saad asked.

"My friend, we have tens of thousands of applications. It will take at least four weeks to process this—they need to be thoroughly examined by military intelligence. By that time he will have only a week in which to travel—it won't be worth it."

"I can spend a week traveling!" I butted in.

"It's not up to you, young man," the official told me. "If we

say it's not worth it, it's not worth it." He handed the papers back to me.

"But it's only late because we were delayed by the official in Samarra . . ." I started to argue, but he had already moved away to join his colleague.

Crestfallen, I turned to Saad. "Come on, Sarmed," he said quietly. "We're wasting our time here. Let's go home."

Saad tried to approach his high-ranking contact once more, but that door seemed shut to us. "This is the second favor," my uncle was told. "I have a job to do—I can't keep sorting out your problems."

Saad looked demoralized as he put the phone down. "I'm sorry," he said. "I feel as though I've let you down."

I shook my head. "I've been let down," I told him, "but not by you." We sat in silence for a while. "It was my father, wasn't it? He tipped off the official in Samarra about my application and asked him to delay it."

Saad nodded. "It can't have been anybody else."

"No wonder he was so relaxed about me leaving. Why does he have to be like this? I thought he *wanted* me to study medicine."

"He had his reasons." Saad muttered the platitude, unwilling to speak badly of my father in front of me; but the steel in his eyes told of less forgiving thoughts.

"There must be something I can do," I almost whispered. "I can't stay here—this place is making me mad."

Saad looked at me closely. "I'd hoped that you would be able to get out legally," he said after a while. "There is another option, but it is very dangerous."

"What is it?"

"You would be taking a great risk."

"I'm not a child anymore," I said impatiently. "What do you have in mind?"

He still seemed reluctant to tell me. "I have heard that there are Kurds who are willing to smuggle people north into Kurdistan. They would forge a document saying that you are their son. From there they would get professionals to create false papers and take you over the border into Turkey."

We were silent for some time. Both of us knew the implications of what he was suggesting. If I was caught trying to leave the country without the proper permissions, the chances were that I would be escorted to Abu Ghraib. Once there, I would hope that the guards did not decide to become creative in their dealings with me. I did my best to dispel those thoughts. "Do you know anyone who does this?" I asked Saad.

He shook his head. "Not directly. And it will take a while to find someone—I can't just approach people in the street and ask them if they are willing to smuggle my nephew to Turkey. It could take some weeks. You'll have to start at university in the meantime."

I shrugged. "If it's only for a few weeks . . ."

"You can't make this decision lightly, Sarmed," my uncle told me almost with impatience. "It's not a game, and you know what will happen if you get caught. Maybe you should think about staying—get your degree and see how you feel then." His piercing eyes looked straight at me. "I understand why you want to leave, but everybody wants you to stay."

"I know," I replied, humbled by the affection my uncle was showing me. "But please, Uncle Saad, find out what you can."

"Okay, Sarmed. I'm not promising anything, but I'll do my best."

With a heavy heart, I enrolled at university to study accounting and finance, hanging on to the hope that Saad would find someone who could help us, and soon. I did not consider what would happen

if I was caught—such thoughts were too unpleasant to dwell upon—and in any case I was single-minded in my determination not to stay in Iraq for a day longer than was necessary.

My attendance at university was poor. As I look back now I realize I should have made the most of it, but thoughts of escape were foremost in my young mind. I was not to know that my actions would precipitate everything that followed, but my enthusiasm for the course was nonexistent, and in any case I did not expect to be around long enough to make it worth my while to even show up. Once my nonattendance hit a certain level, I knew that republican law dictated that a letter be sent to Samarra—probably to the same official with whom I had had dealings before—and I would be tracked down and called in. I would then be given a choice: find another course and attend it properly, or enlist in the army. But by the time that happened, I was convinced, I would be well on my way to Turkey.

I saw Saad every day. Sometimes we played chess; other times we just sat and chatted. Every day I asked him how his inquiries were going; every day he skirted around the issue. "I need a few more days," he would say. "Be patient, Sarmed. I'm working on it." And I knew he was.

It was acknowledged without words that Saad was more of a father to me than my father had ever been. He was beginning to look pressured, however, and although he would not admit it, it was clear to me that he was having trouble finding one of these mysterious Kurdish smugglers. Most of the Kurdish population was centered around Mosul, and Saad had no contacts in that part of Iraq.

One morning, the local Ba'ath party official knocked on our door, and my mother answered. "Sarmed Alsamari must report to the military headquarters in Samarra." There was no point asking questions: it was couched as a request but was very much an order, and if I failed to show up, then the Red Berets would soon come

asking for me. Once more, Saad and I found ourselves on the route to Samarra. "It's okay," Saad told me. "They will offer you another course—you had better attend this one!"

The same military official was dealing with my case. "It appears your attendance at university has been poor," he told me with more than a hint of satisfaction.

I could not deny it. "I didn't find that I was suited to it," I lied. "I would like to find a different course to study."

"It's too late for that," the official told me. He handed me a sheaf of documents. "These are your call-up papers. You are to report immediately to Baghdad military training center. You will undergo three months' training before being assigned to your unit." His words fell upon me like body blows as he turned to Saad. "And there is no point asking your friends to rap my knuckles this time," he told him. "If he fails to attend university, he joins the army. Republican law, and there is nothing you can do about it."

CHAPTER 3

THE ROAD TO AL-MANSOUR

Every month we were granted leave from the army. Papers would be issued by an *arif,* stating how long the leave period was and the date on which it ended. Leave periods were dictated by the army. You could request time off under exceptional circumstances such as the death of a close family member—after inquiries had been made and only if the death was not politically connected—but otherwise you could go home only when you were told.

In the absence of genuinely exceptional circumstances, some soldiers went to the most extreme lengths to engineer them. I saw desperate young men deliberately open fire on their feet—often causing the loss of toes and legs—in order to be awarded temporary or permanent leave from service. I saw them breaking their own arms or cajoling others to do it for them. I saw them firing their AK-47s close to their eardrums so that they could sustain deafness and be sent home to recuperate.

Whenever any soldiers were granted leave—for whatever reason—I envied them with all my being. The wake-up call would be blown about half an hour after the early-morning call to prayer, which itself

was about half an hour before sunrise so that the faithful could complete their prayers before daylight. But everyone who was going home for a few days would be up well before that, preparing their bags and getting ready to leave. I would pretend to sleep through the noise, not wanting to listen to their good-natured gloats about what they would get up to at home.

When it was my turn for a break, however, it was a different matter. I too would be up before the sun, hastily collecting my things and checking more than once that I had my leave papers all in order. They were thin, easily crumpled pieces of parchment, and the stamps were often blurred and unreadable. Checkpoint guards relied more on the fact that a color-rotation system was used than on their ability to read the stamps, but it was common for soldiers to be escorted back to their unit simply because their perfectly valid leave papers were illegible.

Once outside the gates, the soldiers who had been granted leave bought watermelon or bottles of water for the journey. The richer ones flagged down a taxi to take them to the bus station. The rest of us had to walk, but the hour-long trip to the station was always completed with a lighter heart than the trip back. The journey to Baghdad took a good six hours, and I counted every kilometer impatiently, desperate to get back to the comforts of home, such as they were. Once there, I spent a glorious five or six days in the little house my mother shared with my siblings and grandparents, simply relaxing, away from the regimented horrors and brutality of the army.

My mother would ask me what I had been up to, but I would answer her only vaguely, keen to protect her from the realities of what was going on. Uncle Saad, on the other hand, had no need to ask. He had been through army life and he knew of its bitter realities. I did my best to speak to him regularly from the unit, but all our calls were monitored so there was no way I could ask him about

the one thing that was constantly on my mind: his attempts to smuggle me out. Back home, it became clear that things were not going well. Smugglers did not advertise their services on street corners, and they had every reason to be suspicious of this ex–army officer making inquiries about their illegal activities.

The night before I had to return was always a time of bitter despair and anguish, but there was nothing I could do to avoid the inevitable fact that I had to go back. My farewells to my mother and my brother and sister were emotional; my grandmother cried, while my grandfather, who seemed older every time I saw him, sat quietly in the corner of the room, his head nodding. I knew I could not allow myself to prolong the moment, however: if I was late getting back to the unit by even an hour, it would mean the loss of a whole day when my next leave came around.

The first evening back at the base was always the worst. I felt lonely and far from home, somehow divorced in every way from the bustle of activity around me. Sometimes I walked to one of the farthest corners of the camp, where nothing but a thick wall of barbed wire separated us from the expanse of the desert, and I watched the sun set; other times I lay on my bed and played one of my cassettes of Western music, closing my eyes and thinking of happier times. It was on one of these occasions that an *arif* walked through the dormitory. I can't remember what music I was listening to, but instead of reprimanding me he took a sudden interest to it.

"Do you understand what they are singing about?" he asked curiously.

I nodded. "Yes, sir."

"You speak English?"

"I spent some time living there when I was younger." He nodded attentively, then left me alone to spend the rest of the evening as I saw fit.

The next day I was summoned to see the commanding officer of

the camp: to his face we called him "sir," of course, but behind his back we always referred to him by his real name, Taha. I walked into his office and saluted; he continued to scribble on a piece of paper before looking up. "At ease," he told me.

I let my arm fall to my side, but my body remained rigid. Summons to this office normally led to a punishment of some kind. I didn't know what I had done wrong, but I needed to make sure I was on my best behavior. "How's your English?" the officer asked out of the blue.

I was caught momentarily off guard—it wasn't the question I had expected. "Good, sir," I replied hesitantly.

He turned to a radio on his desk and switched it on. An English news program crackled into life. "What are they saying?"

I listened briefly, then translated what I heard into Arabic. The officer nodded slowly to himself. "Good," he muttered. "Good. Where in England have you lived?"

"Manchester," I told him.

"Ah," he said with a nod of the head, "Manchester United! You like it in England?" His face was expressionless as he asked me, and I hesitated, unsure as to whether this was a trick question or not. "It's okay," he encouraged me. "You can answer me honestly."

"Yes, sir," I replied quietly. "I like it in England."

"I would like to visit there myself. If I were to do that, could you arrange people for me to stay with?"

It was such an unusual request. Although Taha maintained his superior demeanor, this was a conversation that I might have had with a casual acquaintance on the streets of Baghdad. "Of course," I replied. "I have family there. I would have to ask them first, but . . ." My voice trailed off.

"Naturally," he replied. Then, suddenly: "You are dismissed."

I saluted and left.

Over the next few weeks I received more of these curious sum-

monses. Each time, Taha would ask me more about England, sometimes sounding as if he was merely wanting to satisfy his own curiosity, at other times firing questions at me in quick succession as if trying to test the truth of what I was saying. "Who did you live with in England?" he asked.

"My parents and my brother and sister, to start with," I replied. "Then just with my father, when my mother went home."

"Why did she not stay?"

I stared ahead, impassively. "Their marriage ran into problems, sir."

"What sort of problems?"

I had no desire to tell this man the full truth. As I stood there considering his question, I could not help but remember the sorry image of my mother weeping in the corner of a room, distraught by whatever furious words had been exchanged between her and my father. It happened so many times that even I did not know the full truth of what had gone on behind closed doors, but these images had remained locked in my head for too long for me to start discussing them now, especially here. "Just the usual problems couples have." I shrugged it off. "It often happens in the West."

On other occasions, Taha would ask me in more detail about whom I knew in England, and about the lifestyle, and he would listen to my answers with what seemed to me to be great interest. I would be asked to translate songs and news programs, and I gradually became aware of the fact that I was turning into teacher's pet. My interviews did not go unnoticed. My colleagues started to tease me—"Hey, don't mess with him. He's got special contacts now!"—and even the *arifs* started to treat me with less disdain, clearly unaware of the content of our conversations.

Some time after our first meeting, I was summoned to see Taha once more. He had in front of him a file that he casually flicked through. "I see you live in Al-Mansour," he commented.

"Yes, sir."

"How would you like the opportunity to be based back there?" I felt a shudder of excitement. "I would like that very much, sir."

"Excellent," replied the officer. "Then you will be pleased to hear that I have arranged for you to transfer to the military intelligence compound. I'm sure they will find your skills to be of great use."

Al-Mansour military intelligence compound was a stone's throw from my grandparents' house. The officer was offering me a ticket out of the unit I hated so much, straight into the arms of my family. It was very rare for a soldier to be transferred to intelligence—the privilege was almost unheard of for a lowly recruit like me. As a member of *Al-Istikhbarat,* the intelligence services, I would occasionally be allowed to wear civilian clothes and would start to earn a decent wage. If I worked hard, I could even become rich, driving expensive cars and brandishing exotic weapons just as I had seen important people in Baghdad do. I don't deny that I had sometimes considered that path—in a society where power was everything, everybody dreamed of having a little. The only way you could ensure a high standard of living for yourself and your family was to become part of the system, a cog in the massive machine of terror that Saddam had constructed to keep himself in a position of omnipotence.

But I knew my success would come at a high price. No doubt they wanted me for my interpreting skills, so that I could listen in to Western messages intercepted via radar and satellite and translate them for my superiors. But inexorably I would be dragged into a den so deep I might never come out of it. Al-Mansour was a fearsome place, and those who worked there more fearsome still. As a member of military intelligence, it would not even be called into question that I would betray my friends, even my family if need be, for the greater good of the country and its glorious leader. The transfer was a prison sentence in itself, one that would last for the

rest of my life as I was turned into the very symbol of everything I wanted to escape.

Indeed, escape would be farther from my reach than it had ever been. As it stood, the dangers involved were too terrible to think about; but if a member of the intelligence services was caught betraying his country, the consequences were unimaginable. If I was caught absconding from Al-Mansour, I would be tortured and killed, certainly, but the retribution would not stop there. Whether the authorities apprehended me or not, they would without question go after my family. My parents and grandparents would undergo horrific cruelty—they would perhaps even be murdered—and I could not be sure that my little brother and sister would not be brutalized in some way.

These were not idle fears: they were part and parcel of life in Iraq—accepted facts that touched every family across the land. I remembered talking to my friend Kamall one day. The heat of the summer was beginning to subside, and heavy clouds in the distance threatened one of the tumultuous deluges that sometimes fell upon Baghdad, turning its wide streets into rivers. Out of the blue, I decided to ask Kamall the question that had been nagging at me ever since we had met: "Where's your father?"

Kamall was silent for a moment. "I don't know," he told me, looking intently down the street at nothing in particular. For a moment he didn't elaborate, and I sensed that it would not be tactful to press him; but gradually he opened up. "He was a pilot."

"In the air force?" I asked quietly, thinking that perhaps he had been one of the many casualties of the war.

Kamall shook his head. "No," he replied. "For the state airline." *Al-Khutoot Aljawiyaa Al-Irakia*—Iraqi Airways.

It transpired that he and another pilot had spoken out against part of the airline's safety policy and were arrested. The other pilot

agreed to retract his objection, but Kamall's father wouldn't. Only a few days later, the authorities came for him. Kamall remembered two white security vehicles pulling up outside the house. There was a knock on the door; Kamall's father opened it to see three or four men in civilian clothing brandishing handguns. They did not need to say anything. They just looked at Kamall's father and then at Kamall himself, who was no older than ten, and gestured that they should follow them to one of the security vans. Kamall's father held up his hands. "Okay," he said. "Take me. I'll come with you now without any struggle. But please, leave my family alone."

"Our instructions are to take you and your son," one of the intelligence officers replied.

A horrible silence ensued. "Please," Kamall's father begged quietly, "he's only a little boy."

Suddenly, Kamall's mother started to scream. "Don't take my little one!" she shouted. "Please, don't take my little one!" She held her son tight to her body.

The intelligence officers looked around nervously. They had no wish to be recognized by other members of the general public for what they were, and the screams of Kamall's mother were bound to attract attention. "All right then," one of them said to his father, "just you. But move quickly."

Kamall's father nodded. He held his wife for a few brief moments, then bent down to hug his son, but no words were spoken. And then he walked out of the door with the guards. He was never seen again.

At home that evening, I told Uncle Saad the story as we sat playing chess. "Yes," he said. "I knew Kamall's father. He was at school with me."

I wanted to know more about what I had heard. "Would they really have taken Kamall?"

"Who knows, Sarmed. I suspect not. More likely, I think, that

they were saying that to make his father come quietly. The officers would not have wanted a fuss. They wouldn't have wanted neighbors to see their faces—much better for them to keep their identities under wraps as much as possible."

"What do you think happened to his father?"

Saad shrugged. "A bullet in the head, if he was lucky. Something more inventive if he wasn't."

"Inventive like what?"

Saad slowly moved one of his chess pieces. "You don't want to know, Sarmed."

"Maybe they just put him in prison. Maybe he's still there."

"Maybe," replied Saad with an indulgent smile. "But there aren't enough cells in Abu Ghraib to house everyone who has disappeared in the last ten years. Not by a mile. And besides, who's to say that a bullet in the head isn't preferable to what goes on there?"

"Like what?"

"I don't know, Sarmed. It's just rumors. Forget about it." He obviously didn't want to talk about it anymore, so the fate of Kamall's father was left to my imagination, as it had been to Kamall's these past few years.

In a horrible, warped kind of way, Kamall had been lucky; I had no reason to assume that my family would be so fortunate.

"What if I say no?" I asked Taha.

He was evidently surprised—he thought he was offering me a tempting promotion, perhaps by way of recompense for my agreeing to introduce him to people in England should he ever visit. He was giving me a way out of being a simple soldier, looked down upon by everyone, and the look he gave me was quizzical; but of course, he had no inkling of my escape plans.

"If you say no," he replied slowly, "then I will inform the authorities that, having been allowed to spend time in England as a result of the government's generosity, you have now declined to serve

your country in return." He held his hands out and shrugged. "They will decide what action to take."

I remained silent as we both considered the ominous threat implicit in his last statement.

"I take it you want me to proceed with the transfer?" Taha asked finally.

"Yes, sir," I replied in a small voice. "Thank you, sir."

My telephone call to Saad that evening was urgent. I could not tell him explicitly of my fears, of course—no doubt somebody was listening in—but he immediately understood the implications of what I told him. "They are transferring me to *Al-Istikhbarat* in Al-Mansour," I said as soon as the pleasantries were out of the way.

Saad fell silent. "How long have you got?" he asked.

"I don't know, they haven't told me."

My uncle quickly directed the conversation elsewhere. Some minutes later, however, quite out of the blue, he said, "Next time you're home on leave, we'll pay that visit to your family in the north." There had been no plans to visit anybody, of course. Saad was trying to tell me something else.

I spent the next few days in a state of the highest anxiety. The summonses to see Taha had come to a halt, and I felt in a state of limbo. I called Saad again a few nights later.

"You know that thing we were talking about?" he asked.

"Yes," I replied apprehensively.

"I've found out another way to go about it. We'll try it next time you're home."

It was two weeks until my next leave, but I started to make my preparations long before that. Saad's comment had been ambiguous, but I fully expected that I would never see the unit again. I pre-

sented my leave papers to the *arif* for stamping in good time. "Please," I asked him, "stamp it carefully." It was a bold request, and he gave me an irritated glance but stamped the flimsy piece of paper slowly and forcefully. I took special care to wait until the ink was dry before stowing it away with my military ID—I could not risk it smudging. The night before I was due to leave, I packed my bag with no feeling of nostalgia: I would not be sorry in the least to leave this place.

The following morning I did not loiter. At sunrise I left the barracks, and as I passed through the gates I breathed the cool morning air deeply, barely able to suppress the excitement I was feeling. Without looking back at my unit, I walked straight to the bus station as quickly as I could—the hour-long trip took me no longer than forty-five minutes—and boarded a bus to Baghdad. The bus was almost full, but I managed to find myself a seat toward the back.

We passed the first couple of checkpoints without being stopped. As we approached the third, a number of my fellow passengers were snoozing—we had all been up with the sun to catch the early bus—but I was in no state of mind to sleep. We were still two hundred kilometers from the capital, and already my mouth was dry with anticipation. I did not know what Saad had lined up for me, but the quiet confidence in his voice the last time we had spoken had given me reason to expect that things had been put into motion.

The driver sent his assistant—a young boy of about fourteen— around the bus to shake the slumbering passengers. "Checkpoint," he told them. "Have your papers ready so that we can pass through as quickly as possible."

Everybody fumbled around for their documents; mine were already held tightly in my fist, although I made sure I did not touch the stamp to avoid any risk of it becoming smudged by the sweat from my hand. As we approached the checkpoint, the bus slowed

down, coming to a halt at a gesture from one of the Red Berets. The doors opened, and a large, unsmiling border guard walked on. His skin was dark—swarthy, almost—and he had a thick and immaculately groomed mustache. Nobody spoke. The Red Berets were vile: often they reminded me of the villagers from Hamam Al-Aleel—vicious and uncaring. Ordinary Iraqis referred to them as *zanabeere*—wasps—because of the way they swarmed threateningly the length and breadth of the country. No good could come of a conversation with a *zanboor*. Slowly he walked the length of the coach, scrutinizing every passenger's papers carefully before handing them back and moving on. I had no reason to be nervous—all my papers were in order—but somehow the silence in the coach was enough to make even the most law-abiding citizen feel edgy.

Finally the man reached me. "Papers," he said curtly, and I handed him my documents. He gave them only the most cursory of glances before putting them in his pocket. "Go down," he instructed me.

"Why?" I asked. "I've got . . ."

"Don't ask any questions," he interrupted. "Just go down."

I left my bag in my seat—I was confident that I would not be detained—and asked the person sitting next to me to save my seat. But the guard interrupted again. "Take your bag with you," he told me.

The side of the road was swarming with people—both guards and ordinary citizens, who sat in the dust eating food or talking animatedly. None of them paid me any notice as I stood by the side of the bus waiting for the guard to finish his checks. Eventually he alighted from the bus and indicated to the driver that he could leave.

As the bus left, my hope left with it. The guard told me to walk over to a square concrete building. Once there I was led into his office, where he took a seat, leaving me to stand opposite his desk. Another Red Beret sat in the same office, not even bothering to conceal his interest in what was going on.

"Haven't I seen you before?" my captor asked.

"No," I replied.

"Yes, I have," he insisted. "I saw you only last week. You're forging papers for leave."

I shook my head as I felt my stomach twisting. "No," I assured him, "these are genuine."

"Forging papers," the guard repeated as though he had not heard me. "Very serious." He looked at me expectantly.

I could not decide what he wanted me to do. My instinct told me that he was waiting for an offer of a bribe, but I could not be sure, and I did not want to land myself in more trouble by trying to bribe somebody who was not as corrupt as I perceived him to be. Even if I wanted to bribe him, I had no idea how to go about it. What should I say? How should I say it? I had never found myself in this position before; and besides, I didn't have a great deal of money.

"I'm going to conduct some inquiries," he persisted, "make a few phone calls. I know you're forging papers, so you might as well confess now. If you do, I'll send you back to your unit for three months' solitary. If you don't, you know where you're going to end up: military tribunal, then Abu Ghraib. You'll probably be there for fifteen years."

"I'm not confessing," I said weakly. "I haven't done anything wrong." Then it struck me that maybe I had a trump card to play. "I'm to be transferred soon to Al-Mansour military intelligence compound."

The guard scoffed. "You? At Al-Mansour? Don't make me laugh." He called through the thin door of his office, and another guard appeared. "Put him in the cell," he ordered.

The cell was housed at the other end of the building. The small metal door was opened, and I was pushed inside. I had never been in such a filthy place. In one corner was a communal lavatory— little more than a foul-smelling hole in the ground. There was a

flushing mechanism above it that clearly hadn't worked for years, and a small bottle containing water for cleaning yourself. Two fans hung from the ceiling, providing a little welcome coolness but also circulating the putrid smells from the lavatory. Graffiti covered the wall, and a few glum-looking prisoners sat at one end, hunched up with their arms around their knees. I stood for a few moments, not quite able to believe what was happening to me, before, in despair, I sat down to join them. My face fell into my hands in utter desperation.

Some hours later, the door opened again, and the guard who had detained me put his head into the cell. The moment he appeared, my fellow prisoners rushed up to the door like hungry children to a sweet-seller. They started begging him to let them leave. "I can get my brother to send you some money! Please, let me out," one of them implored.

The guard sniffed the air dramatically. "I'm going home now," he told us. "When I get there, I'm going to sit under the shade of my vine and eat cold watermelon while my wife cooks me a delicious meal. You know," he said regretfully looking directly at me, "all this could have been avoided if you had simply rustled up a few notes." He smiled an insincere smile, then slammed the door.

I stayed in that stinking cell for a week while the army's interminably slow internal mail system verified that my leave papers were in fact genuine. During that time, other prisoners came and went, and as I talked to inmates more experienced than myself, I began to understand why the guard had picked on me particularly. I was neatly dressed, for a start. I took pride in my appearance, but all the guard saw was a young man from a good home who probably had a bit of money. The Al-Mansour address on my papers had confirmed this impression. My leave was for eight or nine days, and that too counted against me. The guard knew that I had to be returned to

my unit before the end of the leave period. If I had only a couple days of leave, the threat of one day in the cell would not have been enough to encourage me to pay a substantial bribe.

I listened to what I was told, but I took very little of it in. After a while I even stopped noticing the revolting conditions. All I could think of was Saad and my mother. They were expecting me back home, and they had made arrangements. What those arrangements were I did not know, but they had probably cost money and they were most likely time-sensitive. My uncle and my mother had no way of knowing what was delaying me: my mother would be sick with worry that some accident had befallen me, and driven to distraction by the constant questions from my brother and sister—"Mama, when is Sarmed coming home?" Saad, I was sure, would be expecting something more sinister. And every day I spent in the cell, my chances of leaving the country were becoming more and more remote as I became increasingly desperate: the longer I stayed there, the less chance I had of being able to get to Baghdad.

After a week, tired and dirtier than I had ever been, I was released into the custody of a military guard. Confirmation had come through from my unit that my leave papers were not in fact forged, but it had been decided that there was no point in my going on to Baghdad as I had only a couple days of leave remaining. Wordlessly I was ushered into the back of a military truck with a heavy camouflage canopy with seven or eight other soldiers. Two Red Berets sat at the back keeping watch over us.

I wanted to cry with frustration as the truck headed back south, trundling along the road that took me inexorably farther from the place I had to be. My companions kept their distance—I assumed it was because I smelled terrible after my week in the cell—and the Red Berets eyed me suspiciously. Clearly they had not bothered to find out why I was being returned to my unit, so they assumed the

worst. As I sat there, driven to distraction by my situation, crazy es-cape plans formulated in my head. Perhaps I could bribe the Red Berets to leave me by the side of the road. Perhaps I could act with more bravado, charge to the back of the truck, and hurl myself out. But my wild plots were the stuff of the Western movies that occa-sionally found their way onto Iraqi television. This was real life.

After about an hour of traveling, the truck approached a road-side service area. As well as oil and water for the cars that had stopped, there was a mosque and a restaurant. A line of coasters—small coaches that acted like buses—lined up ready to take their passengers away. The place was humming with people going about their business as the driver and his assistant went to freshen them-selves up. They came back with a jug of water and a steel bowl, and the Red Berets allowed us all a few gulps. I was the last to be offered the water. Having drunk deeply from the bowl, I turned to one of the guards. "I need to use the toilet," I told him.

"Go and crouch down and piss in the desert." Soldiers were per-fectly used to doing that.

"No," I said. "I need to shit."

The two Red Berets looked at each other. "Okay," one of them said. "You've got ten minutes. If you're not back then, I'll tie a rope around your neck and drag you all the way back to your unit." He opened the back of the truck.

As I jumped down from the truck, I heard my fellow soldiers clamoring "I need to go! I need to go!"

"*Ukulkhara,*" the Red Beret shouted in no uncertain terms. "Eat shit!"

I walked into the main restaurant area. It was teeming with people, and I soon became lost in the crowd. In the far right-hand corner was the door to the lavatory; to my left was a partitioned-off area for praying. I weaved my way toward the lavatory, where I freshened myself up and splashed cold water on my face in an effort

to wash away the grime and sweat of the past week. As I walked back into the restaurant, I looked out the front window. The Red Berets were standing by the truck smoking cigarettes; there was no way that they could see me from that distance in the hubbub of the building.

What happened next occurred as if in a dream. It suddenly struck me that the coasters were leaving every couple of minutes. If I could board one without the Red Berets seeing, I could be speeding away from the service area before they even knew I was gone. It didn't matter too much which direction I went in. Once I was away from them, they would have no means of finding me. My leave papers still had a couple of days to run, so with the luck I was surely due by now I could get through any checkpoints and be in Baghdad by the end of the day. It was dangerous, but I had only a split second to make the decision either way. I determined to make a run for it.

With my head bowed, I hurried toward the prayer area, intending to walk out of a side entrance to where the coasters were lined up. To my right were three men, kneeling with their faces to the floor, deep in prayer. On pegs by the door were their robes. Checking that nobody was looking, I quickly grabbed one. As I pulled it down over my uniform, I realized it was far too big for me, so I pulled up some of the extra material and held it between my teeth, as was the custom in the south of Iraq. My army boots were visible beneath the robe and must have been a curious sight; but I reasoned that if the Red Berets were to come looking for me, I would have more chance of melting into the crowd like this. I took a deep, tremulous breath and stepped outside. I headed for the coaster at the front of the line, noticing that there weren't too many passengers and that there were seats free at the back. Out of the corner of my eye I saw the Red Berets: they had finished their cigarettes and were looking impatiently toward the restaurant. I bowed my head once more, stepped onto the coaster, and found myself a rear seat.

Gradually passengers started to return to the bus, having gone about their business in the service area. One man approached me. "Is that your seat?" he asked me curtly.

"No," I apologized. "I only just boarded."

"Well it's my seat. I was sitting here." He pointed to a free place by the door. "You can go and sit over there."

"Please," I whispered, not wanting to make a scene to attract attention, but equally wanting to stay well hidden at the back of the vehicle, "let me stay here."

The man looked pointedly at the boots below my robes. He raised his voice. "I'm not giving up my seat for some shitty little soldier," he shouted. I cringed as he did so and looked out the back window, where I saw the two Red Berets scouring the area, talking to other members of the military with urgent looks on their faces. Please, I silently implored the driver, please just go!

"Why can't you sit over there?" One of my neighbors started standing up for me, but it only infuriated the man more. Before I knew it, a shouting match was taking place around me. As it reached a peak, I saw the heart-stopping sight of a Red Beret approaching the bus. It wasn't one of my two guards, but I most certainly didn't want him to start asking me questions. I pulled the huge robe tighter around me, even partially covering my face, and tried to make myself as inconspicuous as possible. It took only a brief glance, however, for the Red Beret to see how suspicious I was looking. The second he noticed me, he jumped off the bus and called to his colleagues, my guards who had clearly enlisted his help in looking for me. Within seconds one of them was on the bus, striding down the aisle with a grim look.

He grabbed me roughly by the front of my robes and shoved me toward the door. The passengers on the bus were shocked into silence by his vehemence. He kicked me hard from behind as I approached the door, and I fell heavily onto the dusty ground,

where he continued to kick me in the stomach until I had to beg him to stop.

"Get up!" he shouted. I scrambled to my feet. "Where did you get the robes?" he asked abruptly. I pointed to the side door. "Take them off!" I rolled the robes into a bundle and handed them to him as he pushed me toward the truck. Once I was there, the second Red Beret threw me inside. He climbed in himself, locked the back door, and sat there, his finger resting on the trigger of his Kalashnikov while his colleague returned to replace the robes.

The truck continued its slow, uncomfortable journey south. The nearer we came to my unit, the more sick I felt at what awaited me. My fate would depend on the whim of the officer in charge, and although he had treated me well in the past, I had no reason to believe he would look at all kindly on my attempts to abscond. All the horror stories I had heard about soldiers in my position rang in my ears, and even though the heat of the day was strong, I felt myself occasionally shiver as a cold sweat broke out across my body. I knew that as soon as I got to the camp I would be hauled up in front of Taha and told to explain myself, so I desperately tried to construct some sort of excuse for my actions. My head was muddled, though, and I found myself unable to think straight.

The journey seemed to pass more quickly than usual, and when we stopped outside the base, an *arif* was called. "He tried to desert," one of the Red Berets told him as he threw me down off the truck.

The *arif* said nothing; he just pointed toward the door of Taha's office. The Red Beret led me there and knocked respectfully. When we were called in, he explained in a dead voice what had happened. "Leave us," Taha said when he had finished his explanation.

Taha must have seen the fear in my face, and he did nothing to ease it. The look he gave me was cold, and for a while he didn't speak. "You understand how serious this is, I take it?" He uttered the words without emotion.

"Yes, sir," I mumbled.

He sat there playing with his pencil. Suddenly he let out a deep sigh. "I don't understand. Why are you so reluctant to take advantage of your promotion?"

"I just wanted to see my family," I lied, before explaining the events of the past week. "I wasn't trying to desert. I just wanted to see my mother while I still had a couple days of leave left." It was an unconvincing story, I knew, but it might be enough to spare me from the full force of the army's brutality.

It was impossible to read from Taha's face what he thought. I assumed he was weighing up the fact that I had been unfairly treated with the fact that I had tried to desert. I closed my eyes and let up a silent prayer to Allah that he would believe me.

"Okay," Taha said after a while. "As you've already been imprisoned, I'll do you a deal. The very least you should receive for this is three months in solitary. I'll give you three days, and all leave is canceled until you are transferred to Al-Mansour. But any more games like this, and you'll be up before a military tribunal. Understood?"

"Yes, sir. Thank you, sir."

"Good. Now get out of my sight."

CHAPTER 4

A SHOT IN THE DARK

S olitary confinement does strange things to your head. I was in the small, bare cell for only three days, and compared to my previous accommodation it was positively luxurious, but after the events of the past week each day seemed like a lifetime. I went through periods of genuine rage: rage against the corrupt Red Beret who had thwarted my plans; rage against the *arifs* on guard outside who pelted my door with stones to keep themselves occupied; rage against anything and everything. I hurled my shoes at the wall, and if I heard laughter from the base in the evenings as my fellow soldiers started winding down, I literally yelled with frustration. As the evening wore on, a few less charitable soldiers used the door of my cell for target practice with their slingshots and stones.

Other times were spent more introspectively. I examined the graffiti that previous incumbents of the cell had carefully carved into the wall using their belt buckles, and as I did so, my mind became focused, obsessed even, on deciding what the best way was to deal with my situation. I was desperate to call Saad and let him know what had happened; but more important, having got away

lightly with one escape attempt, I was emboldened to try another. I had to get away before I was enlisted at Al-Mansour. As I was denied all leave until that point, I would have to be more robust in my plans and make my escape directly from the unit. I also knew I did not have the leisure to consider things at length. The *arifs* would know what Taha had instructed, and I would be under more careful observation. They would not expect, though, that I would make any attempt to break out the night I came out of solitary, especially considering what I had just been through. I decided to use that to my advantage.

I was let out of the cell at six o'clock, and I made my way straight to the living quarters, where I had my first shower since leaving for Baghdad ten days ago. I wanted to call Saad and tell him in some roundabout way that he would be seeing me in the next few days, but the waiting line for the telephone was too long. I couldn't exactly start packing a bag in preparation to leave, so I wandered to the outskirts of the unit. The barbed-wire fence stood between me and the desert, and about a hundred meters away, halfway to the road, was a pile of old, burned-out military vehicles that had been dumped there. In the distance, patches of bamboo rose out of what I knew were small pools of water. I gazed for a while, calculating the distances, and then examined the fence. It had been dug deeply into the ground, but I found one small area where it looked as though a small animal had been burrowing. The barbed wire had slightly curled up from the bottom, leaving a small opening. It was by no means big enough for me to get through, but if I could find something to cut it with, I could make the hole just big enough.

I did not want to be caught loitering, so I went back to the dormitory. Keeping myself to myself, I rooted around in my locker and found my old leave papers. They were crumpled, and some of the stamps were not as clear as they could have been, but this time they suited my purposes well. I took a black pen and, as carefully as I

could manage, doctored one of them so that it appeared to have a current set of dates on it. It would not stand up to close scrutiny, I knew, but I had to trust to hope that it would be glanced at briefly if at all. My plan was to break through the fence, make my way to the road, and flag down a car to give me a lift to the bus station. Once there, I would board a nighttime bus to Baghdad in the hope that the checkpoint guards would be less thorough at that time.

I needed one more thing. I wandered out along the edge of the parade ground until I came to the unit workshop, where small repairs were done. It was still open, and a few soldiers were working inside. I wandered up to someone I vaguely knew who was sweeping the floor. "You're working late," I commented.

"Fucking *arif*," he said with venom—he was clearly on some sort of punishment. I stood by a workbench chatting with him. He kept looking around to check that nobody could see him slacking, and while his head was turned, I surreptitiously grabbed a pair of pliers and slipped them into my pocket. "I heard you got solitary," he said.

I gave him a rueful smile.

"What was the reason?"

"There has to be a reason?" I feigned surprise. He laughed and started sweeping again as I wandered out.

And then I waited.

The dormitory lights were switched off at ten, and I lay there for at least an hour until the usual round of banter died down. Gradually people started to fall asleep, and the quiet babble of the few radios that were still switched on faded away. Every few minutes somebody would get up to go to the lavatory, but by about eleven o'clock it sounded as though most people were deep in slumber. I lay on my back, my eyes pinned open, my breathing steady but deep, as I prepared myself for what was to come.

Noiselessly I removed my covers and slipped out of bed. I had

placed my uniform neatly under the bed, and now I gathered it up in my arms. The jacket contained everything I needed: my papers, what little money I had, and the small pair of pliers; I had also packed a small nylon bag containing an apple and a flashlight. I left my Kalashnikov where it was. Although it would have been comforting to have it with me, I knew it was too cumbersome for what I had in mind. Swiftly I walked out of the dormitory, knowing that anyone who was still awake would assume I was going to the lavatory, and stood silently at the door that faced toward the parade ground.

All was quiet. A light shone onto the center of the parade ground where the Iraqi flag was raised, but there was no wind so it simply drooped limply at the top of the flagpole. Beyond it I could just make out two guards chatting to each other. I took advantage of the fact that their attention was diverted and walked toward the bare room that was used as a mosque. Every part of my body screamed at me to run, but I knew that if I did so I would only draw attention to myself. I moved swiftly, but even so it seemed to take an age to move those few meters.

Once inside, I removed my pajamas and put on my uniform; then, clutching my nylon bag, I slipped out again. Keeping close to the walls, and stopping at any corners to check whether I could hear footsteps, I hurried toward the boundary of the camp. When the buildings ended, I got down on all fours and crawled toward the barbed wire. It took me a few moments to find the hole, as I did not dare turn on my flashlight and attract attention to myself in the darkness, but once I reached it I stopped to regain my breath and look around.

At one corner of the perimeter fence stood an observation post. Searchlights shone down from them, but for now they were all directed inside the camp, and although I couldn't make them out from that distance, I knew that the observation post was occupied by

heavily armed guards. Beyond the fence, the desert was still. I stared out to allow my eyes to become accustomed to the dark and could just make out the pile of burned-out vehicles that I had decided to head for. I took the pliers from my pocket and went to work on the barbed wire. It took a good fifteen minutes of effort to make the hole big enough to squeeze through. In places I managed to break the wire; elsewhere I simply rolled it up as far as I could force it, doing my best to ignore my bloodied hands and all the while checking behind me to be sure no guards were anywhere near. My luck held, and I slowly managed to wriggle my way through to the other side.

Once I was out of the unit, I saw no reason not to hurry. I crawled under the barbed wire—as they had taught me—heading as fast as I could in the direction of the vehicles, twisting my head occasionally to keep one eye on the observation post and its searchlight, knowing that if it were to fall on me, I would be lit up like a firework—and shot down just as noisily. But its beam stayed safely inside the camp, and I continued crawling.

Suddenly I heard a gunshot crack loudly into the air. I froze, not daring to move an inch. It was followed by another one, which seemed to ring through me, and then silence. I remained still as I allowed myself time to regain my composure, and I told myself over and over again that what I had heard was nothing out of the ordinary. Guards fired random shots into the air every night: it quieted the stray dogs that fought each other in the area surrounding the unit, it maintained the threatening military presence, and it gave them something to do. We just learned to sleep through it.

I started crawling once more, doing my best to keep quiet so as not to attract the attention of the wild dogs. The distance to the burned-out vehicles was deceiving in the darkness, and it took longer than I expected to get close. When I reached them, I would stop for a few minutes to gather my thoughts before moving on to

the road. I was only a few meters away when guns started firing yet again. This time the sounds were different: not the familiar sound of single shots being fired into the air but the steady repetitive thud of a machine gun. I looked back: the searchlight on the observation post was moving frenetically, illuminating not only the inside of the compound but also the surrounding desert. I started to crawl more quickly toward the vehicles; then suddenly I heard the high-pitched whiz of bullets speeding past my ear. Some of them became lost in the desert; others hit the metal chassis with a sickening clank, and I could see the occasional spark caused by the impact. I raised myself up onto my knees and started to head around to the other side of the military vehicles, where I would be protected from the shower of ammunition.

All of a sudden, I felt my right leg collapse beneath me, and a sudden, pounding pain coursed through it. I let out a shout before putting both hands over my mouth to silence myself. I felt my pulse pumping in my leg as my face creased with the pain.

"You've been shot!" I stated the obvious fact to myself in disbelief under my breath as I fumbled for the wound with one hand, my other hand still covering my mouth as I bit deeply into the fleshy part of my palm. The inner thigh of my trousers was wet with blood. I felt around the other side to see if there was an exit wound. There didn't appear to be, which meant the bullet was still lodged somewhere deep inside my leg. My every instinct was to shout out, but I knew that to do so would be suicide, so I bit harder on my palm as I forced myself to battle with the pain and lunged to safety on the far side of the vehicles.

I sat on the ground, trembling as I waited for the firing to stop. I did not think I had been seen—the searchlight had not illuminated me—but it seemed they had probably discovered my absence earlier than I would have thought possible. Perhaps they were firing

randomly into the darkness of the desert, knowing that was my most likely means of escape. Or maybe they were using their binoculars to survey the desert landscape more carefully. Generally they used them to pass the time spotting wild dogs at which they could take potshots, but tonight they appeared to know they had a more interesting target. In either case, I had no option but to make it to the road as quickly as I could and desperately try to flag someone down. I had no idea whether the guards from the base were out looking for me on the road, so I had to trust once more to the luck that had not served me well so far. By now my leg had gone numb, but it was still bleeding heavily and making me feel dizzy and light-headed. I knew I had to stem the bleeding, so I took my beret and stuffed it down my trousers, covering the wound with it. I then removed my belt and, panting heavily, tied it tightly around my leg, hoping that the pressure would ease the flow of blood until I could get proper medical attention. When that would be, I had no idea.

I could not linger long. The pile of scrap cars was an obvious place to hide, so I knew I had to move away as quickly as possible. I went back down on all fours, and as my leg hit the ground it felt as though it had been stabbed with a needle-sharp dagger before going numb again. Then I crawled for my life, through the dirt and the dust toward the road. How I made it there I don't know. The final few meters were the worst, as I had to climb up a bank of rubble, boulders, and old, discarded bits of car engines; it took all of my rapidly sapping strength to pull myself up. When I finally reached the side of the road, I collapsed into an exhausted heap.

By now my leg had started to throb again; when I checked the beret I felt that it was saturated with warm, sticky blood. I was on a main highway, so cars were passing with some frequency. I couldn't risk being spotted by one of the military vehicles that I was sure would have been dispatched to find me, so I crouched down and

huddled myself up with my head bowed in the hope that an incurious passerby would mistake me for a rock or not notice me at all. All the while I kept looking for a taxi.

It took fifteen minutes for one to approach, the slowest fifteen minutes of my life. When I did eventually see the familiar white light, I pushed myself painfully to my feet and furiously waved my arms. As the car slowed down, I saw that the interior of the taxi was highly decorated, as was the custom of the south: a picture of Hussein, the disciple of Muhammad, was surrounded by little fairy lights and multicolored garlands. The car came to a stop, and the driver wound down his window. He was an old man, his face deeply lined and weathered, and he wore a traditional white headdress. "I need to get to the bus station," I told him from behind clenched teeth. "As quick as you can."

The cab driver looked my uniform up and down. "What are you doing sitting on the side of the road?" he asked suspiciously.

I had not even considered what I would tell him, so I said the first thing that came into my head. "I was cleaning my gun in the barracks and I shot myself," I lied.

"Why aren't they taking you to the hospital?"

"No vehicles," I gasped. It was not as unlikely as it sounded—it wasn't a life-or-death situation, and that's how badly ordinary soldiers were treated. The cab driver seemed to accept my story. "Please, take me to the bus station."

"Okay," he nodded. "Get in the back."

"I need to lie on my leg to stop the bleeding," I told him.

"No!" he shouted. "The blood will get everywhere. Wait there." He got out of the car and retrieved a blanket from the trunk. Silently I urged him on, terrified that the sight of a car stopping for any period of time by the side of the road would attract unwanted attention. He laid the blanket over the backseat before allowing me to climb inside. He drove off to the sound of my heavy, shaking

breathing in the back. "Why don't I just take you straight to the hospital," he offered. "It's okay—I won't charge you."

How could I tell him that the hospital was the last place I wanted to be? Hospitals meant impossible questions and awkward answers—he might as well drive me straight back to my unit. "No, please," I said weakly, "no hospitals. The bus station is fine." I don't know quite what I was thinking—there was no way I would be allowed onto any bus in this state. But amid the pain and the confusion, I remember thinking to myself that Allah had sent me this taxi just when I needed it the most, and that he was protecting me and would continue to do so.

The taxi driver drove on in silence for a few moments. "*Ibnee,*" he said suddenly, "son, you need to get that wound looked at. I don't know why you won't go to the hospital, but you must have your reasons. But at least let me take you to a doctor I know in the next village. He is discreet, and he'll look at the bullet for you."

By now, I was sick with the pain, and deep down I knew that the wound needed urgent attention. I did not know for sure if I could trust this man, but I didn't really have much choice. "Okay," I whispered. "Take me to the doctor."

The village was a good half hour away, but once we got there it did not take the driver long to find the house he was looking for. All the while I remained lying down in the back of the car, steeling myself against any bumps in the road that would aggravate the pain of my injury. When the car came to a halt, the driver spoke again. "Wait there," he told me. "I'll go in and get him."

I lay in the backseat for ten minutes becoming increasingly nervous. What was taking him so long? Were they making phone calls? Where they alerting the authorities? By now, though, I had put my trust in the driver, and there was little I could do in this strange place. Eventually, to my relief, he came back with another man. The stranger peered into the car, but because of the darkness I did not

get a good look at his face. He opened the door before quietly and efficiently removing the belt I had strapped around my leg and then my trousers. I shouted out in pain as he pulled the beret away from the wound and briefly examined it.

"You didn't shoot yourself" were his first words to me. "You've been shot."

"No," I insisted, "I was cleaning my gun . . ."

"My friend," the doctor interrupted, "if you had shot yourself at that sort of range with an AK-47, I would not be removing the bullet. I would be removing your leg. There's not even an exit wound. This bullet rebounded off something before it hit you—that's probably what saved your life."

I remained silent, too scared to admit that he was right as I remembered the sight of the bullets sparking against the metal of the burned-out military vehicles.

"I don't know who you are or where you've come from," he continued, "although I have my suspicions, but your very presence here puts me and my family in danger. I'll remove the bullet for you, but I'll do it here, not in the house. You don't ask my name or anything about me. When I've finished, I never want to see you again. Do you understand?"

I nodded.

"Wait there, then," the doctor told me. "I'll need some implements."

He returned with a small bag, a flashlight, and a steel bowl of orange liquid. The taxi driver held the light in place over the wound while the doctor rubbed his hands with the liquid, which he then smeared over the bullet hole. It stung horribly as he applied it, and I tensed my leg. The doctor removed something from the bag. "This will hurt," he told me. The object in his hand was a large pair of metal calipers with flat feet pointing outward. "Ready?" he asked. I nodded, and swiftly he plunged the feet of the calipers straight into

my leg, then pulled them apart so that the wound was held wide open. The pain was indescribable—ten times more intense than the actual feeling of being shot—and I shouted out.

"Be quiet!" the doctor barked urgently as he poured more of the orange ointment straight into my leg. It burned almost as if he had poured boiling water. "This will help stop any infection," he informed me. Once more I shoved my palm into my mouth and bit hard.

Leaving the calipers in the wound, the doctor rooted around once more in his bag. He pulled out a thick swab, which he soaked with the contents of a bottle of clear liquid. "Hold this to your face and breathe it in," he told me. "It will help the pain."

I breathed deeply. The smell was sweet and pungent and made me feel slightly queasy.

"The bullet went in at an angle," the doctor told me. "You're lucky it didn't hit the bone, but it has lodged itself several inches into the leg. It may take some time to remove. Are you okay?"

I nodded quickly and breathed a little deeper. The doctor brought out a pair of long, pointed forceps. I felt him tentatively insert the tips of the forceps into the wound. As the cold metal touched my bleeding flesh, I felt my whole body shivering and shrieking with pain. The bottom half of my leg went numb once more, and my head started spinning.

It took nine or ten minutes to pull out the bullet. All I remember was the light of the flashlight and the constant, muttering prayers of the taxi driver: "*La hawlah wallaa kuwatta illa billah.* There is no greater help than that of Allah." I did not even see the bullet when it came out. The doctor flicked it onto the road almost contemptuously before stuffing a clean swab inside the wound, soaked with yet more of the agonizing orange ointment. He slowly removed the calipers and, taking a needle, slowly but carefully made a few small stitches in my leg. Then he dressed the wound with a

clean bandage, ignoring my short, heavy whimpers with the professionalism of a man who had clearly done this sort of work many times. When he finished, he quietly packed up his tools and walked back inside, muttering a brief farewell to the taxi driver.

The driver closed the back door before sitting in the front. He said nothing for a moment, as though deciding what to do next. "I don't want to know the details," he said, "but tell me where you need to get to."

"Baghdad," I told him. There was no point keeping anything secret from this man now.

He nodded. "You can't make the journey in this state. You need rest. Come to my house—you can sleep the night in the guest room."

"What about tomorrow?" I asked. "Can you take me to Baghdad?"

He closed his eyes as though I had asked him the one question he wished I would not ask.

"I'll pay you double," I pleaded.

The taxi driver looked straight out of the window. I knew I was asking a great deal, but it did not seem to me that I had very much choice.

"Very well," he said finally. "I will take you to Baghdad."

CHAPTER 5

BAGHDAD

B aghdad: the center of Saddam's power. The one place in the world
I was trying to escape was the one place in the world I had to get
to. It wouldn't take long for the military to come looking for me, and
the only people I could trust to help me now were my family.

We had passed several checkpoints on the way, where the taxi
driver had shown my altered leave papers. One look at me laid out
in the back of the car, white-faced and sweating and covered in blankets, combined with the fact that a taxi from the south up to Baghdad was seriously expensive, made the checkpoint guards believe
that I was very ill, and we were waved through without problems.

The heat of the sun was becoming intolerable, and the bullet
wound in my right leg—bandaged under the white *dishdash* the taxi
driver had given me to wear—throbbed as a result of the bumpy
roads and the taxi's poor suspension. As we drove through the sub-
urbs of the capital, I tried to distract myself by watching the ordinary Iraqis going about their daily business. Gradually we muddled
our way through the traffic-filled streets as we headed toward the
central region of Al-Mansour—my home. I gazed out of the window,

staring blankly at the familiar sights, lost in my own thoughts. My mother had expected me home on leave a week ago. She would be worried—angry, probably—having no idea of the trauma I had undergone. She would find out soon enough, though, when the military police came knocking on her door asking where I was. I had a couple of days' grace—it would take time for the inefficient Iraqi communications network to get word to the capital that I had deserted—but when they came, I knew I had to be far away.

The taxi driver—he had not told me his name, and I knew better than to ask so I just called him *Hajji,* a term of respect to an older person—pulled up outside my grandparents' house, and for a moment we said nothing as I looked straight ahead preparing myself for the explanations to come. To wake me from my reverie, he coughed and, with a gesture of apology, I fished out the money I had promised him—double fare, and the last few notes I possessed. Once he had the money safely stowed away, he turned to look at me. Although we had not spoken of it, he knew that my actions were those of a man with something to hide. "*Allah wiyaak. Bilsalameh,*" he muttered quietly. "God be with you. Safe journey."

"*Shukren,* thank you." I nodded at him and got out of the car, then watched the vehicle disappear into the midday haze. He was clearly eager to put some distance between us, and I didn't blame him.

Through the door of my house I could hear the sound of my brother and sister, Ahmed and Marwa, playing in the hallway. They were often to be found there in the heat of the day as it was the coolest part of the house. The sound of their banter instantly comforted me, a reassuring reminder of the fact that no matter how dangerous my life had become, at home everything was as it had always been. I rapped on the door, aware that my arrival was about to change that.

They opened the door, and their shouts of enthusiasm were like

a balm. There was no look of shock on their faces, no concerned questions—just joy at seeing their elder brother again. "Mama, Mama!" they sang as we hugged and kissed. "Sarmed is here! Sarmed has come!" I hugged them once more and then left them in the hallway while I went to find my mother.

She was sitting alone; the look she gave me was puzzled. She raised a questioning eyebrow but, in accordance with the traditions of the Middle East, she refrained from asking me any questions just yet. It was hot; I had been traveling and was tired. All I wanted to do was have a shower, put on some clean clothes, eat a meal, and gather my thoughts. Questions could wait until later, and my mother sensed and respected that.

It felt good to wash the dirt and blood off my body, rinse the mud from my hair, and pull on some clean clothes. My mother prepared a hot meal of soup, rice, and bread—humble fare but so welcome that it tasted as fine as a banquet in the presidential palace, and I fell upon it ravenously. She watched me as we ate, but still I avoided telling her what had happened. Despite everything, I was still a teenager with a teenager's preoccupations; moreover, I wanted to put my troubles out of my mind for a few quiet moments.

I drank a cup of tea, then sat down in front of the television to relax—not easy given the state of my bullet wound. My leg was throbbing and felt impossibly heavy, and there were shocks of pain running from my thigh all the way up my back. I forget what was being shown—a movie of some kind, I think—but I remember clearly the intermissions. Every half hour the film stopped, and a fat man with a large mustache appeared, singing a song about Saddam, praising him:

> *Sir, we are your servants,*
> *In life you are our prize!*
> *In moments of worry,*

Your hand gives us joy.
Whenever we face difficult times,
By your hand they become easy.
You are the father of generosity and goodwill,
With you we have overcome the difficult times.
We are the joys of your life,
We are the candles of your victories.

The song would be cut with pictures of Saddam in his white suit surrounded by children throwing petals at his feet, images of the army marching by the statue of the unknown soldier in Baghdad, tanks forming part of the procession, and servicemen saluting their leader. Fantasies from the warped mind of a tyrant—there was only so much of this I could watch. I switched off the television in disgust and limped off in search of my sister to catch up with local gossip. There was a girl I was interested in—what news of her? Had my friends come asking about me? What were our cousins and the rest of our family up to? The questions were inconsequential in the grand scheme of things, but it was a relief to me to be able to focus on such trivia at that moment.

And then I called my uncle.

"Uncle Saad," I told him, "I'm at home. I need to see you. Can you come now?"

Saad knew better than to ask any questions. I suppose he could tell from the tone of my voice that this was not a conversation to be had on the telephone. "I'll be there as quickly as I can," he reassured me.

Saad's car pulled up outside the house an hour later. With difficulty, he maneuvered himself out of the vehicle. He did not knock immediately on my mother's door. Instead, he made his way into my grandparents' house to say hello to them. It would have been

unseemly had he not. His parental duties fulfilled, he made his way slowly over to my mother's house. My mother made tea and offered it to her brother along with a glass of cold water, before telling my brother and sister to go to their grandparents' house. And then, as we were all sitting around the table, I took a deep breath and broke the news to them.

As the story of my first, unsuccessful escape attempt unfolded, my mother started huffing and puffing, wringing her hands and displaying the warning signs that I knew heralded an explosive display of maternal rage. I told her that I had injured my leg, having decided to keep quiet about the fact that I had been shot, but it was not enough to stop her shrieks and shouts when I told her the conclusion of my story. "Sarmed!" she shouted. "How could you do this? They could have shot you on the spot."

I kept quiet. There did not seem much to say—other than that I knew full well what would happen if they caught up with me.

My uncle tried to calm my mother down, but she was in no mood to be appeased. It broke my heart to see her in that state because of me, but I could not help but be worried about the danger of her shouting like this. The walls of the house were thin; our neighbors were close and often nosy. A woman who lived in the immediate vicinity had sons who were in the Republican Guard, and I could not risk her hearing the shouts coming from the house and putting two and two together. Saad and I exchanged a glance. "Sarmed," he said quietly but firmly, "come with me. We're going for a drive, just the two of us."

It felt good to be alone with my uncle in the car, good to unburden myself fully of my story. There were a number of checkpoints between my grandparents' house and his, but I knew I'd be safe with him. He was a former high-ranking officer, and officials would treat him with respect.

"I took a bullet in the leg as I was escaping," I admitted to him.

Saad nodded. "I noticed you limping. You need somebody to have a look at that. One of your aunties, perhaps . . ."

I shook my head. "No," I told him. "I don't want anyone to see it. The wound will heal in time. The doctor cleaned it well."

We drove on in silence. "They will come for you, Sarmed. And sooner than you think."

"I know."

"We have to get you out of Iraq. It is not too late to go through with the arrangements I have made for you. You will not be safe until you are beyond the jurisdiction of the Republican Guard. I have found some people who can help."

Saad's four little daughters greeted us with much excitement. We kissed and hugged, and though it was good to see my cousins, I was eager to know what it was that Saad had in mind. We made our way into the guest room and sat down. Saad handed me some documents. There was a passport with my name, complete with an exit stamp to Jordan, and a yellow and green card stating that I had permission to be absent from the army for a period to travel abroad. Such documents did not come cheap—the corrupt officials who provided them knew that they could more or less name their price—and the risk my uncle had run in acquiring them had been considerable. I was suddenly overwhelmed with a feeling of love for this man who treated me like his own son and was seemingly willing to take any risk to help me in my bid to leave Iraq.

"These should be good enough to get you through any internal checkpoints," he told me. "They are unlikely to be checked in any detail. But they won't get you over the border. The guards there are more vigilant. They have the means to verify whether your leave of absence is genuine; it won't take them long to discover that it is not."

I looked blankly at my uncle. "Then what am I going to do?"

"Have you heard of the Al-Shamarry?"

I shook my head. "Who are they?"

"A Bedouin tribe who live near the Jordanian border. Very powerful in that region. I have dealings with some of their relatives who live near here. I've been told that they are willing to help people across the border."

"What about the border patrols? Even if I avoid the border checkpoints, surely the patrols keep an eye out for people trying to cross elsewhere."

"That's why we use the Bedouin. They have been crossing that border for hundreds of years in order to trade with each other. No one would dare strip them of that right."

"Can we trust them?"

"It's in their interest to get you across the border. If you don't make it into Jordan, they don't get the money I will have to pay them." He looked me straight in the eye. "I'm not pretending it isn't dangerous, Sarmed. It is—very. But I think it is your only chance."

I had to make a decision, but in truth I knew the decision had been made for me. My options were few. "When do we leave?" I asked him.

"Tomorrow. You have to get to Jordan, and you have to get there quickly. If they apprehend you in Iraq . . ."

"What?"

Saad looked away. "You will face the firing squad. And there will be nothing I can do to help you."

We sat in silence for a few more minutes while I considered my uncle's plan.

"What if I meet a corrupt internal checkpoint guard like before?"

Saad gave me a mysterious look. "I don't believe that will be a problem."

"Why not?"

He smiled. "Because I will be coming with you."

. . .

. . .

I slept badly that night, although I relished the coolness of the primitive air-conditioning system as I lay on one of the gray metal beds in the bedroom I shared with the rest of my family. My thoughts were a whirlwind. Finally I had a chance—a real chance—of getting out. Over the years I had watched my peer group dwindle as, one by one, unhindered by obstacles as I was by my father, they disappeared to make new lives for themselves elsewhere. Gradually all that remained of my group were the ones who simply had to stay in Iraq because of their family, and the ones who were too scared to take the risk. And me. Now, despite everything, I was being given the opportunity to make a new life for myself as my friends before me had done.

My excitement was tempered by fear. Not a vague, unfocused fear but genuine knowledge that there was still so much that could go wrong. I didn't know quite how many military checkpoints there were between Baghdad and the Bedouin village, but each one was dangerous—I knew that well enough from my past experiences. My uncle's chilling reminder of what would happen if I was apprehended resounded in my head. I would be placed against a wall with other absconders, my hands tied and a blindfold covering my eyes, and shot down by a firing squad. Then an officer would shoot me in the head at point-blank range to make sure I had been fully dispatched.

Even if we made the journey to the Bedouin village successfully, how did I know I could trust my guides? I would be putting my fate into the hands of people I had never met, and that made me nervous. And there were dangers even closer to home. I did not really expect that the military would come knocking on my mother's door just yet, but in the dark quiet of the night even my most unlikely fears were compounded tenfold.

But there was also cause for relief. When Saad had told me that he would be accompanying me to the Bedouin village, it was as if a weight had been lifted off my shoulders and I felt more optimistic than I had for weeks. He would be wearing his decorated military uniform and a suave, confident smile. Surely, if the first of these was not enough to get us past the internal checkpoints, the second would be. I could not wish to be in safer hands.

My leg throbbed. Medicine was hard to come by, and painkillers were especially scarce. All I had been able to lay my hands on had been some acetaminophen, but it certainly wasn't enough to stop the pain of a bullet wound. I tried to put it from my mind by running over the events of that evening. I had stayed late at my uncle's house, going over and over the plan for the following day. Around midnight he had driven me back to my grandparents' house. My mother, brother, and sister were still up when we returned, and the house was shrouded in the nervous quiet of anticipation. I could tell from the look on my mother's face that she was still angry with me. I hated to see that expression, but I knew there was nothing I could do or say to make her feel better. My uncle took her into the guest room, and they remained there for some time. I heard the gentle murmur of voices through the door, and I knew that Saad was explaining to her what it was that we were intending to do. Gradually my mother's voice became louder; Saad's, by contrast, remained perfectly calm. Once she had fallen quiet, he came out of the room and smiled at me. "You'd better go and get your stuff together," he told me. He glanced at my mother's anxious face. "Take your brother and sister."

I took Ahmed and Marwa by the hand and led them across the courtyard to the separate flat they shared with my mother. There I began the business of putting together the things that I would be taking with me out of the country. I would not have room for much—there was no way I could carry huge bags with me across

the desert. But my possessions were few in any case, and I limited myself to photographs, cassettes, and other trinkets, items that would sustain me in a foreign land away from my family, as well as the small amount of money that I had.

My brother and sister watched me pack. "What is happening, Sarmed?" Marwa asked me. "Where are you going?"

I knew I had to tell them the truth, so we sat down together. "I'm leaving Iraq," I explained to them. "Saad has arranged it. We go tomorrow."

"How long will you be gone for?" they asked.

I shook my head. "I don't know."

"Are you going to go and see Uncle Faisal in Manchester?"

"I'm going to go to Jordan first. From there, I'll see if I can make my way to England." I didn't tell them that what I was doing was illegal.

"Will you write to us?"

"Of course I'll write to you."

"Will we see you again?"

I looked into the inquiring eyes of my brother and sister. How could I tell them that I did not even know if I would make it as far as the border? "Of course we will see each other again," I told them. "I promise."

I finished packing and walked out into the courtyard. I needed a few moments to myself, time to say good-bye to the place that had been my home when I was a young boy. Standing in the moonlight of that hot night, I remembered happier times that I had spent there. I remembered the hours I had spent caring for my menagerie of animals—the dogs, the parakeets, the tortoises, and the pigeons. I remembered the happy days I had spent climbing our date tree when its branches had become heavy with fruit, gathering its harvest in a small basket. I remembered the times I had spent with my

family digging holes for flowers, trying to create our own little patch of color in the huge sprawl of Baghdad. I allowed myself a smile as I remembered my grandmother, bent with age, vigorously hurling a raw egg against the inside of the front door before anybody brought a piece of electrical equipment across the threshold. It was a common custom—where its origins lay, nobody knew—meant to ward off evil spirits and bless the equipment, but it brought great hilarity to the household every time it happened.

Suddenly it seemed very difficult to leave this little house, and perhaps if circumstances had been different, when it came to this moment I would have made the decision to remain. Being surrounded once more by the love and care of my family made the rest of the world seem lonely and dangerous, but now I had no option. I allowed my hands to linger upon the whitewashed walls, trying to absorb something of the place before I left it, most likely never to return.

The lone voice of a *muadhin* penetrated my slumber as it floated around the rooftops like a tendril of smoke disturbed by a gentle breeze. Its quiet, monotone drone was punctuated by moments of lilting musicality: "*Allah u Akbar,*" it sang. "Allah is great! I bear witness that there is no divinity but Allah! I bear witness that Muhammad is Allah's messenger! Hasten to the prayer! Prayer is better than sleep! Allah is great, *Allah u Akbar!*" A similar sound would be emanating from every mosque far and wide across the Middle East, calling the faithful to prayer. There was no time for me to visit the mosque, but my prayers that morning were fervently, if silently, said nevertheless.

My mother had prepared breakfast. As we ate, the tension between us was still strong and we spoke only a few words. When we

did speak, we avoided the matter at hand, talking instead of more mundane things. Suddenly I heard a shout from my grandparents' house. It was one of my little cousins who was staying there. "Sarmed, Sarmed!" he called. "Uncle Saad is here!"

I felt a momentary hesitation, a reluctance to go through with our plan that had so many potential problems, but I put those worries firmly from my mind. I knew how limited my options were. Without saying a word, I stood up from the table and went about gathering my things. Then, my small case in my hand, I made my way over to my grandparents' house, my mother, brother, and sister following behind me. Saad had given my grandparents a bag of peaches. He always brought them something, some small gift to cheer their day—a watermelon, perhaps, or some dates. My uncle was wearing the trousers and shirt of his military uniform—the jacket, with its medals and honors, he had left in the car—and he had attached his false leg rather than have to move around clumsily with his crutches. He and my grandparents sat in the front room of the house, waiting for me.

It was a quiet farewell. Although my grandparents did not know the full details of my situation, they knew I was making a bid to leave Iraq, and they clearly felt the need to help me in whatever way they could, whether it was by a kind word or with something more material. My grandfather sat nodding in the chair in which he always sat. He gestured to me to approach him.

"Yes, Jidoo?"

"Good luck, Sarmed," he muttered in his quiet voice. "May God be with you, and *inshallah*—God willing—you will reach your uncle Faisal in England. Do not forget your family." Few words, but well meant.

My grandmother had been preparing food for Saad and me to eat in the car on the way—kebabs and fruit, traditional Middle

Eastern fare—and as she finished packing the meal up, she signaled to me: "Come here, Sarmed. Come with me." I followed her into her bedroom. In her bedroom was a cupboard that, when I was a child, had always been a place of great mystery to me. In this cupboard my grandmother kept what seemed to my childish eyes to be great treasures: sweets, old letters, gadgets, tools, videos and a VHS player, jewelry, packs of cigarettes. With a twinkle in her eye, she started to rummage through the cupboard. She had clearly hidden something in there, and hidden it well because it took her some time to find it. Eventually, and with a smile, she pulled out a woolly sock containing a thick wad of notes—American dollars.

"This is your auntie's money. It is what she earned from selling her gold." Carefully she peeled off a hundred dollars. "This is for you. It is only a loan, but it will help you get started."

I did not want to take money from my family, but I knew my grandmother would not be refused, so I gratefully placed the notes in my pocket. "Thank you, Bibi," I said. A hundred dollars to start a new life. It was nothing, really, but at the time it seemed to me like all the riches in the world.

My grandmother placed the remaining money back in her cupboard and then turned to give me a big hug. "The world is a dangerous place, Sarmed," she whispered. "Be careful."

"I will, Bibi," I told her.

Back in the front room, Saad was anxious to begin our journey. It was a long way to the border, and we couldn't afford too much delay. I hugged my mother and my brother and sister, and then we walked out to my uncle's automatic car—the only type he could drive given that he was an amputee. Under other circumstances, the sight of uncle and nephew limping together might have been comical. But there was no comedy here. My mother started to cry. I knew nothing I could say would make our farewells any easier, so I just

held her tight before climbing into the car. Through the window I could see that my sister was also crying, and I felt the tears well up behind my own eyes. I wound down the window. "I'll be in touch as soon as I can," I told them gently.

Then I turned to Saad, who was sitting behind the wheel waiting for me to give him the word. "Let's go."

CHAPTER 6

A JOURNEY AT NIGHT

I did not look back as we drove away, and Saad was discreet enough not to speak to me until long after my home had disappeared into the distance.

The road out of Baghdad was long and busy. It was early, but the sun was already hot, and I was glad Saad's green Toyota had air conditioning. He didn't use it all the time, as it would be expensive to replace; but this was a special occasion, and the fact that he had it would give him more authority if we were stopped by any check-point guards. As we struggled down the congested streets, flustered pedestrians looked hopefully at Saad. In Baghdad there were lots of official taxis, but never enough to satisfy demand at the busy times of day. Today I saw only the occasional familiar sight of the white and orange taxis, the battered TEX'E signs on their roofs—as if the gaudy coloring were not enough to make it clear that they were for hire. Some of them were decorated with garlands and religious symbols in the same fashion as the taxi that had brought me up from the south. Others had a photograph of Saddam fastened to the dash-board—either an expression of the drivers' Ba'athist sympathies or

the result of a threatening word from a passenger who had happened to be part of the security services. "I see you have a picture of Muhammad. What about our leader, may God protect him and bless him? Why do you not have a picture of him?" More often than not the terrified taxi driver would waive that particular fare.

When cabs were scarce, anyone with a car would suddenly switch professions and become a taxi driver for an hour. Saad's air-conditioned Toyota was popular, and he could always be sure of a good fare if times were lean. He would pull up to a crowd of people waiting for transport and see who was going in the direction he was headed. A moment of intense negotiation would follow. Money would be discussed, certainly, but the potential customer would also want to be sure that this opportunist chauffeur had the right intentions and was not some bandit with a false smile, fully prepared to murder him in the backseat for the price of the few dinars in his pocket. This was an alarmingly common occurrence. While the penalty for deserting from the army could be horrifically severe, the punishment for murder—if you could show that it was done in self-defense (easily enough achieved with a few bogus witnesses)—was six months' imprisonment.

But there would be no fares today, nobody to hinder us in our objective. Our journey would take us first around the outskirts of Fallujah, and the road that would lead us there was good and full of traffic. It was unlikely that we would encounter any difficulties on that early stretch. Once past Fallujah, however, things would become more problematic. It was about four hundred kilometers from there to the village where we were heading. Although the highway that continued west to the Jordanian border crossing was relatively new, in places where heavy military vehicles had made their mark on the road, it was in poor repair and the going would be slow. We did not expect to get to our destination until the following day.

The state of the highway, however, was the farthest thing from my mind. I could think of nothing but how we were going to talk our way through the internal checkpoints. I asked Saad how many there would be. "Three, perhaps four," he shrugged.

I kept quiet. I did not want Saad to know how scared I was about approaching them, but I think he sensed my fear in any case. "Don't worry about it," he told me calmly. "If they stop us, leave everything to me."

I was dressed neatly in a pair of jeans and a T-shirt, and together we looked perfectly respectable. "We want to give them the impression that you are my son." He gestured at the jacket of his military uniform, which was neatly folded in the backseat. "When they see that, it will instill some kind of respect into them," he told me. "If they assume that you are my son, that respect will rub off on you. Let me do the talking."

We passed the busy town of Ar-Ramaadi and a few miles later approached a fork in the road. The right-hand fork would take us up to Al-Haglanya and then on to the Euphrates River, but our path did not lie that way. Instead we continued straight on, into the desert region of Al-Anbar. From time to time, to our left and right, the roads branched off toward poor desert towns—replicas of any number of the faceless communities I had seen near Mosul or Basra. Houses were built using huge lumps of concrete covered over with mud; cows roamed the streets. Kids played in the dirt tracks with sticks, and colorful market stalls belied the poverty of these places. Inhabitants eked out a living selling homemade drinks on the streets, but only those with the strongest immune systems would be wise to risk them.

It did not take long for us to approach a checkpoint. My uncle slowed down, and a look of intense concentration passed his face. "Give me my jacket, Sarmed," he said. I reached into the back and

handed him the jacket, and he wriggled his way into it, keeping one hand on the steering wheel. "Good," he said. "Now, open the glove compartment."

I did so. Stashed inside was a 9mm Beretta handgun. This was not an ordinary Beretta. For a start it was an Iraqi-made *tarek*, and it had been given to the officers of the Iran-Iraq war who had been awarded bravery medals as a "gift" from Saddam. It bore a small insignia on the handle that identified it as being a special-issue weapon; the owners of such items were afforded special respect by other members of the military. Saad took the gun from me and placed it prominently on the dashboard where it could be easily seen.

As we approached the checkpoint, I saw the usual hubbub of activity. Buses were parked by the roadside, as were white and orange taxis—more modern than the one in which I had journeyed the previous day. Their occupants were hanging around outside, talking, drinking, cooling down, and generally just taking a break from their journeys. The checkpoint itself was little more than a bunker on the side of the road, there to protect the guards from the sun. The Red Berets gripped their AK-47s firmly, and their light-armored vehicles stood nearby as they looked through the papers of those drivers they had decided to stop.

I saw all this from a distance. My uncle continued to slow down and as he did so I felt my heart in my chest. I did my best to look straight ahead and appear calm. But as I strained my face into a look of somber innocence, I could not help but feel that to the trained eyes of the Red Berets I showed all the signs of a guilty man. For a split second I thought I caught the eye of one of them. He had noticed me. Surely the look of fear on my face would arouse his suspicions. I breathed deeply.

"*Let-khaaf,* Sarmed," said my uncle. "Don't be afraid." He kept looking straight ahead as if he didn't have a care in the world, but I

could not take my eye off the guard. As we passed him, I foolishly turned my head, and our eyes locked; I saw him begin to raise his arm before I quickly jerked my head away. My uncle kept the car moving slowly forward, ignoring the guard's attention and, suddenly, the checkpoint was behind us. I looked in the rearview mirror, fully expecting to see one of the light-armored vehicles pull away. I wanted to tell Saad to drive more quickly, but I knew that would just arouse suspicion; and gradually the checkpoint faded behind us, without any guards appearing to follow. We had passed our first obstacle, it seemed, without incident.

As we drove farther from Baghdad, the traffic became less and less heavy. From my point of view, this was not good. The fewer vehicles there were along the road, the more chance we had of being stopped at the next checkpoint. Although the Red Berets would be more likely to stop buses or taxis, they would still pull over a substantial number of ordinary vehicles, and that could mean us. Perhaps I should have felt more relaxed having made it through the first checkpoint safely; in fact I just grew more terrified.

Later that afternoon we approached a second checkpoint. It was less busy than the first, but our luck held and we were waved past with no questions asked.

We stopped for the night in one of the small, run-down complexes that lined the road at irregular intervals. Part restaurant, part garage, part mosque, these places catered to the most basic needs of the travelers along the road. We ate a meal in the restaurant, which was the least filthy part of the whole complex, and then made our way to the car to spend the night. I tried to sleep, but without much success.

We left early the next morning. Gradually the traffic, which had been sparse, became more heavy. It did not take long to see why this was happening: there was a checkpoint up ahead, and to my horror they were stopping every car that passed. Terrible scenarios flitted

through my brain. Did they know Saad and I were on the road headed west? Had the military police been to my mother's house and extracted some sort of confession from my family? Why would they be stopping every car that passed if not to look for us? Whether such thoughts were going through Saad's mind, I cannot say. He simply put his military jacket on once more and made sure his Beretta was in full view. We were silent as we sat in the line of cars awaiting our turn, but the time we spent in that queue gave my mind the opportunity to imagine increasingly awful explanations for this delay.

Eventually, two Red Berets walked up to the car in front of us. They stood there for some minutes asking questions of the driver, before asking him to pull his car over to the side of the road. As he did so, one of the guards followed him; the other unsmilingly waved us forward. He appeared at the driver's door and gestured at Saad to wind down the window. He took one look at his military uniform and saluted him, but there were no pleasantries. "Where are you going?" he asked.

"We are going to see family in Rutbah." My uncle smiled at him.

"Is this your son?"

Saad nodded.

"Your papers," the Red Beret said to me.

Nervously I handed him the fake military pass. He studied it carefully. The seconds ticked by. Out of the corner of my eye I could see the driver of the other car being frisked and then taken into the guards' hut. There was an anxious silence; even Saad could not think of anything to say. The Red Beret looked at me, looked back at my papers, and then handed them back.

"Do you always keep your Beretta on the dashboard, sir?" he asked my uncle.

Saad flashed him a grin. "Why?" he said. "Are you looking to buy one?"

That was all that was needed. The Red Beret smiled for the first time at my uncle's joke. "You can go, sir," he told us. Saad inclined his head politely, they saluted each other; and we were waved on. As we passed the checkpoint, I let out an explosion of breath, and Saad and I laughed with relief. We were through.

We arrived at a small Bedouin village at around seven o'clock that evening. There were perhaps twenty houses made of mud and brick. We knew that the tribesman we were looking for lived in this area, but we had no means of finding him. There was nothing for it but to go knocking on doors.

"Do you know Abu Mustapha?"

At first we were met with blank faces—either they did not know this man, or they did not want to let on to somebody in military uniform that they did. But eventually we found somebody who was willing to help. He pointed to a small road leading away from the settlement. "Take that road," he told us. "It will lead you to another village. He is well known there. Ask anybody and they will point you to his house."

We returned to the car and followed the road he had indicated. As we drove, the silence of the desert gradually impressed itself upon us, and we grew quiet ourselves. Sure enough, after about half an hour, we came to another village. A group of children were playing in the street, so we stopped and asked them the same question: "Do you know Abu Mustapha?" With typical childish exuberance they shouted that they did and pointed us in the direction of what seemed to me to be a more modern house than the others. As we made our way toward it, a few children who, barefoot and filthy,

had been playing their games in the driveway at the front of the house came out toward us.

"What do you want?" they shouted. "Who are you?"

Saad limped up to them. "Is your father at home?" he asked.

The children scurried indoors, calling for their mother, who soon appeared at the door. "Who are you?" she repeated, suspiciously.

"My name is Saad Al-Khatab," my uncle replied politely, "and this is my nephew Sarmed."

"What do you want?"

"We are here to see Abu Mustapha."

"Are you sure it is him you want? What makes you think he lives here?"

"I am a friend of relatives of his in Baghdad. They described to me the place that he lives. I have a business proposition for him."

Reluctantly, the wife nodded and went inside. "Wait here," she said as she disappeared.

We stood outside the house and waited for several minutes before a huge figure appeared at the door. He had a thick white mustache and white hair and was wearing a black robe; he was an impressive sight in the failing light of the desert evening. He stood in the doorway and said nothing, so my uncle repeated the introduction he had already given to his wife: "My name is Saad Al-Khatab, and this is my nephew Sarmed."

Suddenly a smile lit up the tribesman's face; it was clear that he understood in that instant why we were there. He clapped his hands and shouted at his children to stop playing and make themselves scarce. Then he called to his wife. "*Ya marr'a!* Prepare supper!" he shouted. He extended his arms to Saad and me, and he ushered us inside. Our presence did not seem to surprise him. Maybe he had been forewarned of our arrival; maybe people like us arrived on his doorstep out of the blue on a regular basis.

We were led into Abu Mustapha's guest room. It was a peaceful place: there was no television, and the walls were covered with embroidered religious texts. The seating, of course, was all Bedouin style, with cushions scattered across the floor. We sat down, and tea was brought in to us, along with sherbet—concentrated fruit juice diluted with water. We were thirsty after our long journey, and the drinks refreshed us. The tribesman sat opposite Saad and me, a huge imposing figure shrouded in his flowing robe. I glanced at my uncle and saw on his face a look that I recognized, a calm, almost humble aura he emanated before he was to start engaging in any kind of negotiation. As we sat there, there were frequent moments of silence as my uncle and the tribesman smiled and nodded toward each other. Each knew what the other wanted, but there was a ritual to such meetings, and nothing was spoken of the real reason for our presence just yet. Tradition dictated that we should wait until after we had eaten together—or at the very least finished our first round of drinks—before we even began to discuss business.

Abu Mustapha fingered his *sibbha*—a string of beads—and continued smiling knowingly at us. Every few minutes he shouted, "*Allah bilkhair*—Welcome! God is good!"

"*Allah bilkhair.*" We intoned the traditional reply.

Gradually my uncle engaged the tribesman in small talk. He explained that he was acquainted with his relatives in Baghdad, that he had had business dealings with them before now.

"You are interested in guns?" the tribesman asked out of the blue.

My uncle shrugged. "A little," he replied.

The tribesman stood up suddenly, left the room, and returned with a *berrnaw*, a rifle with an extra-long barrel. It was the traditional weapon of the Bedouin of that area and could shoot over hugely long distances—even up to two miles. The tribesman had a look of pride as he handled it, mixed with a glint in his eye that

spoke volumes: he was, he was demonstrating, a man who could take care of himself. .

We admired his gun for a short while, and then food was brought in. His wife presented a steaming dish of *baagillah.* It was a favorite of mine, an Iraqi dish of lamb, bread, and beans traditionally served on Fridays after prayers. Saad and I fell upon this feast as hungrily as politeness would allow.

When we finished eating, more tea was brought. This was the sign for us to get down to business. I had expected my uncle to explain the situation in more roundabout terms than he did; after all, we did not know yet that we could fully trust this man sitting opposite us. He was full of smiles, but who knew what those smiles could be hiding?

"My nephew here, Sarmed, has deserted from the army." I gave Saad a sharp look, but he held his hand up to me and continued. "He needs to leave the country, and he wants to go to Jordan. Your relatives told us this might be something you can help with."

For a while the tribesman said nothing. He just sat there expressionless. The silence in the room was thick, broken only by the sound of the tribesman fingering his *sibbha* and the constant whir of the fan above us. We had come all this way, and I had never imagined that this man would say no to our request—but he certainly did not seem to be jumping at the chance. I had an uncomfortable feeling that we were about to have to drive back to Baghdad that night. He looked carefully at me, and then at my uncle. It was impossible to read his eyes. Finally he spoke. "I do not recommend that you go to Jordan."

In that moment I knew we had a chance of persuading him. He had not turned us down outright, so it was clearly something he was prepared to do. But why not Jordan? And if not Jordan, where? As if in response to my unspoken question, the tribesman intoned "Syria."

Saad shook his head. "Syria will be too dangerous for him." He was right. The relationship between Iraq and Syria at that time was bad. For starters, Iraqis were not allowed to work in Syria; in Jordan, there was at least a chance. More worryingly, if I was apprehended in Syria, the likelihood was great that I would be taken for a Ba'ath party spy and imprisoned for I don't know how long.

Abu Mustapha shook his head. "The stretch of land between here and the border to Jordan is much smaller than the land between here and Syria," he explained. "There are many border patrols. The government spends a great deal of money on surveillance in that stretch of desert. The Syrian border police are poorly paid, and there are fewer of them. There are land mines in that area too. We think we know where most of them are, but . . ."

Saad was adamant. "It is a risk we are prepared to take."

The tribesman looked uncomfortable. Maybe he was more familiar with the crossing into Syria, I don't know. He let out a heavy sigh. "If you choose that route, we will have to make the journey at night. And I cannot guarantee you safe passage. There are wild animals in the desert." He looked straight at me. "They do not much care what they eat."

I shuddered, but Saad stood his ground. "If he is captured in Syria, the treatment he will receive will be just as bad as any he can expect in Iraq. Jordan is more civilized, and from there he has a much greater chance of finding his way to the West."

Again there was a silence. Finally Abu Mustapha closed his eyes and slowly nodded his reluctant acquiescence.

He shouted for one of his children to come. Almost immediately one of his sons entered the room. "Go and find your uncle," his father told him almost dismissively. The boy said nothing and left the room swiftly. The three of us remained seated; barely a word was spoken between us.

From the corner of my eye I looked at Saad. He seemed as calm

as ever, his expressionless face indicating none of the rising panic the tribesman's reluctance to take the route to Jordan had instilled in me. The Bedouin knew this stretch of land better than anyone— certainly better than Saad or I. They had crossed these borders all their lives, and their ancestors before them had done so for hundreds of years. They knew where the dangers lay. If they were worried about our plan, should we not also be? I tried to push such worries from my mind. I had trusted my uncle this far; he had not let me down. And as I looked at the imposing figure of the tribesman before me, I could tell that he was a person who would be able to look after himself—and me. That, at least, was some small comfort.

After about half an hour, the door opened again and another burly tribesman walked in.

"This is my brother," our host introduced him. We shook hands in greeting as more tea was brought. "My young guest," he gestured toward me, "is of a mind to travel to Jordan."

Immediately his brother shook his head. "No," he said emphatically. "Too dangerous. We can't take you all the way into Jordanian territory, but we can take you into Syria."

It felt like we were back at square one. His look was stern, and he did not appear to be open to negotiation. I think my uncle must have seen that in him; without delay he played his trump card.

"My nephew is not going to Syria. It is Jordan or nothing. If you are unwilling to take that route, we must leave now. It is a long way back to Baghdad." He sat back without taking his eyes off the Bedouin, and sipped his tea.

The two men looked at each other, aware that their lucrative business arrangement might be disappearing before their eyes. Eventually the brother nodded in agreement. "We have details to discuss," he told Saad.

My uncle nodded. "Wait here, Sarmed," he told me as the three of them stood up and went outside. I heard the murmur of hushed

negotiations through the door, and I knew that they were discussing what Saad would pay them to undertake this illicit venture, along with payment terms and guarantees. My uncle would then have to persuade them that I would not be a liability to them in the desert—that I knew how to take care of myself. When they returned, there were smiles all around: a deal had been struck.

"The arrangements have been made," Saad told me simply, his voice altered now from one of concern to one of confidence. "You will stay here tonight, and you will make the journey after sundown tomorrow."

"What about you?"

"I must leave," he told me quietly.

"Now?" I asked him. The moment seemed to have come upon us very quickly.

"There is no reason for me to stay, and I have business to attend to in Baghdad." He smiled at me. "Don't worry, Sarmed. You are in good hands. Everything will be fine." He turned to the tribesman and his brother. "You have my thanks, and the thanks of my family. *Inshallah,* as soon as we hear that he has made it across the border, I will give the remainder of the money to your relations in Baghdad." With that he left the room.

I followed my uncle to the car in silence. To say good-bye to this man who had risked so much for me was almost more than I could bear. Neither of us had spoken of the one thing that was foremost in our minds throughout this eventful journey: we might never see each other again. And now, standing by the car in a strange village somewhere in the Iraqi desert, the time had come to say our farewells. As I removed my things from the trunk of the car, Saad fished a piece of paper out of his pocket, on which he had scribbled a name and an address.

"When you arrive in Amman, find this person. His name is Wissam, and he is a friend of mine from many years ago. He will

help you in any way he can." My uncle put his hands on my shoulders. "Be strong," he continued, "and trust no one. You have to have your guard up all the time."

He went to the car and came back with something wrapped in material. "I want you to have this. Handle it with care."

I gingerly unwrapped the package. Inside I felt cold steel. It was a black Beretta handgun—not the special-issue Beretta that he had positioned on the dashboard but another weapon from his collection. "You might need it to protect yourself after the Bedouin leave you," he explained. "You know how to use it, of course."

I said nothing while Saad hugged me tightly, holding me close to him and breathing deeply, smelling me as if trying to absorb something to remember me by. "Good-bye, *habibi* Sarmed," he whispered, "and may Allah be with you. You are my son, and you always will be. I will miss you very much." For the first time ever, I heard his voice wavering and I saw his eyes filling up. I did not trust myself to say anything; nor could I think of anything to say.

How long we stood locked in that embrace, unwilling to leave each other, I couldn't say; but eventually, and reluctantly, Saad climbed into the car and started the engine. He wound down the window and looked me straight in the eye. "Be careful," he told me solemnly. "And remember, the genuine man never forgets his family. We are sending you to freedom so that one day you may rescue them from this place." Then he slowly pulled away.

I stood on that weathered track in the near-darkness, my eyes full of tears and a small bag by my feet containing everything that I now possessed in the whole world, and I watched my uncle's car as it became a cloud of dust settling in the distance. Then I turned back to look at the Bedouin house where I was a stranger.

I had never felt so alone.

· · ·

. . .

I made my way back to the guest room. Abu Mustapha and his brother were still there, and I tried, half-heartedly, to make conversation. But it was clear to them how upset I was at having said goodbye to my uncle, and that now was not the time for polite chitchat, so they made their excuses and left me alone. I was grateful to them for that: I needed time to compose myself.

I knelt in front of a picture of Mecca that adorned the wall, and prayed. I prayed that my uncle would make it back to Baghdad safely; I prayed for my family; and I prayed that the next thirty-six hours would not be filled with the dangers that haunted me. I opened my bag and looked through my things. The trinkets I had brought with me seemed out of place in such a remote location so far from home, but it was a comfort to have them with me as a reminder of the place I had left behind. I took a pen and a piece of paper and started trying to write a letter to Saad, but somehow I could not find the words to express what I wanted to say, and the letter was abandoned almost before it was begun.

Behind me I heard the door open, and Abu Mustapha entered with his wife. She lay a mattress on the floor for me to rest. "It would be best if you tried to sleep," the tribesman told me. "We wake early, and there is much to do tomorrow in preparation."

I nodded and thanked his wife for her kindness. Alone again, I redressed my wound with some clean bandages I had taken from home, wincing as I removed the doctor's professionally inserted swab and replaced it with the limited skill my military training had afforded me. It still hurt beyond belief, but I had other worries to occupy my mind now: as I lay on the mattress and closed my eyes, I knew that when sleep came—if it came—it would be fitful and disturbed.

Sure enough, I awoke early the next morning. The tribesman

entrusted me to the care of his nephew—the son of his brother who had been with us the previous evening. It was explained to me that the three of them would be accompanying me that night, and I was to spend the day learning as much about them as I could. If we were stopped by border patrols, it was essential that I was believed to be one of them.

The Bedouin are nomads of the desert. Divided into tribes, each tribe historically led by a sheikh, traditionally they herded and traded livestock—sheep and goats—moving across the desert according to the seasons. The restraints of international boundaries meant nothing to them. They had—and still have—a disregard bordering on contempt for anything or anyone that attempts to influence their centuries-old traditions, and especially governments that try to impose nationalities that mean nothing to the Bedouin. Their concern is not with the outside world. They are traders, wandering across the desert from village to village to buy and sell their livestock, crossing borders at will, often traveling at night to avoid the scorching heat of the desert sun. They are, as they have been for hundreds of years, an accepted feature of the Middle East landscape, and nobody—not even Saddam—would contemplate removing from these desert wanderers the right to travel where and when they please. The Al-Shamarry tribe especially had a number of villages dotted around the desert between Iraq and Syria, although there were fewer across the Jordanian border.

This did not mean, however, that the Bedouin were above suspicion. The authorities were not so naive that they did not realize that certain Bedouin tribesmen took advantage of their nomadic status to earn themselves extra money. The border guards in this region allowed the Bedouin to wander at will but nevertheless kept close tabs on them. There was no guarantee that we would not be stopped and questioned as to our movements, and if this happened, it was essential that I look and act like a member of their tribe.

Abu Mustapha's nephew was a little younger than I—perhaps sixteen—but the ravages of life in the desert had not been kind to his features, which were weathered beyond his years. We sat together in a communal courtyard around which the village's houses were built. In the middle of the courtyard, the burned-out shell of an old car lay in a pool of mud and water, and thin-looking sheep and goats wandered around at will. The nephew quizzed me about myself and my life in Baghdad and Mosul, and I did my best to answer his questions patiently, aware that the world I was trying to escape may well have seemed strange to him, just as his world did to me. But my mind was focused on the path that lay ahead, not that which lay behind, and I was eager to talk to him about our evening's work. "What will I have to wear tonight?" I asked him.

"Come with me," he said. We went inside and he found me a dark, embroidered *dishdash*. He also gave me another, heavier robe. "This is to protect you from the cold," he explained. "In the desert, the temperature drops at night. You will freeze if you are not properly dressed."

I put the garments on. They had a heavy, musty smell to them, but they fit well enough. He then handed me a long stick. "This is what we use to herd our sheep," he explained. "It's not difficult. If you tap them on the right, they will turn left; if you tap them on the left, they will turn right. Come with me, we can practice."

We returned to the courtyard, and he identified the sheep that belonged to his family. Families marked their animals on a particular part of their bodies, either with henna or with some other dye, so that they could distinguish which beasts belonged to whom. Together we practiced herding the sheep that we would be taking with us that night, while the nephew explained to me that if I was spoken to I would have to try to speak in his dialect. This would be difficult for me—the difference in the accent was extreme, and I did not believe I would be able to fool anyone. I did my best to practice with

the nephew, but I could tell by the look on his face that I was at best unconvincing. I would have to hope no border guards spoke to me.

The day passed slowly. As the sun was setting, I sat in the guest room waiting for my guides to tell me it was time to leave. When Abu Mustapha arrived with his brother and nephew, I saw that they were wearing headdresses tied tightly around their heads and their chins, and they had strapped bullet belts in the shape of an X around their bodies. Both of the older men were carrying their evil-looking *berrnaw*. I looked at them inquiringly. "In case of wild animals," Abu Mustapha said by way of explanation. "Come, we need to get moving."

I put on my Bedouin garb, grabbed my bag, and followed them outside. My belongings were strapped to one of the sheep, and the place was full of activity. Primitive bells around the necks of the cattle clinked as they wandered freely, children ran around, and the wife was cooking bread in the courtyard. It was a heady, homey smell, and under other circumstances it would have made me hungry; but even though the journey ahead was long, my stomach was churning from apprehension and I had no thought for food. We left the bustle behind us and set off into the silence of the desert night, four Bedouin tribesmen and seven sheep, a common sight in the deserts of Jordan and Iraq and one that I hoped would pass unnoticed.

As soon as we were clear of the village, the tribesman spoke to me. "In that direction," he pointed away from him, "if you walk for twenty miles, you will hit the Syrian border. But the border with Jordan lies this way." He pointed straight ahead. "We are heading for an area where there are fewer Iraqi patrols," he told me. "I hope we do not encounter any, but if we do, you must leave it to me to do the talking. Busy yourself with the sheep, and do not attract attention to yourself."

"What if they ask who I am?"

"We will simply tell them that you are our relative and you are coming with us to sell some sheep."

It didn't seem very convincing to me, but I could do nothing now but trust my guides. I nodded and looked ahead. Even in the twilight I could see the desert stretching out before us, and I wondered how on earth these people would be able to navigate their way through such a featureless expanse of land. Behind us, the lights of the village twinkled in the distance; ahead was a barren, hilly landscape. Small bushes dotted the desert sands, spiky cacti of various sizes, some small and unassuming, others huge and gnarled. "We will take you across the border and point you in the direction of the road that will take you to Amman," the tribesman continued.

"Can't you take me to the road itself?" I asked him. I didn't relish the idea of being left alone in the desert.

He shook his head. "It would be too dangerous. The Jordanian border guards know that we would never travel along that road— we need to make them believe we are traveling between villages, and the road is completely out of the way. If they catch us heading toward it, they will be sure to start asking questions that we do not want to answer, and they will check us out thoroughly. It won't take them long to find you."

As the light failed, it became impossible to see what lay in front of us, but the Bedouin seemed in no way unsure of their route. Soon it was very, very dark. It was not the darkness that I was used to in the city, or even in the desert surrounding my unit; here we had only the light of the moon. We could still just see the village behind us, and somewhere, far away, the distant lights of another settlement. The tribesmen used these landmarks as points of reference and occasionally consulted a compass by the light of a match, but their most important navigational tool was their own knowledge of the desert.

It quickly grew cold—I was glad of my heavy overgarment—and

I became aware of the engulfing silence, the stillness of the desert. The Bedouin talked in low voices ahead of me, and occasionally the sheep bleated; apart from that, other than the sound of our own footsteps, there was no noise.

Suddenly the silence was broken. In the distance I heard an unfamiliar sound, somewhere between a bark and a high-pitched whine. It shocked me, and I stopped walking for a moment. "What is that?" I asked nervously. "What was that howling?"

Slowly Abu Mustapha turned around to look at me. He was smoking a cigarette, and the light from the tip vaguely illuminated his face, giving him a sinister aspect. "They are wolves," he said quietly and in an almost singsong voice.

"If they catch you," added the nephew as if sensing my tension, "they will rip you into little bits!" He grinned at me.

I gave him a flat look. For some reason he was clearly enjoying my discomfort, but I did not let him relish it for too long. I turned away and continued walking; but though I tried to seem nonchalant, beneath my studied calm was a terrible sense of panic. As we continued our slow march, the noise of the howling grew nearer. Whether the wolves had sensed our presence, I couldn't tell; but it was not something I felt I wanted to find out. The tribesman clearly had the same thought. He raised his hand, and we came to a stop. Swiftly he raised his rifle toward the direction of the howling and fired a warning shot. It seemed to do the trick and the howling receded, for now, at least.

The later it got, the more edgy I became. The sound of the wolves had worried me, and in the dark I became increasingly aware that there might be any number of other hidden dangers in the desert that night. I was wearing my army boots, which was a relief because I trod on all manner of unknown, unseen objects and textures. My great fear was that I would tread on a slumbering snake. Had I been wearing my army trousers, it would have been less of

a worry as they were made from tough material; but under my Bedouin *dishdash* I was wearing only thin jeans, which were by no means robust enough to withstand a snakebite. Snakes had always been my greatest phobia, and I do not think I would have been able to continue my journey if I had encountered one.

Every so often, the wolves grew closer, and the tribesman fired a shot toward the sound of the animals to ward them away. The sound of the *berrnaw* was twenty times louder than any handgun, so it encouraged them to stay clear. But I also had reason to be nervous about the gunshots. Each time the tribesman fired, the noise announced our presence to any border guards who happened to be in the vicinity. It seemed unlikely that we were going to avoid being noticed by them for long.

It had been fully dark for about an hour when we first saw the lights of a patrol vehicle. Rather than head straight for us, it drove around us in a circle and then disappeared from sight. "Perhaps they didn't see us," I said to the tribesman.

"No," he replied. "They saw us. They will be back."

He was right. We continued through the desert, and sometime later we saw lights coming from a different direction. Whether or not it was the same patrol, I couldn't tell, but it seemed likely that they had been circling us, either to make us nervous or for some other, more obscure reason. Eventually what looked like a pickup truck approached us straight on, stopping directly in front of us with the headlights beaming straight into our eyes. In the back was a large spotlight, and a guard sat there operating it. I froze momentarily but then remembered what the tribesman had told me: "Busy yourself with the sheep, and do not attract attention to yourself." I took my staff in my hand and started herding the animals, which had started to wander. The tribesman's nephew did the same, calling to the animals as he did so; I kept quiet so as not to attract attention to my accent. Abu Mustapha approached the patrol vehicle as I

made some pretense of checking the luggage strapped to one of the sheep. *"Allah bilkhair! Allah bilkhair!"* he called congenially into the night.

Three patrol officers got down from the car. They did not look friendly. "Who are you?" the driver asked roughly.

"My name is Jaffar Mohammed Hassan, known as Abu Mustapha, from the Al-Shamarry tribe," the tribesman replied smoothly.

"I see," replied the driver. "One of my brothers-in-law married into your tribe. Where are you going, Abu Mustapha?"

"We are taking these sheep to a village nearby to trade, but we have no truck to transport them, so we travel on foot."

The driver did not seem to find this odd—it was common enough for the Bedouin to travel in this way. He turned his attention to the rest of us. "And who are these people?"

"This is my brother, and these are his sons who are helping us."

The driver looked closely at us; I continued to busy myself with the sheep, worried that if I caught his eye he would ask me a question.

"You should come to our house," the tribesman said suddenly to divert the driver's attention. "On behalf of my village, you are most welcome!" It did not seem an odd invitation—such gestures of hospitality are central to Bedouin tradition—but the other two border guards seemed particularly unmoved by it. It served its purpose, however, as he turned his attention away from me and back to the tribesman.

"Abu Mustapha, I expect you all to return to your village, and I do not expect any of you to go missing."

The tribesman smiled. "Of course," he told the driver. "If only my vehicle hadn't broken down." The two other border guards eyed him suspiciously; then they all climbed back into their vehicle. "You are welcome anytime in our village," he called after them as they screeched away across the sands.

I watched them disappear behind a hill. "Do you think they will come back?" I asked the tribesman.

He shrugged. "Who knows?" he answered me noncommittally. "We had better keep moving. The border is very close."

We walked for another hour, and gradually in the distance I started to notice moving lights. "What are they?" I asked nervously. I was still terrified that the patrol would return, and any sign of movement compounded those fears.

"That is where you are headed. It is the road into Amman. We must leave you soon."

Slowly the lights ahead grew imperceptibly closer, and once more the tribesman raised his hand to call us to a halt. "We can't take you any farther," he said. "We have bypassed the two main checkpoints on the road. All you need to do is continue in that direction toward the lights and you will be okay."

I nodded.

"If you hear the wolves, fire some warning shots into the air. It should scare them off."

"Thank you for your help," I said. It seemed inadequate, but what else could I say?

"*Bilsalamah,*" he replied in acknowledgment. "Be safe." He hugged me perfunctorily before quickly kissing me on each cheek. The others followed suit, before silently turning to retrace their steps. It did not take long for my guides to disappear into the blackness, leaving me with nothing but my bag and my gun.

Never had I felt so vulnerable. As the sound of the bleating sheep disappeared, I stood perfectly still and tried to accustom myself to the solitude and the silence. It took me some minutes to compose myself, but with renewed determination I started to make my way toward the road. Now I was alone, and my senses became

more heightened as I strained my eyes and my ears to judge if any unknown danger was close by. Occasionally I looked back and thought that I caught a glimpse of the patrol cars' headlights; but if I did, they were distant—the patrol officers would not be able to see me from so far away. I could just see the road from where I was, and there were no patrols ahead. I would be very unlucky to meet anybody now, but all seemed reasonably silent around me. Unless I was forced to fire the Beretta, I was determined not to do so.

I soon realized, however, that sounds in the desert could be deceptive. More than once I stopped still because I thought I heard an unfamiliar noise alarmingly close, but I told myself over and over again that it was a faraway sound carried to me by the gentle but fickle night breeze. I kept the pace as fast as my wounded leg would allow, keeping my eyes fixed on the occasional light from the road ahead. I realized that it was not only sounds that could be deceiving, but distances also. Although I had no conception of time, the road did not appear to me to be coming any closer, and the longer I hurried through that dark expanse, the more unnerving my solitude became. As I walked, I could feel the swab around my bullet wound become wet—clearly the stitches had opened slightly from the movement.

Then, out of the darkness, I heard a sound I could not ignore, a sound that immediately stopped me dead. It was not new to my ears—it was unmistakably the same howling that I had heard with the tribesmen—but it was shockingly close. I stood perfectly still for some moments, aware only of the trembling whisper of my own heavy breath, before hearing another howl that made the blood stop in my veins. It was as loud as the first and no less desperate. But it was not its closeness that filled me with a sickening sense of horror; it was the direction from which it came. The first howl was somewhere to my right, the second to my left.

I have never known fear like it. A cold wave of dread crashed

over me; I felt nauseous and all the strength seemed to sap from my body. I know I should have fired my gun in the air, but in that minute some other impulse took over, an impulse that forced any faculty of reason from my head and replaced it with blind panic. Foolishly, I ran.

I could never have outrun them. They were lean, desperate, and hungry; this was their territory. I was limping and terrified. The more noise I made, the more I attracted their attention. I became aware of other animals around me—I don't know how many, but it was clear they were hunting as a pack and I was their quarry. Blinded by my tears, I stumbled, and their baying became more frenzied. Then, as if by some prearranged signal, the pack fell silent.

About twenty meters ahead there was a bush. In the darkness, I could scarcely make it out, but I could tell there was movement in there. I stood absolutely still. Vaguely I saw silhouettes ahead, prowling toward me. There were three, maybe four of them. I handled my Beretta nervously; despite my fumbling I managed to release the safety catch, but my hand was shaking too much for me to be sure of an accurate shot even if I had known precisely where I was aiming.

Suddenly the moonlight caught in the eyes of one of the animals, and for a moment it was illuminated. I will never forget its appearance: these were not the furry white wolves I had seen in pictures; they were thin, bony almost, and dirty. There was a madness in their eyes that suggested they were riddled with rabies, and they were more vicious than anything I had ever witnessed, or hope I ever will again. The eyes seemed disproportionately small for the animal's face, but there was something almost human about it; as our glances briefly locked, it snarled and pawed at the sand, baring its teeth and preparing to attack me. I wanted to run, but I knew there was no way I could get away from these fast, hungry beasts; and in any case my legs had frozen to the spot in fear.

Then, as one, they started to run toward me, the momentary silence broken by the wicked sound of their barking and snarling. Almost by reflex, I opened fire.

The magazine of the Beretta contained only fifteen bullets. In quick succession I fired several shots blindly as the wolves ferociously hurled themselves toward me. The first few shots disappeared into the night. Although the noise of the gun stopped the charge of the animals for a moment, they were clearly worked up into a frenzy by the prospect of fresh meat so close; rather than turn and run as I had hoped they might, they scampered around in a circle before continuing their approach. They were close enough for me to smell—a sickening, rotten stench.

Once more I fired, all my skill with a gun dissolved by fear; it was more by luck than judgment that I hit at least one of the animals when they were only meters away from me. I heard them yelp as the bullets seared into their flesh, but I knew I was not safe yet. There was at least one more out there, and suddenly everything had fallen silent once more. I spun around, my arm outstretched and my quivering hand gripping the handle of the gun with all the strength it had, trying to spot whatever wolves remained as I stepped backward away from the bodies of the animals I had hit. How long I continued like that I cannot remember, but gradually I became aware of another sound. I stood listening for some moments before I realized what it was: the noise of one or more wolves biting into the carcasses of their injured—but not yet dead—colleagues.

The animals had been distracted by easier meat, and I had no option but to run. I circled around where I thought the beasts were and headed as fast as I could toward the road. I was shivering from the cold and sweating from fear; the wound in my leg made me limp and slowed me down completely; at one point I stumbled and, thinking in my near-delirious state that I had fallen upon a sleeping snake, I started shouting into the darkness for help. I lay on the

ground trembling for about five minutes; then behind me I became aware of the noise of more wolves fighting over the dead animals. I did not know how long it would take them to strip the meat off the bodies, but I wanted to be well away when they did so. That was the impetus I needed: I pulled myself up and continued to hurry—half running, half limping, always glancing behind me, and occasionally firing one of my few remaining bullets in the direction of the wolves—toward the road.

For forty-five minutes I ran, stopping only occasionally to catch my breath and to vomit onto the sand through fear, propelled more by horror of the wolves than by any desire to reach the road. Eventually I arrived. There were very few cars, and I was in no state to tell whether those that passed were military vehicles or not. I collapsed. The wound in my leg hurt more than ever, and I could feel the sticky wetness of the blood beneath my trousers. I was in shock. I was freezing cold. I was unable even to speak. The lights of the cars in the road blurred before my eyes into a sea of movement, and as nervous exhaustion and delirium set in, I became vaguely aware of what looked like a white border-control vehicle stopping a few meters past me. I heard a confusion of voices around me but could not make out any faces. Out of the confusion I heard a man's voice: "Get him in the car," he said in an accent I didn't recognize, "and we'll take him back to the border crossing."

"No," I rasped, not even knowing who I was talking to. "I can't go back to the border. I need to get to Amman . . ."

But as I spoke the words, my head fell heavily to the ground and blackness engulfed me as I passed out.

PART TWO

NO GOING BACK

CHAPTER 7

AMMAN

When I regained consciousness—perhaps seconds later, perhaps minutes—they were looking over me and talking in hushed tones. I could tell they were male by the sound of their voices, but their faces blurred in and out of focus as I lay there stretched out on the road, and I heard myself repeat the words I had already spoken: "Please, I can't go back to the border. *Don't* take me back to the border."

The blurred faces looked at each other. "What are you doing by the side of the road?" one of them asked without hiding the suspicion in his voice. I tried to answer, but the words that came out of my mouth were confused and incoherent, and suddenly I felt myself being picked up by the arms and dragged along the road toward the car. The wound in my leg throbbed as my heels scraped along the rough surface, but soon enough they gently lowered me back down to the ground.

I looked around me, my head starting to clear. It was still dark, and the lights of the car seemed overly bright to my tired eyes, blinding me and still preventing me from seeing exactly who these

people were. I felt a knot in my stomach as the thought returned to my mind that they must be border patrol guards, and the conversation that followed did nothing to ease my concerns.

"We'd better search him?"

"What for?"

"Find his papers, see who he is. Look at him—he's in no state to tell us himself."

Almost involuntarily I clutched the bag I was holding. I didn't want anyone to start rifling through my things, although I was hardly in a state to deny these officials—if indeed that was who they were.

"We haven't got time for this," one of the men said impatiently. "The sun is coming up soon, and it's a long way to Amman. I don't want to be driving in the heat. Let's just take him back to the border and let them deal with him."

"No," I whispered hoarsely, causing them to look around in surprise that I had spoken again.

The other man bent down in front of me. He was wearing a *dishdash,* and I remember his dark eyes sparkling in the beam of the headlights. "What's your name?" he asked me quietly.

"Sarmed," I told him.

He nodded mutely. "And what are you doing lying by the side of the road, Sarmed?"

I peered more closely at the man. If he was an official, everything about his demeanor was wrong: his clothes, the way he spoke in a concerned voice rather than harshly demanding immediate answers to his questions. But still I couldn't tell him the truth: it would have been reckless of me to come clean especially when his companion—the driver, presumably—seemed so keen to get rid of me and continue with his journey.

As I decided how to answer him, I heard one of the car doors

open. "What's going on?" a voice asked—a woman's voice, which instantly put me more at my ease. Suddenly it seemed much more likely that this was just a family journey. "Who is he?" She walked around to where I was sitting and gently put her hand on my cheek. "You need water," she told me. "I have some in the car." Seconds later she was handing me a bottle, and I drank from it gratefully. The driver was pacing infuriatedly in the background, clearly wanting to be off, and as I finished drinking, his friend repeated his question: "What are you doing here?"

I looked straight into his eyes with all the sincerity I could muster. "My car was stolen," I told him shortly.

He raised an eyebrow, as if urging me to tell him more.

"There were two guys by the side of the road," I continued lying with a little more confidence. "They flagged me down and I pulled over to give them a lift, but they had a gun and they forced me out of the car, beat me up, and then drove away. That's why I'm in such a state."

The man nodded his head, scanning my face for any signs that I was not being truthful. Whether he found any or not, I can't say, but I felt that there was still an air of mistrust around him. "So why don't you want to go back to the border? It's not far—you can report the crime there."

I shook my head violently. "I'm Iraqi," I stated, though it was clear that he already knew that from my accent. "Those guys stole all my papers. If you send me back to the border, I'll never have any chance of finding my car again, and I won't be allowed to stay in Jordan." In the end, I knew, I would simply have to appeal to his better nature, and that of the woman who seemed to have taken a shine to me. "Please," I begged. "I can't go back to Iraq."

"But . . ." he started to protest, but I interrupted him immediately.

"Give me a lift to Amman. *Please.*"

"We can't give him a lift," the driver barked from the darkness on the side of the road. "The car's too full of people as it is. Where are we going to put him?"

The others were quiet. Awkwardly I pushed myself up onto my feet, wincing as a shock of pain ran through my gunshot wound, then peered into the car. The driver had a point. In the front passenger seat was a small, sleepy child—clearly he had been traveling on the lap of whichever adult was sitting there—and in the backseat was a girl of about eight, another older man, and a young man of about my own age. It was full to capacity, but I knew I had to persuade them to take me. My only other option was to wait for a bus, but it was a long, almost empty road. I had no idea how long it would be until a bus passed, and even if one did I was worried about how I would flag it down. I walked around the car, desperately trying to come up with a solution. As I did so, I heard the woman start chanting a prayer in a light, monotone drone. When she had finished, she started entreating the driver. "Don't send him back to the border. Can't you see how scared he is?"

"No." The man was adamant. "There's no room."

"We can squeeze up," she offered.

"Don't be foolish." The driver glanced over at me and then turned back to the woman. "Look at him," he said distastefully. "He stinks."

He was right. I looked down over the heavy *dishdash* the Bedouin had given me and saw the stains where I had vomited in fear. Added to the fact that I had been sweating like never before, I can't have been an appealing prospect. But I couldn't let that get in my way. "I'll hold on to the roof rack," I told them.

The three of them stared back at me uncertainly. "It'll be easy," I said, trying to persuade myself more than them. "I'll sit here," I indicated the small metal frame that was attached to the trunk at the back of the car and on to which their luggage was strapped, "and

hold on to the roof rack here." I climbed onto the luggage to show them. It was uncomfortable crouching there, but I felt that I could manage it for a while.

The man who had been questioning me walked over. "What if you fall? I could bind your hands to the roof rack with rope," he suggested. "That way you'll be safer."

I shook my head. "It's okay," I told him. "I'll be able to hold on." I didn't much like the idea of being shackled to the car. I was used to being on the run now, and I didn't want anything to hinder my escape if that was what was required.

"This is stupid!" The driver stormed back into the fray. "I can't drive to Amman with him clutching on to the back of the car like that. I'll have to drive slowly, and it will take us all day to get there. He'll fry in the heat."

"We won't have to take him all the way." His colleague started to back me up. "Just until we find another vehicle on the road to take him. A taxi or a bus—there's bound to be something coming along soon."

The driver looked pointedly along the road. There were no other cars along the long stretch. "Whatever," he shrugged. "*Yella.* Come on. We haven't got all day." He stomped off, and after a few seconds I heard the unmistakable sound of him urinating against one of the low scrub bushes that lined the road.

The woman looked after him with amusement in her eyes. "Now we've stopped," she said lightly, "we should eat something. Are you hungry?"

I nodded keenly, then sat down again to reserve energy for my next ordeal. Meanwhile, the others got out of the car and eyed me suspiciously and without speaking. The woman placed two bowls in front of me, both wrapped in muslin cloth and tied together at the top with a heavy knot. She unwrapped them and offered me the food they contained. In one bowl was *kofte*—ground meat mixed

with onions and herbs—and in another was bread. "*Tafadel.* Go on," she said, encouraging me to help myself. "Eat." I took some food and devoured it quickly while she offered it around to the rest of the party.

We had been there for about half an hour by the time my rescuers decided to start off again. "Are you sure you'll be able to hold on?" the woman asked me, worry etched on her face.

"He had better be," the driver muttered. "I'm not going to travel along at a snail's pace on his account."

"I'll be fine," I assured the woman. I climbed up onto the back of the car once more, hitched my bag onto my shoulder, pulled my Bedouin robes tighter around me, then clutched the roof rack as firmly as I could while the others clambered back into the car. I closed my eyes, mumbled a quick prayer, and we set off.

At first it seemed as if the driver had been a bit disingenuous. He drove slowly and carefully, taking care not to drive over any bumps in the road. But as his confidence, and mine, increased, so too did his speed. Grim faced, I held on as the wind blew in my face, my eyes half closed to protect them from the elements. It didn't take long for my arms and the rest of my body to become stiff and uncomfortable, so I occasionally allowed myself to let go with one hand as I shuffled myself into a less stressful position before holding on tightly again as the car shuddered at high speed over the less-than-perfect road surface.

As we drove, my mind was doing fireworks. How had I got myself into this position? The wolves were still fresh in my thoughts, and as I squinted out at the bleak expanse of desert that was just starting to lighten up with sunrise, I wondered how many more of those awful beasts were out there. It wouldn't do to find myself alone again at the side of the road—I clutched on to the roof rack with renewed vigor and tried to put all thoughts of falling from my mind.

The road remained fairly empty. Occasionally a car would pass us traveling in the opposite direction, its headlights announcing its presence on the long, straight road a long time before it was actually upon us. Whether their occupants found the sight of a frightened young man clutching on to the back of the car they passed a strange one, I can't say. Nobody stopped to look, and the driver of our car was traveling too fast for anyone to overtake us from behind. It was a far cry from how things would be a few miles up the road in Iraq, where the fear of checkpoints and border guards would have made this way of traveling an impossibility for me. The scenery around me might have been practically identical, but already I could sense the differences between the two sides of the border.

We drove like this for nearly an hour, by which time my arms and wrists were aching from the exertion of holding on so tightly, and nausea was encroaching on me. Every time we hit a bump, I felt the shock, unsoftened by the car's shoddy suspension, reverberate through my whole body. Occasionally my mind wandered as I reflected on the almost dreamlike sequence of the night's events; but I was brought harshly back to reality when I realized that my grip on the roof rack was not as firm as I thought it might be.

Suddenly I felt the car slow down slightly, and the driver veered into the middle of the road, forcing me to steel my body against the force in the opposite direction. I swore under my breath—what was he playing at?—but then I noticed that the driver had put his hazard indicators on. I peered over my shoulder. Behind me were the unmistakable lights of a bus's headlights, and in the instant I became aware of them, there was a deafening noise, a screeching siren of a horn as the bus driver tried to stop the strange car ahead from driving so dangerously. My nerves already frayed, I wanted to close my ears with my hands, but that wasn't an option as I had to maintain my grip on the car; instead I scrunched up my face and tried to calm my body from the shock the noise had given me. The car's

driver, however, remained firm. He stayed in the center of the road, gradually slowing down and waving his arm out of the window to indicate to the bus driver that he should pull over. Whether it occurred to the bus driver that this was strange behavior—more befitting a bandit trying to hijack the bus or a couple of drunks fooling around—I don't know; certainly I remember simply feeling relief that I might soon be able to find myself a more comfortable mode of transport. After ten minutes of driving like this, the two vehicles gradually came to a stop in the middle of the road.

The two men climbed out of the front of the car and walked toward the bus. "Stay there," one of them told me as they passed. "We'll do the talking." I did as I was told.

There was a hiss as the bus doors opened, and after a few seconds' pause, two men climbed out of the bus—the driver and conductor, I presumed. One of them, a short, squat man with an ugly face, was carrying what looked like a piece of heavy metal piping strapped to his hand with a sturdy length of leather. The way he was holding it made it perfectly clear that this was something that had been specially adapted to be a weapon, and that he was perfectly prepared to use it without any qualms. For a moment nobody spoke, and the threat of violence hung in the air.

"What do you think you're playing at?" the man holding the piping finally growled at my two new acquaintances.

The man who had been sitting in the passenger seat pointed at me. "He needs a lift. We can't travel with him like that for much longer."

None of the suspicion left the other man's face. "Does he have any money?"

"I don't know. I'll ask him." He walked back to me. "Well, do you?" he asked.

"A little," I said warily. "American dollars."

He reported this back to the coach driver, whose eyes softened

slightly although he maintained his grip on the metal piping as he walked up to me. "Okay," he asked, "what's your name?"

I told him.

"You're from Iraq?"

I nodded.

"Which tribe?"

"The Alsamari."

"And what happened to you?"

I repeated the story about my car being stolen, taking care to make sure the details I relayed were the same as those I had told earlier. The driver listened without much interest. "Where do you want to go?" he asked when I had finished.

"Amman."

"It will cost you thirty-five American dollars."

Thirty-five dollars. A sizable chunk of the money my grandmother had given me only three days before, but I wasn't in a position to haggle. I immediately fished inside my bag and brought out a handful of crumpled notes, counted them out carefully, and handed them to him. He nodded curtly and indicated to me with a flick of his thumb that I should board the bus.

Painfully, but with some sense of relief, I climbed down from the car and approached the two men who had given me the lift. "Thank you for your help," I told them simply.

The driver didn't respond—he just walked back to the car. But his friend gave me a little more time. "*Bilsalamah,*" he said. "*Inshallah* you'll find your car." We exchanged a meaningful look, and as our eyes met I realized he probably hadn't believed a word of my story.

"Thank you," I said again as he walked back to the car. I stood there for a minute, watching the car head off along the road, before I was hurried onto the bus by the conductor.

The bus itself was packed with maybe forty people. They all

looked at me curiously as I climbed on, but by this time I was too exhausted to allow their stares to worry me. There was no chance of a seat—even the conductor was sitting in the aisle—so I dumped my bag on the floor and prepared myself for a long, uncomfortable journey to Amman.

It didn't take much time for the other passengers to grow used to the sight of me, for the mild excitement caused by my arrival to subside. And now that it was clear to the conductor that I was not a threat to him, he started to become a bit more friendly, asking me questions that I didn't really want to answer. What was my name again? How many people were there who robbed me? What did they take? What was I going to do? His questions were well-meaning enough, I suppose, just intended to pass the time, but I was in no mood to answer them with anything but the curtest responses, and eventually he fell silent and left me to my own thoughts.

Everything had happened so quickly in the last few days that I had scarcely had the chance to organize the events in my head. It seemed impossible that only five nights ago I had still been in the confines of the army barracks near Basra, a place that seemed a million miles away from me now. As I thought back over the events that had followed my escape, I realized how lucky I had been. Had the coin fallen differently on any number of occasions, I would have been enjoying circumstances very different from the ones in which I found myself. It made the discomfort of the cramped bus seem a bit more bearable. Every time the vehicle slowed down, though, I had to suppress a shudder of fear, and I realized that I had been living with constant terror of being stopped and searched. Just because I had managed to cross the border didn't mean that I could simply shrug that terror off. My passport, with its fake Jordanian entry stamps, would not stand up to prolonged, professional scrutiny, and although checkpoints and security guards were not a part of daily

life in Jordan as they were in Iraq, I did not find it easy to escape the paranoia that had been with me for most of my life.

It was not just fear of capture that knotted my stomach; it was fear of the unknown. Up until now I had focused solely on making it across the border into Jordan. All my energy had been channeled into that one aim, but I had not given much thought to what I would do once I arrived here. I had very little money and I knew nobody. Had anyone asked me, I would have told them that my plan was to travel to England to live with my uncle; but at that moment England seemed like an impossible dream.

The bus trundled on, and I remained lost in my thoughts.

I was awakened from my daydream by the sound of a woman's voice. I looked up to see her sitting there—an old lady, clearly an Iraqi, next to a young child—telling him to move and let me have his seat. I shook my head. "It's okay," I told her. "I'm fine. Don't worry."

But with quiet firmness, she insisted. "Come and sit here. You're tired; you've had a rough day. The boy can swap with you—he'll be fine." The child looked at me with wide eyes and nodded, so I gratefully accepted the old woman's offer and took the seat by the window. We started chatting, but somehow I did not find her questioning as intrusive as the conductor's. I told her my name and repeated the story of my car being stolen, and even proudly told her that I was traveling to Amman en route to England. It made me feel better to tell her that, almost as if I was making the plans in my head more concrete. I refrained from asking her too many questions about what she was doing in Jordan, because I knew she was unlikely to have had much difficulty being granted permission to leave Iraq. It was the way with elderly people—too old to be of any use in the country, they were allowed to leave so as to be less of a burden. Saddam had no use for old ladies; it was fit young men like me that he wanted.

It was much lighter by now, and as we journeyed on I found

myself gazing out of the window. Every few minutes we passed a hostel of some description on the side of the road, and only then did it suddenly sink in that I was not only in a different country but almost in a different world. It was small things that spoke to me, things the Jordanians no doubt took for granted, but they jumped out to me as sights that I would never see in Iraq. Some of the hostels were advertising ice cream; others had bananas hanging from the walls. I was astonished. Bananas on display? Nobody would be so idiotic in Baghdad as to do that—someone would steal them within minutes and probably attack the owner for good measure. But the thing that made my eyes pop out more than anything were the crates of Coca-Cola, full of one-liter bottles piled high outside the hostels. Flashing signs advertised the distinctive logo. I hadn't seen Coca-Cola for years, not since the sanctions had been established against Iraq in 1990, just before the first Gulf War, and the sight was as curious to me as piles of gold bars would have been to a Westerner. If crates of Coke had been spotted in Baghdad in such numbers, they would have been fallen upon by thirsty young Iraqis like vultures pouncing on dead meat. It was that, more than anything else, that brought home to me the fact that I was no longer in a military state. This was a place where tourists came, with their sunglasses and their disposable income to spend on luxuries like ice cream and Coca-Cola. I found the sight vaguely comforting. Resting my head against the window, and watching these places as they sped past, I soon fell into a deep sleep.

By the time I awoke it was about nine o'clock, and the scenery around me had grown more urban as we drove through the outskirts of Amman. The road was better here, and modern-looking buildings were intermingled among the white tenement blocks and the colorful domes of the many mosques. Expensive cars shared the road with run-down vehicles, and I even saw other buses full of

tourists. It was an unfamiliar sight: very few people came on vacation to Baghdad.

Eventually the bus pulled up outside a line of white buildings. "The hotel," my newfound companion said shortly. I looked at it through the window. There was nothing to indicate that that was what it was, but as I looked, the passengers started to get their belongings together and head for the door. I realized that this was some sort of package that included accommodations at the hotel, which suggested to me that a room would be cheap. If I was going to stay there, it would have to be—my money was already dwindling and I had been in Jordan for only a matter of hours. I approached the hotel with the old lady and her young companion, and we waited our turn at the reception desk.

"How much for a room?" I asked the bored-looking hotel employee when our turn came.

He quoted me a figure much too high for my meager budget, and the concern must have shown clearly on my face because the old lady instantly came to my aid.

"It's okay," she told me. "You can stay with us."

My eyes flickered toward the desk clerk, but he was perfectly uninterested in my sleeping arrangements.

"Thank you," I told the old lady. "I'll give you some money . . ."

But she dismissed my offer with a wave of her hand as though she were brushing off a troublesome insect. "For a night or two it will be fine. But perhaps you would be good enough to help us carry our luggage upstairs."

The hotel was far from glamorous. A small elevator took us up several floors to our room, which was sparsely furnished—a couple of beds and a wooden table. I put the old lady's luggage down, then rather sheepishly laid my putrid robes on the floor as a makeshift mattress.

"You look tired," the woman said, and she was right. My few hours' snooze on the bus had done nothing to alleviate the desperate fatigue I was feeling, but I knew there was no chance of sleeping now. My mind was dancing with the excitement and apprehension of being in a new city, but I also had something urgent to attend to.

My bullet wound had not received any attention since the Bedouin's house. Since then I had gone through a punishing amount of physical exertion, and I knew from the sinister throbbing in my leg that the wound needed cleaning. The last thing I wanted to do was take myself to a doctor or a hospital, so I realized I would have to attend to it. I excused myself to my benefactor and went in search of a pharmacy. It didn't take long to find one, and I spent a few of my precious dollars on clean bandages and an alcohol solution to disinfect the wound. Back at the hotel I was relieved to see that my roommates had gone out, so I sat on one of the beds and removed my jeans. The wound was as bad as I expected: blood had seeped out and stained the bandage a dirty brown, then dried in streaks down the length of my leg. I gingerly unwrapped the bandage, wincing slightly as it unpeeled from the wound, then steeled myself for the inevitable sting as I dabbed the alcohol solution onto the raw, exposed flesh. As I did so, the memory of falling in the desert, not knowing if the wolves were ahead of me or behind me, flashed in front of my eyes; I felt suddenly giddy as the enormity of what I had gone through in the last twenty-four hours hit me yet again. It took a moment for me to regain my composure; then I tightened a clean bandage over the wound and pulled my dirty jeans on once more.

Again it struck me how tired I was, that perhaps I should try to get some sleep. But time wasn't on my side. I couldn't stay in this room forever, no matter how benevolent the old lady might be feeling. I had to make arrangements for myself, and to do that I needed to get my bearings and make inquiries. I needed to head to downtown Amman.

CHAPTER **8**

THE COMFORT OF STRANGERS

A mman is a city of refugees—Palestinians from the west, Iraqis
from the east. It is a melting pot of cultures. For some it is a new
home, for others simply a staging post on the way to somewhere
more hospitable. For me it was ideal: I could blend into the scenery
and, without the constant fear of the Republican Guard around
every corner, perhaps even allow myself a little breathing space. But
I couldn't become complacent. My passport was fake, as were the
stamps on it that allowed me access to Jordan. Even if they fooled
people, I was allowed to be in the country for only six months, after
which time, if anybody scrutinized them I risked deportation back
to Iraq and all the horrors that awaited me there. I needed to start
work immediately on gaining passage to the West, to a place where
I could claim political asylum from oppression. To England.

I was a stranger in a strange country. I had no friends, little
money, and no idea where to go to get the help and information I
needed. I had overheard some of the Iraqis on the bus saying that
when they arrived in Amman they would head immediately for an
area called Hashemite Square, and the hotel desk clerk confirmed

with something of a sneer that this was where the Iraqis in Jordan tended to congregate. His manner suggested that he had opinions of his own about such people, but he kept them to himself and I followed his directions to find this place.

Hashemite Square seemed a lively, built-up area. Along the side of the main road was a vibrant collection of shops, behind which rose a hillside covered with a crowded jumble of white houses and tenement blocks. On the other side was a verdant parkland with trees and lakes. A stark white, modern clock tower stood in the middle, and at its base groups of young men sat talking animatedly. The whole area was full of people milling around, and the air was thick with the distinctive Iraqi dialect of Arabic. Nobody paid me any attention whatsoever—to them I was just another face, and I found that blanket of anonymity a comfortable one. I realized how thirsty I was, so I took a seat in a nearby fast-food joint and ordered a milkshake—cold and sweet, just what my body was craving. After my first few thirsty gulps, I slowed down and pulled out a piece of paper from my pocket. Crumpled and dirty, it was the scrap on which Saad had written the name and phone number of his friend Wissam. I remembered Saad's words: when I arrived, I was to hunt up Wissam.

I felt uncomfortable making the call. I had no idea who this man was, and I didn't even know what I was going to ask him. Surely my call would seem suspicious—the chances were good that he would want nothing to do with this unknown Iraqi boy with nowhere to stay and hardly any money, never mind who his uncle was. I didn't know what kind of favor Saad had afforded this man to make him so sure he would help me, but I did know that some favors were soon forgotten and reluctantly repaid.

Still, experience had taught me that I could trust Saad's judgment in these matters, and besides, I didn't have any other choice. That crumpled-up piece of paper was the only collateral I had. I

slurped the remainder of my milkshake and went to find a telephone.

I dialed the number. The phone rang several times. I was on the
verge of hanging up when someone finally answered. "Hello?" The
voice at the other end growled its greeting rather unenthusiastically.

"Good afternoon," I replied as politely as possible. "My name
is Sarmed Alsamari. I'm the nephew of Saad Al-Khatab from
Baghdad."

The sound of his voice was like the sun coming out. "Saad Al-
Khatab!" he exclaimed. "Of course! How is he?"

"He's well, and he sends his regards."

"Saad is a good man. What can I do for you, Sarmed?" His voice
was booming and jolly.

I lowered my voice slightly, though for what reason I can't say—
probably out of habit. "I've just arrived in Jordan from Iraq. I don't
know anybody here, so Saad suggested I call you . . ." My voice
trailed off.

"Of course." His voice became more sober. "Where are you
now?"

"In Hashemite Square."

"And where are you staying?"

"In a hotel on the outskirts."

I heard him sucking on his teeth in thought. "Okay," he said
finally. "I'll tell you where I live." He recited an address in an
unfamiliar-sounding area, before explaining which bus I would need
to take to get there. "It's a little way outside of Amman," he told me.
"Let's meet tomorrow and we'll see what we can do for you."

I thanked him profusely and put the phone down feeling more
confident than I had in days.

Before I could walk away, there was one more phone call I had
to make. I lifted the receiver, dialed the operator, and for half an
hour waded through the bureaucratic red tape that was necessary to

make a call to Baghdad. Eventually, a familiar voice answered. As I spoke, I could hear my own voice cracking. "Uncle Saad," I said quietly. "It's me."

Saad was silent for a moment, as though he did not dare hear the answer to the question he had to ask. "Where are you?"

"In Amman," I told him, unable to withhold a grin even though I knew he couldn't see it.

Saad let out an explosive breath. "Thanks be to Allah," he whispered. "Did you have any trouble?"

"A little," I told him, not wanting to worry his mind with the realities of what had happened since I last saw him. "I am meeting with your friend tomorrow."

"Excellent," Saad replied. "He is a good man. I'm sure he will help you." I couldn't help feeling that he did not sound entirely confident about that. "I'll tell your mother that you are well. In the meantime, keep your head down and don't get into trouble. And Sarmed."

"Yes, Uncle Saad."

"Don't forget what I told you."

His parting words echoed in my mind. *The genuine man never forgets his family. We are sending you to freedom so that one day you may rescue them from this place.*

"I won't forget, Uncle Saad," I told him sincerely. "Hug my mother for me."

The conversation lasted no more than a minute.

I spent the rest of the day simply enjoying being able to walk around without fear. As evening fell and the heat of the sun dissipated, I noticed more and more crowds of young people appearing in the area. There were all sorts of nationalities there—Jordanians, Iraqis, Syrians, Lebanese, Saudis—and they congregated in groups, laughing, eating ice cream, having something to drink. Not having eaten since early that morning by the roadside, I approached a stall

selling street food. A group of young men about my age were hanging around there, and somehow we fell into conversation. "Where are you from?" one of them asked me.

I looked around nervously. In Iraq, you entered carefully into conversations with strangers on the street, because you never knew who had the ear of the authorities. The idea of spilling my secrets to some person I had just met was anathema to me, but there was something about this guy's demeanor—a lack of interest that suggested he was making idle conversation rather than pumping me for incriminating information—that made me feel I could trust him. "Baghdad," I told him. "I arrived today."

"Staying long?"

I shrugged. "I don't know. I want to get to England."

"To claim asylum?" He sounded as if it was the most natural thing in the world, and I nodded a little warily.

"Have you been to the UN yet?"

"The UN?" The question surprised me. "No. Why would I want to do that?"

The guy smiled at me as if indulging a naive child. "To get yourself on their lists. Sometimes they provide refugees with passage to a safer country. You never know, it might be quicker than whatever else you had in mind."

Just then one of his friends interrupted. "Be careful, though."

"What for?"

"There are all sorts of rumors going around that the place is watched." Without taking his eyes off me, he took a slurp from the glass bottle of Coke he was drinking through a straw.

"Who by?"

"Spies," he said shortly. "Military police from Iraq or wherever, put there to keep an eye out for people who skipped the country illegally. Not that I'm saying that's what you did." He smiled and winked knowingly.

"What about the Jordanians?" I asked, a bit disconcerted by this news. "Is it worth asking them to grant me asylum?" It wasn't something I had particularly planned to do, but I figured that it was best to know what all my options were.

The guy laughed, a short, ugly bark that betrayed his contempt for the Jordanian system. "Sure, you can try," he told me. "They'll put your name on a list and you'll never hear from them again. At best you'll be forgotten; at worst you'll be alerting them to the fact that you're here illegally. Don't let yourself feel too welcome in this town, my friend. They only tolerate our presence because of the cheap oil they're getting from our country—if it wasn't for that, we'd be out of here faster than you can say 'Abu Ghraib.'" He laughed again, at his own joke this time, before wandering off with his friends.

It had been a sobering conversation. In my overwhelming desire to get to Jordan, it had not really crossed my mind that such tensions would be something I would encounter, but now that it had been spelled out to me it made perfect sense. And as if to confirm my newfound discovery, as I was wearily making my way back to my hotel an incident occurred that underlined how careful I needed to be. I had just left Hashemite Square and was looking around, drinking in the sights and sounds of the quarter where I would clearly be spending a fair amount of my time, when I passed a group of young men and women not much older than myself. Suddenly one of them called out to me, and it was clear from his accent that he was Jordanian. "*Alaa waaish bidahik*," he shouted. "What are you looking at?"

I stopped, suddenly frozen by the aggressive sound in his voice, and didn't answer.

I shook my head. "I'm not," I mumbled.

"What is it? Do you want to fight me?" He was walking toward me now, his gait lurching in a way that suggested he had been drink-

Above: My mother and me in our garden in Iraq.

Left: With my sister at home in Iraq in 1981.

Left: My beautiful mother in happier days when we first arrived in Manchester.

Below: With my mother, brother, and sister on a trip to the Arndale shopping center in Manchester.

Below: My ninth birthday party at home in Manchester with my brother, sister, and some friends from school.

BISHOP BILSBORROW PRIMARY SCHOOL

Princess Road
Manchester
M14 7LS

J.4.

Mathematics	C+	A satisfactory result but Samad finds problems quite difficult. He must concentrate more and when in difficulty seek teacher help and not rely upon his friends
Reading and Language Development	B	Has made good progress in his reading which has been reflected in his written work
Science	B	Samad works well in a group situation and takes an active part in discussion and investigation activities
Environmental Studies		Has enjoyed the visits and produced some good work which has been displayed.
Physical Activities		Always tries hard and applies himself well to team games. Progress has been made in his swimming.
Creative Activities		Has potential in art and craft showing a special talent in modelling in clay. Has used this talent in other subject areas.
Social and Personal Development		A pleasant boy who enjoys school. Samad will talk about any problems he has and not become anxious about them.
General Comments on Year		A reliable and trustworthy boy who has worked hard this year to do well. If he continues this approach he will progress at St Thomas Aquinas.

Teacher ....A.M.Roman..........

Top and left: The party to celebrate our last day at primary school in Manchester.

Background: My report from my final year at primary school.

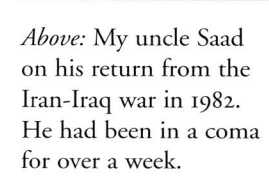

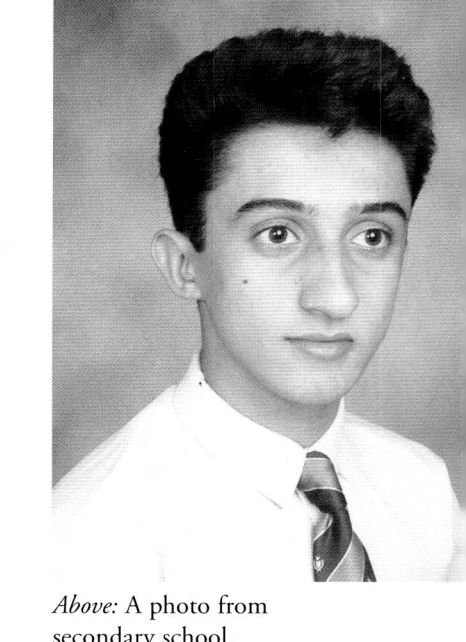

Above: A photo from secondary school.

Above: My uncle Saad on his return from the Iran-Iraq war in 1982. He had been in a coma for over a week.

Right: With my physics teacher and high school classmates in Mosul.

Below: The counterfeit student ID card I used to get out of Iraq in 1994.

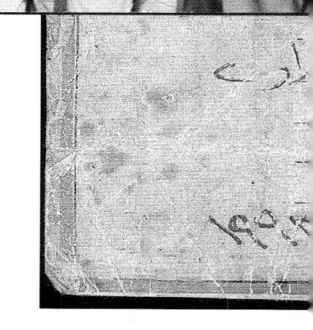

هوية الطالب

الاسم الثلاثي : سعيد .. السامرائي
الصف والشعبة : السادس العلمي .ب
اسم المدرسة : الاعدادية الشرقية
المديرية العامة للتربية في : نينوى

نافذة لغاية ٩/٣٠ / ١٩٩٤

Left: With two of my friends in Mosul at the medical clinic in the College of Agriculture and Forestry.

Below: With my biology teacher and two of my best friends in high school.

Below: My military ID card.

Left: At work in Jordan.

Right: My ID card with the fake name from the counterfeit UAE passport that I used to travel to Malaysia.

The British Council

LIBRARY
ADULT MEMBERSHIP

Family Name ; *MOHAMED AHMED*

First Names : *MR. AADEL*

Expiry Date : *27. 11. 96*

No. **0664**

Below: In the office at the company I worked for in Jordan.

Left: Working out at the gym in Amman—a home away from home.

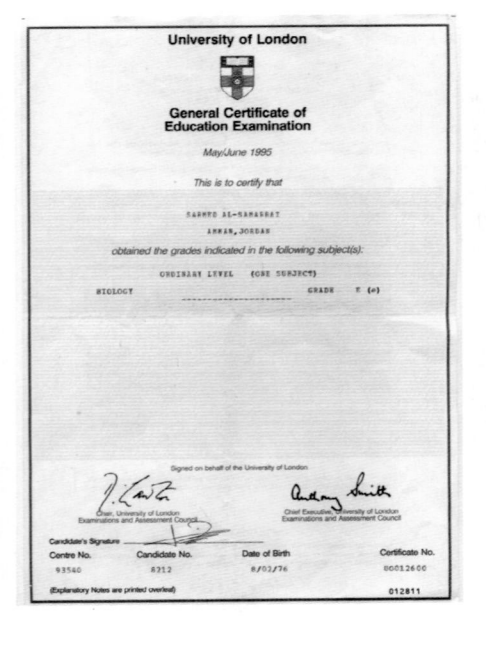

Right: In Hashemite Square in 1995, just before I left Jordan.

Below left: The picture of myself in Amman I sent home to my family in Iraq.
Below right: The certificate from my biology O-level, which I took in Amman in preparation for medical school.

Left: In *United 93*, playing the role of the lead hijacker.

Diploma

ASSOCIATE ACTING DIPLOMA

ALAM

awarded to

LOUIS ALSAMARI

Summer 2003   Head of Examinations

Patron: H R H Princess Alexandra, The Hon. Lady Ogilvy GCVO

Below: My first reunion with Uncle Saad in Syria in 2007.

Right: Outside my house in London.

ing. I took a step backward, but he continued to bear down on me. He pushed me heavily against my chest and I stumbled.

"Look, my friend," I started to say. "I'm not looking for trouble . . ." But as I spoke I saw the sight of a uniform at the other end of the street. Immediately my fear of the confrontation was supplanted by my inbuilt horror of uniforms. Every instinct in my body shrieked at me to get away, to avoid being asked questions I didn't want to answer by a figure of authority.

I walked briskly away with the words "Fucking Iraqis!" ringing in my ears.

First thing the following morning, having showered at the hotel so that my body at least was a little cleaner, I made my way to UN headquarters. I had not forgotten the warning I had heard the previous night, but I had decided to take a calculated risk. If these talked-about Iraqi spies were real, how would they spot me from among the tens of thousands of other Iraqis in Amman at the time? My passport was good enough to pass a cursory examination, and after all this was the UN. If I didn't feel safe there, where would I?

The headquarters was housed in a quiet residential area of Amman, surrounded by pretty gardens and tall metal railings. A number of people were milling around outside, but as I approached the gate with as great an air of confidence as I could muster, I avoided meeting anybody's eye because I didn't want to betray my nervousness. I have legitimate business, I kept telling myself over and over again. I have a right to be here.

Nobody approached me as I walked in. The scene inside could not have been more different from the calmness of the exterior. It was bedlam. Despite the early hour, all sorts of people were there, refugees from Sudan, Somalia, and all over the Middle East, chattering loudly to one another in languages that I did not understand.

I stood there for a moment in a daze, not quite sure what to do, before joining a line marked "Asylum Requests" and awaiting my turn to be interviewed.

When my turn came, I sat down at the desk nervously. "Fill this in," the official in charge said without even looking at me. I scrawled the few details that were required of me on the sheet, then handed it back. Finally the official looked me in the eye, his contempt and boredom written plainly across his face. "Where are you from?" he asked me in a tone of voice that immediately reminded me of the corrupt checkpoint guard who had detained me on my way back to Baghdad.

"Iraq," I told him, shifting uncomfortably in my seat. This was not the welcome I had expected from the UN.

"Do you have permission to be here?"

I shook my head.

"Why do you need political asylum?"

"I believe my life is in danger if I return to my home country." I thought this sounded dramatic, but the official had clearly heard it a thousand times before. He looked at me with suspicion, as if deciding what to do with me—though in truth I don't suppose he had the authority to do anything other than process me as he had everyone else. Finally he stamped my form and gave me a date several weeks hence when I was to return for further interviewing. He beckoned the next person in line before I even stood up to leave.

I left the room feeling slightly bemused. I had expected UN headquarters to be a haven, a place where I would feel safe, where my past would be something to invoke sympathy, not suspicion. In reality, I was just another number, an illegal alien, a statistic. Nobody was interested in me as an individual. With a start I realized that I could rely on nobody but myself to ensure my safety—and the fulfillment of my dream to make it to England.

Hitching the small bag that contained everything I owned far-

ther up on my shoulder, I stood at the gates of the UN for a moment to gather my thoughts, this time taking in my surroundings in greater detail. There seemed to be more people outside now than when I had gone in, and I took a brief moment to scan the faces of those around me. Some of them were hanging around in groups, others sitting on benches across the road. On the street corner I noticed one man just standing there, loitering. He was wearing Western clothing, and he would have been entirely unremarkable had it not been for the fact that he was staring directly at me. I tore my gaze from him and tried to look nonchalant, but when I glanced back his eyes were still fixed on mine. Immediately I found myself short of breath, with nauseous waves of panic crashing over me as the warning I had received the previous night rang in my head. I started walking briskly away in the opposite direction. Desperately I tried not to look back so as to avoid calling attention to my nervousness, but in the end I couldn't stop myself.

The man was no longer on the street corner.

I stopped, turned around, and scanned the crowds to see if he was still among them. No sign—until suddenly he walked out from behind a group of people. He started ambling coolly toward me, and even though I had no way of knowing whether he really had any interest in me or not, I was overcome by a paranoia that would let me do only one thing: run. Not caring how conspicuous I made myself, I turned and fled, losing myself in a maze of backstreets. I ran with a painful limp for five or ten minutes, all the while glancing back over my shoulder to check that I wasn't being followed. I invited curious glances as I hurtled down the streets in my filthy clothes, seemingly running from nothing and with sweat moistening my skin. But when I stopped, it was not out of a desire to stay still. Out of the blue I was almost floored by an excruciating, burning sensation in my stomach. I stumbled to a halt, then bent double as I gasped for breath—half on account of my exertions, half on

account of the terrible, piercing pain that was ripping through my abdomen. I collapsed on the side of the road, unable to move, and waited until this sinister pain had subsided.

The relief I felt when it had done so was like a balm. I touched my hands to my cheeks and realized they were wet from unnoticed tears, so I wiped my face with the back of my hand and tried to regain my composure. Part of me felt foolish, as though I had been running from shadows; but I knew that in the same situation, I would do the same thing again. I had come too far to throw everything away through carelessness. What the pain in my stomach had been I had no idea. Probably just hunger, or maybe stress, but I couldn't worry about it now, as there was too much to do. I went to find someone of whom I could ask directions back to Hashemite Square, from where the buses out of Amman departed. It was time to meet Saad's friend.

Wissam lived with his wife and children in a well-to-do Christian area some miles out of Amman. After an uneventful bus journey, I approached his house with a certain amount of trepidation. It was a large, beautiful place draped in grapevines and with fruit trees in the courtyard, not the sort of place I expected to find myself on my second day in Jordan. I knocked rather timidly at the door, unsure what to expect. The man who greeted me was friendly, if formal at first, tall and good-looking with piercing green eyes. He introduced me to his family, his wife brought us some tea, and we sat down to talk. As we dealt with the necessary pleasantries, I immediately gained the impression that despite his friendliness, he was a firm man, somebody who knew what he wanted in life and was comfortable with the position he had achieved. I could trust him, I knew; but I would not be able to overstep the mark. He would help me so far, and no farther.

"Now that I think about it, I remember you," he said mysteriously when we had made ourselves comfortable in the shade of the

vines forming a canopy over the courtyard. I looked at him questioningly. "When I came to Baghdad to study in the seventies, you were just a little baby." He smiled at the memory. "Your uncle took care of me when I was a stranger in a strange land. He showed me where to go and what to do, and even let me stay with him for a while. I would be repaying him poorly if I did not do the same thing for you."

"Thank you," I said sincerely.

He sat back in his chair. "Why don't you tell me everything?" he asked.

I closed my eyes, took a deep breath, and started to tell my story: how they had wanted me to join military intelligence; how I had escaped the barracks; how Saad had helped me to get out of Iraq. Certain things I kept to myself—the shooting, the journey across the desert with the Bedouin—so as not to make myself sound too dangerous a charity case. All the while I spoke, Wissam stayed silent, nodding gently, and I realized that although some Jordanians—like the youths with whom I had had a run-in the previous night—resented the presence of Iraqis in their territory, others, like the man in front of me, understood what the reality of life was like in our country and were prepared to help us. It was a reassuring moment.

When I was finished, he was silent for a while as if he was mulling my story over in his mind. Finally he spoke. "Do you have money?"

"A few American dollars. Not enough."

"And what is your plan from now on?"

"To get to England and study to become a doctor."

He nodded silently. "And how do you propose to do that?"

"I don't know. There must be a way, but I'll have to make inquiries . . ." I knew it sounded feeble even as I spoke the words, but it was the truth.

Wissam waved his hand as if to indicate that he didn't want to hear about such things. He knew that I was alluding to an underground world of false documents and people-smugglers, and he clearly didn't want to go down that path. He clapped his hands briskly to divert me from the subject. "You'll need a job, then," he said in a businesslike fashion. "What can you do?"

Of all the questions he could have asked me, that was the one for which I was the least prepared. I had never really had a job, and my academic qualifications, such as they were, seemed next to useless now. "I can speak English," I told him with a shrug.

"Okay," he told me. "That's good. Tomorrow I'll take you around, speak to a few friends. We'll see if we can find you some work. In the meantime, until you get a place for yourself, you can sleep here."

As he promised, the following day he started taking me around to places he knew that might be able to offer me a job. We started out at a baker's shop, but when they found out that I had never worked in a bakery before, they rejected me out of hand. "I'm sorry," Wissam was told. "He has no expertise. We've got Iraqis who know how to bake bread lining up for jobs." Everywhere we went it was the same story, and as the day progressed I started to grow demoralized—and so, I think, did Wissam.

"It looks like there are a lot of Iraqis trying to find work," I said to him at one point. "Too many. What if I'm not successful?"

He didn't answer.

Eventually he took me to the last place on his list. "It's a company I know," he told me vaguely, before explaining that it was run by three Iraqi brothers. The law stated, however, that you had to be Jordanian in order to own a company, so foreigners paid Jordanians to front their affairs for them. The man we were about to meet was the Jordanian front for the company.

"Their business is imports and exports, and they have offices in Baghdad. I'm sure they'll be impressed that you speak English, but I imagine they'll want to know if you have any degrees or more advanced qualifications. Just tell them you have."

I nodded. Dissembling was becoming second nature to me now, and I knew that if I could lie my way through Iraqi checkpoints, I could lie about a few examinations. Besides, I liked the sound of this place. A proper company. There would be desks and carpets, people doing business—it sounded a lot better than the sweltering kitchens of the bakery that I had been to see, and maybe I would learn something useful. I wondered why Wissam had left this place till last.

The man we were led in to see was enormous—one of the fattest people I have ever witnessed—with a long, scraggly brown beard. He had the unusual and slightly off-putting habit of placing his left thumb under his left armpit and digging it into his ribs, almost as if he was massaging his overstrained heart. His name was Khalil Bakir, and he looked at me with utter disdain. I had the impression that Wissam was a client of his and that that was the reason I was being given so much as the time of day.

"Can you make tea and coffee?" he asked in response to Wissam's inquiry about job openings, surprising me because I had been preparing myself to answer much more complicated questions.

"Yes," I replied meekly.

"Good. You can start the day after tomorrow. One hundred dinars a month."

And so it was that I became an employee of the company.

On my first day at work they took a photocopy of my passport without paying it much attention. It was little more than a formality to them. Wissam had vouched for me and clearly his word was trusted, and in any case they were in no position to tell a genuine passport from a fake one. My job was to make tea and coffee for

Bakir and his brother, do a bit of cleaning up, and run a few errands, and it wasn't long until I started to learn more about the company and its workings.

The first thing that struck me was how little work everybody seemed to do. The office was staffed by Bakir's family as a condition for him fronting the company. Clearly Bakir had told his Iraqi colleagues that if they wanted to set up in business, his nearest and dearest would have to receive paychecks. His family members were illiterate—they neither read nor wrote Arabic, which was not uncommon—and they did literally nothing other than sit around chatting and drinking the tea I made them. I remember thinking, perhaps slightly naively, that the import-export business must be a very profitable one in order to allow the management to keep on such a large number of unused staff. It was not up to me to say anything, however, because Bakir, their benefactor, had me under his thumb.

There was something about his demeanor that terrified me. I can't explain what it was, but I do remember wondering why it was that I, who had escaped the army, been shot, and fought with wild wolves in the desert, was so scared of this one man. Perhaps it was the fact that he now held my livelihood in his hands. Iraqis were treated like scum in Amman. I was lucky to have this job, and it was the only way available to me to earn enough money to continue with my plans. Bakir knew he had a hold on me, and he took advantage of that to make me work hard: his gaze was ferocious, and his eyes followed me around the office as I went about my business, keeping me well and truly in line. I exercised all the politeness I had on him, but most of the time he seemed impervious to it, like a smooth, fat rock that would not shine no matter how many times it was buffed.

Deep down, though, Bakir had a heart. On occasions his sons, who were younger than I—one about fourteen, the other perhaps

ten—used to come into the office. They were well dressed, and their full faces spoke of a healthy, plentiful diet and privileged lifestyle— a stark contrast to my ragged and undernourished features. I used to envy them and wonder why life had not rolled the dice for me a bit differently. Sometimes, after his sons had been to the office, I caught Bakir looking at me thoughtfully, as though the difference in our circumstances was not lost on him. And so, although he treated me with brusqueness, he also did his best to help me.

He knew that I spoke English—he himself spoke very little— and after a while, once it had become clear to him that he could trust me, he started giving me little jobs to do. Writing a letter, translating something—little tasks that an English-speaker was suited to. Then after about nine months and after I had demonstrated my ability, he sacked his secretary and put me in her place. It was a brutal move, and one that did nothing to dispel my fear of the huge man, even if what he had done was in my favor. I felt as if I was strangely favored but had a sword hanging over me nevertheless. I shuddered to imagine what Bakir's reaction would be if he knew the truth about my past. Doubtless nobody in the company really expected this young Iraqi man to be around forever, but every instinct informed me that my story was best left untold.

But now I had more responsibility and a slightly bigger paycheck. Because the company had offices in Baghdad, I was allowed to divert some of my pay there, so that my family—normally Saad—could pick up the money when times were lean. I was not the only Iraqi to do this. It was a common way for my fellow countrymen to send money home, and as a result I met quite a few other Iraqi immigrants. Some of them paid me little attention; others I grew to be friendly with. An architect whose name was Abu Firas seemed to take a particular shine to me. Whenever I saw him at the company offices, we chatted; and now and then I saw him outside his favorite café in Hashemite Square.

Occasionally, when Bakir was not looking, I used the company phone to make calls home and speak to my mother or to Saad. Sometimes they even phoned me. These conversations were short and nonspecific, for we couldn't be sure that nobody was listening in. Personal household telephones could be—and frequently were—tapped; and if you wanted to make a call from a public phone, you had to submit all your details, including your civil registration card, and then wait for two hours before making the call. Anonymous calls were practically impossible. So everyone was careful not to disclose anything that might give away where I was—they just asked after my well-being and thanked me for the money I had sent or told me that they were okay this month and that I should hold on to my earnings. They knew how important it was that I saved up.

As time went on, these phone calls home became more sinister and traumatic. At first all I had was a vague sense of misgiving, the uncertain impression that something was wrong. Gradually, however, I managed to piece together from our coded conversations that a soldier from my unit had, about three months after my escape, arrived at my grandmother's house to deliver notice that I had gone AWOL. A month or two later, things escalated when my mother, my brother, and Saad were apprehended by *Al-Istikhbarat* and taken to Division 5 in the area of Al-Khadimiya.

What happened to them there, I did not know at the time. I had to piece it together from snippets I gleaned from my mother and from what I knew went on in that place. He was told that I had six months to return to my unit. If I did, they said, I would be dealt with leniently. My ears would not be cut off, and I would not face the imprisonment or even worse that I would be expecting; I would just be made to complete my military service in the usual fashion. My family knew, of course, that they were lying, and they remained firm. So they threatened them with economic sanctions. If he did

not help them, Saad was told, they would arrange for him and his family to be cast out of the house in the Al-Zaafaraniya compound, which he had been given as a gift because he was an amputee from the Iran-Iraq war. Still Saad insisted he did not know where I was. So they took his gun from him, held it to his head, and cocked it. "How would you feel," he was asked, "if we shot you with your own gun? Now tell us where he is."

Saad remained silent.

At that point, the interrogation was handed over to somebody else. The two officers who had apprehended Saad had seen him in his home environment, with his parents and his sister. Perhaps they would have been inclined to treat him with undue lenience—to treat him like a human being—if it had been their job to take the questioning to the next stage, so a specialist was brought in to complete the job. Someone who could complete the job without emotion or mercy. Someone who did this kind of thing day in, day out.

My uncle was brutally beaten across the face and chest with a thick iron bar. The fact that he had suffered so much on account of his country meant nothing to his assailant. Whether he asked for pity, I don't know, but I doubt it: his pride was too great for that. His skin was then branded with a hot iron—a common way of reminding people of the pain they had undergone. Then he was released, but not without the demands of the intelligence officers being reiterated: I was to return within six months; otherwise the consequences for my family would be dire.

I found out the details of what had happened to them only later, but through my coded conversations with Saad on the phone, I deduced that I was being pressured to return, and I knew such pressure would be far from lenient. I fell to pieces. I suppose I had always known it was possible that my family would be questioned in some way, but I didn't really expect it to go to that extreme. Saad had filled me with his confidence, and I had felt sure that he would be

able to protect everyone from the most extreme of the security forces' predilections. It seemed I had been wrong. The treatment that Saad had undergone did not bear thinking about, and it was all because of me. There was only one thing that I could ethically do: turn back, return to my unit and hope that I was afforded the leniency that Saad had been promised. But when I made my thoughts known to my uncle, I was shot down in coded flames. "Forget my studies over here," I had told him. "I'm going to come back. I'll finish them another time."

"No," Saad told me sharply. "Think of all the money we've spent sending you abroad to study. Just remember what I told you when you left."

I wanted to ask him how he would deal with this situation, but of course I couldn't. I knew the answer to my unspoken question in any case. It would come down to money. A few dinars in the pockets of the right people, and perhaps he would keep the military police away from my family, for a while, at least. It wasn't foolproof—after all, there was no record of whom he had bribed—so he might have to grease the palms of different people in the future. But for now he sounded confident despite his horrible experiences: "You just concentrate on what it is you have to do," he told me, "on behalf of your family."

With terrible misgivings, I gave up all thoughts of returning; but the terrible prospect of my mother and siblings being harmed did not leave my mind for a single waking moment.

I stayed with Wissam for a couple of weeks, but I soon had the impression that he considered his debt to Saad to be repaid. Nothing was spoken; there was just a vague subtext. I certainly did not want to outstay my welcome, so I asked if I could sleep at the company offices for a while, and arrangements were made for me to do so. After a couple of months I discovered that the company owned an apartment in the prime area of Amman, and I was offered the

opportunity to stay there. Excited by the prospect, and expecting the apartment to be something rather special, I made my way to the place, only to find that what awaited me was quite different from the picture I had in my mind.

The apartment was occupied by *ishroog*, backward and illiterate itinerants from the south of Iraq. It was a three-bedroom apartment with about twenty of them living there. The floor was covered with tattered cushions gathered into makeshift beds, and the occupants seemed to keep their few belongings in old nylon bags. The apartment was not too clean, and as I stepped inside I became aware of the musty smell of too many people living in too cramped a space. Everyone eyed me suspiciously before asking me a barrage of questions. Who was I? Where did I work? Who had given me permission to stay there? I answered the questions honestly and in good humor, not wanting to fall out with these people, who were clearly going to be my roommates, on the first meeting; but they didn't make it easy, closing ranks like a group of frightened criminals. They worked at the head office of the company, it transpired, and because I wasn't working there and wasn't a threat to their jobs, they grudgingly welcomed me into the fold.

As part of my job, however, I occasionally made trips to the head office, running errands for Bakir, and it was there that I started to learn even more about the company's business. It was a large building—eight stories high and owned by the company—and in the reception area was a large picture of Saddam Hussein meeting with King Hussein of Jordan. The company wore its Iraqi origins firmly and even proudly on its sleeve. I had learned from chatting with people in the office where I worked that the driving force behind the company was an Iraqi, a member of the Al-Bu-Nimer—the Tiger tribe from the Sunni Al-Anbar region near the Jordanian border. Although Al-Anbar was a long way from Saddam's power center, the members of this tribe were very loyal to him and received

favors as a result. The main man was called Mushtaq, and he had something of a reputation as a flamboyant character. Occasionally I saw him at the head office—from time to time he came to work in a football shirt, but usually he wore brightly colored yellow or pink suits and a wide smile. Even from a distance he had a magnetic personality—good-looking, confident, and suave—and I was keen to meet him.

One day I got my chance. Running an errand of some sort, I was sent to Mushtaq's office. He was friendly enough, gregarious, but clearly supremely busy and without much time to devote to a lowly secretary from one of his other offices. His own office was huge and richly appointed, but as I stood there answering his half-interested questions, my attention was not focused on the furniture. My eyes fell on something that to me seemed much more sinister. On Mushtaq's desk, in pride of place, was a picture of Mushtaq himself shaking the hand of Uday Hussein, and another picture of him with Saddam. I found myself transfixed. They looked so easy in each other's company—clearly theirs was a relationship that went a long way back. What would Mushtaq do if he knew that one of his employees was here on a fake passport with fake entry stamps, having gone through everything I had gone through in order to leave Iraq? I felt my skin prickle underneath my clothes and realized that I had not taken in a word of what Mushtaq had been saying to me. I made my excuses and left.

That night, back in the apartment, I couldn't sleep. I lay there listening to the heavy breathing and snores of my roommates, unable to get the image of those pictures out of my head. By this time, my bullet wound had largely healed up. It still bled from time to time, but it had crusted over and grown much smaller. It should still have served as a reminder for me to be constantly wary. But in the weeks since starting at the company, I had allowed my guard to drop a little. I hadn't been careless, but I found that I had slipped into this

new life with surprising ease. The picture I saw in Mushtaq's office, however, brought home to me the fact that I could never forget I was on the run. I was grateful to the company for giving me a job, but I knew without question that the business interests of my employers would always come before their charity to me, so I could never let them know the truth about my situation. Part of me wondered if I should look for other work, but I soon dismissed that idea. Having started to make acquaintances with other Iraqis who congregated around Hashemite Square, who had to make do with filthy jobs for scant wages, I knew that I was lucky to be in my position. I was able to put money aside for my ultimate escape from Jordan, and even send a little back home to my family. I would just have to be on my guard.

As I lay there that night, I felt sick. Then I felt scared. Then I steeled myself to continue working hard to earn the money that would buy me my passage out of Jordan.

CHAPTER 9

CAUGHT

The weeks turned into months. I procrastinated, putting off making any calls to my family and feeling terrified whenever I did call
because I dreaded hearing terrible things. As the six-month anniversary of Saad's beating by the military police arrived, I was even more
full of foreboding. But the anniversary came and went, and I heard
no bad news from home. It seemed as though they had decided to
forget about me, for now at least.

I moved out of the company flat and used some of my earnings
to rent a place of my own, deep in the Palestinian quarter of Amman. Here, years before, on the side of one of the hills on which
Amman is built, Palestinian refugees had set up camp and formed
what can only be described as a ghetto. Back then the hillside was
covered in tents; now the buildings were more permanent, and the
area was perfect for me: generally cheap and a place where I could
melt into the background whenever necessary. The room was nothing to speak of: situated by itself on the roof of a high-rise building,
it was a former laundry room with little in the way of amenities, and

it was disproportionately highly priced; but it was my own space, where I could disappear whenever I wanted or needed to.

One morning I woke up to the sound of rain. The rainy season had arrived and such downpours were not uncommon. I lay in bed for a while, mustering the enthusiasm and the energy to get up. It had been a restless night, but that was nothing unusual for me these days—my dreams were filled with gunshots and wild animals and Republican Guards around every insubstantial, shadowy corner, and I awoke several times every night wide-eyed and sweating. Occasionally my dreams were accompanied by the same sinister and excruciating stomach pains that I had experienced the day I ran from the UN, and I lay there in darkness that multiplied my fears tenfold.

But just as the sun dispels shadows, so the daylight banished my nighttime anxieties into a far corner of my mind. I woke up, ate some breakfast, put on my suit, grabbed my umbrella, and left for another day at work. The rain was still heavy, and I was glad of the umbrella as I trod the familiar road to work. Just then, someone walked up from behind me and strode ahead. She was about my height and had long brown hair. As she passed, I caught a glimpse of her face, with its dark skin and the most stunning green eyes I had ever seen. Hers was the kind of beauty that made me catch my breath a little. Almost without thinking I stepped ahead and fell in beside her. "Would you like to share my umbrella?" I asked. My invitation was uncharacteristically forward.

She smiled a modest and appealing smile; I held the umbrella over her head, allowing it to protect her from the rain far more effectively than it did me, and we fell into slightly awkward conversation. Her name was Shireen, and she was perhaps a couple of years older than I. She was studying to be a fitness instructor. I told her that I had a job at a large company and tried to make it sound rather grander than it was. By the time we had made our brief introduc-

tions, we arrived at my work building. I handed her the umbrella. "Take it," I told her.

She smiled that smile again. "But when will I be able to give it back to you?" she asked.

I waved my hand nonchalantly. "It doesn't matter," I told her. "I'll see you around. Give it to me then." She started to protest, but I wouldn't allow her to, and I stood in the pouring rain watching her walk away. Just before she disappeared around the corner, she turned her head and smiled at me.

"You're soaking wet," Bakir barked when I got into the office.

"I'm sorry, Mr. Bakir," I muttered.

"You're also late. I don't pay you to be late. Fetch me tea with honey."

But even Bakir's reprimand couldn't dampen my spirit that day. The picture in my mind of Shireen's smile was enough to ease my other worries, at least for a little while. As the day wore on, I began to curse myself for playing it cool and not arranging to meet her again, so I determined that the following day I would leave my flat at exactly the same time in order to try to run in to her again.

I woke earlier than normal the next day and spent a little longer getting dressed. Stepping out into the street wearing an expression of confidence that I did not really feel, I looked around, trying to see the adorable sight of Shireen walking along the road. She wasn't there. I kept my eyes peeled all the way to work, and by the time I arrived I was crestfallen. It looked as though I had blown it.

I went about my business, making Bakir his tea, shuffling papers without much enthusiasm. It wasn't until midmorning that someone called out to me: "Sarmed, you have a visitor!" There was a slightly mocking, singsong quality to his voice, and as I looked up I saw why.

There was Shireen, holding the umbrella. "I thought you'd like this back." She smiled at me.

I did my best to keep cool, thanking Allah that she couldn't feel the beads of sweat forming on my palms or taste the sudden dryness of my mouth. "I looked out for you this morning," I told her non-committally.

She nodded mysteriously. "I went a different route."

"Do you always go a different route?"

"Not always," she told me. "Perhaps I'll see you another day."

"Perhaps," I grinned and spent the rest of the day walking on air.

A couple of times a week I saw Shireen on my way to work. Sometimes she was with a friend, sometimes alone; but each time we met we fell into easy conversation, and it took no time at all for me to become besotted by my new friend. I learned more about her. She had been born in Jordan, but her family was of Palestinian origin and she still considered herself to be a refugee. Somehow I felt that brought us closer. On the mornings that I saw her, I was happy for the rest of the day; when I missed her, my day was ruined. I even found myself writing poems to her that I knew she would never read. It was an entirely innocent relationship, and looking back I have no doubt that the obsession I felt for this woman was not reciprocated, but to me it was more than just a teenage crush. It was something that made me feel as if I belonged. Now and then I asked her out; she always turned me down with a smile that made me want to redouble my efforts. In a perverse kind of way, her rejections gave me confidence, the impression that I had something to work toward—I was sure that one day she would accept my invitation. Who knows, perhaps when the time came she would join me in leaving the country. But somehow that time seemed a long way off. I had started to feel a sense of community, with my work mates, with the Iraqis in Hashemite Square whom I befriended, and even elsewhere.

One afternoon after work I was walking aimlessly around a sec-

tion of Amman with which I was not familiar when I passed a run-down building that clearly had been a block of apartments. On the roof was a billboard announcing that the building was newly converted into a gym, and impulsively I went in to investigate. The staircase leading up to the gym was horribly shabby—I almost turned back on the assumption that I had made a mistake and people couldn't possibly be working and training there—but I persisted and eventually found myself in a hot, humid room. Mirrors were on the wall, music was blaring, and bodybuilders were working out. No doubt with my mind on the fact that Shireen wanted to be a fitness instructor, I joined there and then.

Gradually the gym became a home away from home. I went there to work out every day after finishing at work, and I started to become friendly with the gym owner, a former Olympic body-builder who seemed to take a shine to me. I think he was impressed with the enthusiasm with which I threw myself into this new hobby, so when I decided that I was spending so much time at the place that I might as well be working there, he was sympathetic to my request.

"You have the right to work here?" he asked perfunctorily.

"I already have a job at a respectable company," I reminded him.

"Very well," he said. "I could use someone to help me clean the gym up at night. I can't give you much, though. Free membership, and a few extra dinars in your pocket . . ." But that was all I wanted—I still had my job at the company, and as I was earning more than most of my fellow Iraqis in any case, I wasn't about to start being greedy.

Gradually, I found myself becoming settled. When the time allowed me by my fake Jordanian entry stamps passed without comment from my employers or anybody else, I suppose I even began to feel blasé. At the back of my mind I knew that this was going to make things difficult for me when the moment came, as it surely

would, to leave; but for the first time ever, I was beginning to enjoy myself a little bit, earning my own money and living my own life free of any interference. And even though I knew I had to be careful, to keep a low profile so that my passport was never requested by the Jordanian police who patrolled the streets, nevertheless I was experiencing the kind of freedom that people in the West took for granted, and it was a genuine liberation. I found that I didn't especially want to leave the life that I had started to make for myself in Amman; I didn't want to leave my friends at the gym; I didn't want to miss out on my morning walks with Shireen.

Despite everything, however, I was illegal, as were many of my acquaintances; as such I could not help but become schooled in the underground business of people-smuggling. Whenever I met with the Iraqis in Hashemite Square, more often than not the conversation would take that direction: voices would become hushed, and people would tell the latest rumors about forged passports and large sums of money changing hands to facilitate border crossings that sometimes were successful and sometimes weren't. I would feel something approaching a sense of peace when I heard of contemporaries who had made it to a safer place; but for every good-news story there was one to go with it of a deportation back to Iraq. It didn't bear thinking of what had happened to the poor souls who were unlucky.

It was a shady, illegal business but not uncommon, and it attracted its fair share of dishonest characters. I had acquaintances who were so run down by the life they were living in Amman—working in bakeries for twelve hours a day in the burning heat for a third of the wage that I was fortunate enough to have—that they threw caution to the wind and listened to the honeyed tones of crooked smugglers who promised them the world. Sometimes you could spot the con men a mile off—young Iraqis who were laboring every waking hour in poorly paid jobs were clearly unlikely to be the

high-flying smugglers that they sometimes claimed to be. Others played the game more subtly. "I can get you to Canada in three weeks," they would state confidently. "It will cost you a thousand Jordanian dinars, but you have to give me the money up front now." They talked a good talk, but anyone foolish enough to pay in advance seldom saw the smugglers—or their money—ever again. Very early on I realized that in such matters it was important to avoid the flashy, confident braggers, the people who spent their time partying and drinking and smoking. As I watched my contemporaries trying to leave, it became obvious that the ones who had the greatest success were those who put their faith in more sober members of the community—religious people, professional people, people who were doing what they did because they truly wanted to help others break free of the political shackles that kept them in that part of the world rather than out of a desire to make a few easy and dishonest dinars.

I learned to be patient. I knew it would take some time for me to be able to amass enough money and find the right person to help me, so I could fulfill my dream and get to England. In the meantime, I determined to make good use of my time—although there wasn't much of that. I finished one job at two in the afternoon, then started my second at four. When I wasn't working at the company or at the gym, though, I spent time at the British Council, learning what I could about English culture and history. They had VHS tapes, magazines, and newspapers that enabled me to learn about the country I wanted to make my home, as well as a large community of pro-Western Arabs: I threw myself wholeheartedly into that environment. While I was there, I made inquiries about the possibility of taking some basic exams with a UK college—I was still determined to study to become a doctor if and when I managed to get to England. "No problem," I was told. "Just write to the college whose course you want to follow, they'll advise you what books to

read, and you can do your exams here. If you pass you'll get your degree." I couldn't believe it was that simple—if I did well, I'd make the grade, unlike in Iraq, where my exam results were compromised by the fact that my parents had no military connections.

I bought the books, I studied hard, and I passed the examination.

The sense of elation and achievement was something I had never experienced before. I had done this on my own, without the need for subterfuge, and I had succeeded. I wanted to celebrate, so the day I received my results I met up with a few friends. Jolly Bee was one of the places where the young people of Amman hung out—a burger joint with MTV screens blaring loudly and a special play area for young children. I spent some time there with Duraid, a new Iraqi friend, and with Muafaq, a Jordanian who worked as an administrator for Mushtaq at the head office of the company. We had a good time, laughing, joking, and feeding ourselves the fast-food treats Jolly Bee had to offer, toasting my recent academic achievement with a succession of milkshakes. When we left, we were in high spirits, boisterous even. I had always made a point of trying to be inconspicuous when I was out and about, but today that caution seemed uncalled for. Duraid, Muafaq, and I ran down the street chasing and shouting at one another, and laughing a bit too loudly. I don't remember what it was that caused such hilarity—perhaps I said something about Shireen to my friends, or perhaps it really was nothing more than high spirits. Whatever it was, for a few moments it caused me to forget myself, to forget that the main focus of my life should have been to keep a low profile.

Suddenly Muafaq and I sprinted around the corner into a much smaller side street. As we did so, we practically ran into a policeman, unmistakable in the summer uniform of the Amman police force. It was as if he had materialized out of nowhere. He had just bought himself an ice-cream cone and was in the process of raising the cone to his mouth when we almost knocked him flat by running into him.

I stood absolutely still. We both did. In the few seconds of silence before the policeman spoke, a panic of thoughts went through my head. Not once in all the months I had been in Jordan had I been stopped by the police. I had been too careful for that. What would he do? We hadn't done anything wrong exactly, so maybe he would just tell us to be on our way with a harsh word. But it was also within his power to question us, to ask for our papers, and to check that we were who we said we were. What would happen next was entirely up to him. I did my very best not to look as though I had any reason to be scared, but no doubt my face was a picture of the concern I was feeling. I had turned from jubilation to desperation in an instant.

He looked us up and down, his face impassive. "What are you two doing?" he asked. His voice gave nothing away.

I was aware of Muafaq quietly making his way to the front of our little group. He was Jordanian, so I suppose he thought that if he spoke for us, the officer might not think he had encountered a couple of Iraqi tearaways. "We're just on our way home, officer," he told him soberly.

The policeman eyed him up and down. "Your ID card." It was an order, not a request.

Muafaq smiled as he pulled his ID card from his jacket and handed it over. "And this is a very good friend of mine . . ." he started to say in an attempt to defuse the situation, but he was instantly interrupted by the officer.

"I'll come to him in a minute," he snapped.

He scrutinized Muafaq's ID card, and as he did so I considered running. The main road was crowded enough for me to be able to lose myself among all the people, but the officer would still have Muafaq. I couldn't put him in the position of having to hide my identity from the Jordanian police. Besides, I had noticed the weapon the officer had swinging from his belt. I would just have to try to

talk my way out of this seemingly impossible situation and pray that he didn't ask me for the one thing I couldn't supply: proof of residence. The officer handed Muafaq's ID back to him, then turned his attention to me. "Can we go now?" I asked, affecting a Jordanian accent as best I could. It didn't fool the officer for a moment.

"Where are you from?" he asked with thinly veiled contempt.

"I live here," I told him, avoiding his question.

"I didn't ask you where you live. I asked you where you're from."

"Iraq."

The officer nodded as though I had confirmed his worst suspicion. "In that case, I'll need to see your proof of residence. Where's your passport?"

"I don't have it with me," I stammered. "Maybe I could bring it to you later."

He shook his head. "Where is it?"

I had to think fast. The passport was safely locked away in my tiny apartment, but I couldn't tell him that. I feared I would have to take him there, and I certainly didn't want the authorities to know where I lived. More important, however, my Jordanian entry stamps had expired. Even if the fact that it was a false passport escaped him, the fact that I was illegal was clearly stated there in black and white. I didn't know what to say. The officer looked at me, one eyebrow raised as the uncomfortable silence between us spoke louder than any excuses I could make up.

"It's at work," I blurted finally, for no reason other than that I thought it might buy me some time.

The officer narrowed his eyes. "And where do you work?"

"I have a job at a company," I said without mentioning the name of the place, then told him the rough area where my office was situated, before adding that I was a secretary to the Jordanian owner. Perhaps that would give me a little leverage.

The officer thought about that for a moment. "Very well," he said finally. "Take me there."

As though in the control of an awful dream that I couldn't stop, Muafaq and I were escorted to a patrol car in which another officer was sitting, and they started driving through the traffic of central Amman toward my office. We stayed silent. We didn't even look at each other, not wanting to betray our nervousness. As we drove, I felt the hotness of genuine fear creeping down the back of my neck. What were my employers likely to do? Sack me on the spot, most likely; leave me to the mercy of this aggressive policeman who clearly had the bit between his teeth as far as I was concerned. There was certainly no reason for them to stick their necks out for me; indeed there were many reasons for them not to. I was popular at work, but they had a successful and profitable business—why on earth would they risk a run-in with the authorities on my account?

As the patrol car edged slowly toward the district where the company had its offices, I became increasingly certain that I was heading into the lion's den, and without really thinking it through properly, I blurted out a change of plan. "Actually," I broke the silence in the car, "my passport isn't there."

The officer who had arrested me looked over his shoulder. "What do you mean?"

"I have another job," I told him. "At a local gym. I had to give them my passport."

"Why didn't you say so before?"

"I forgot," I said rather unconvincingly. "It was a while ago."

I felt scant relief when the policemen directed the car toward the gym. The owner was still a Jordanian, still ran a business, and still didn't want any kind of trouble with the authorities. I just felt slightly more comfortable with the officers confronting him rather than Bakir.

The patrol car crawled toward the gym, but it seemed to my nervous mind as if we arrived there practically instantaneously.

It was about two o'clock when we arrived, and the gym was pretty much empty—the regulars would not turn up for at least another hour, maybe two. Nevertheless, loud Western pop music was blaring through the stereo speakers as I led the way across the gym mats toward the owner's office, closely followed by the officer who had arrested me. Muafaq stayed in the car with the other policeman, which was an extra worry for me: he was not really known for his discretion, and I didn't feel at all confident that he wouldn't say something incriminating. But all that was out of my control; I had to concentrate on the predicament at hand.

I will never forget the look of shock on the owner's face as he watched me through the open door to his little office being marched across the gym toward him. He had been so kind to me over the time I had spent at the gym, helping me out with work and friendly advice—now it must have seemed to him that all was not as I had pretended it was. As we entered, he put down the pen with which he was filling in some paperwork, sat back in his chair, and gazed warily at us both. "Sarmed," he muttered by way of greeting.

I nodded my head; then the officer stepped in front of me. As the gym owner was clearly Jordanian and much older than he, there was no way the officer would speak to him in the same dismissive tones he had used with me, but he was stern nevertheless.

"The boy says he works for you."

The owner nodded.

"How long has he worked here?"

"A few months, nothing more." His eyes flickered toward me as he spoke.

"He's from Iraq." The officer stated what the owner clearly already knew. "We're clamping down on illegal immigrants at the moment, especially young males, so I need to see his residency permissions."

"You think Sarmed might be illegal?" His face gave nothing away.

"Yes," replied the officer. "I do. He's been acting very suspiciously. He tells me you have his passport. Is this true?"

The question hung in the air. Once more I saw the owner's eyes flicker toward me, and from behind the officer's back I slowly made a signal to the owner, visibly imploring him not to give the game away. It was a futile hope, I knew—what could he say when put on the spot like this? Still, my future depended on the answer this burly Jordanian—a former bodybuilding champion—who had no reason to help me gave.

Finally he spoke. "Yes, I have his passport."

"Then perhaps you could show it to me," the officer asked almost politely.

I held my breath.

"I'm very sorry, officer, but I'm afraid I can't do that."

"What do you mean?"

The owner stood up from his desk and pointed to a large safe in the corner of the room. "I keep his passport in that safe. You have to be careful with so many people around, and I wouldn't want to lose it. Anyway, my wife has the key. She's not here today, but I'd be happy to bring Sarmed's passport to you tomorrow whenever it's convenient for you." He smiled, his face lighting up with such honesty that surely nobody would suspect he wasn't telling the truth.

The officer shifted from one foot to the other, glancing from me to the gym owner and back. Then he shook his head. "No," he said firmly. "I'll be back this time tomorrow. Then we'll have a look at these documents of yours."

I inclined my head but didn't say anything. The officer lowered his voice. "Consider yourself lucky I don't take you with me. The cells at the police station are very uncomfortable. Just make sure you're here tomorrow," he told me before turning and walking away.

The owner and I remained silent as we watched the officer walk back across the gym toward the exit, the clomping of his heavy shoes echoing against the mirrored walls. Even after he had closed the door behind him, the owner refrained from speaking. It was as if we were both holding our breath, waiting for the officer suddenly to walk back in and catch us discussing what we shouldn't have been.

Eventually the owner spoke. His voice was quiet, threatening almost. "Can you bring me your passport to show this guy?"

I bowed my head and gently shook it. "No," I whispered. "I can't do that. I'm sorry."

Another pause. Then the owner banged his formidable fist against the table. "Do you have any idea what sort of situation you've just put me in?" he hissed.

What could I say? After all he had done for me I knew he had every reason to be angry, so I wasn't surprised when he pushed past me and stormed into the main area of the gym, striding around furiously for a couple of minutes while I was left there to stew. Now more than ever I was at this man's mercy. He had lied to protect me, but there was nothing stopping him from going back on his subterfuge should he realize that he was in too deep.

Finally he returned to his office where I stood waiting for him. "You're a good boy, Sarmed," he said gruffly. "I don't know why you lied to that policeman, and I don't want to know. But he's going to come back, so you can't be seen around here again."

"What will you tell him?" I asked meekly.

"I don't know." He seemed irritated by the question. "I'll deal with that. You just need to leave this place and keep your head down."

I nodded in agreement.

"I don't blame you for not wanting to go back to Iraq, but you can't live like this forever, Sarmed," he told me, a bit more calmly now. "It's madness. If you're illegal here, they're going to catch up

with you eventually. I don't want to know what your plan is, but if you're going to stay safe, you'd better have one."

"I know," I said. "I'm hoping to . . ." But he held up his hand to stop me giving him any information he didn't want to have. Then I watched as he removed from around his neck a string from which a key was hanging. He walked over to the safe and used the key to open it. I couldn't stop a flicker of a smile from playing over my lips as I remembered the earnestness with which he had assured the policeman that his wife held the key. He took out a small pile of notes and started counting them out. "These are the wages I owe you," he said as he did so, then counted out a few more. "And here is a little extra, to help you on your way." He handed them to me, then wrapped his enormous arms around me in a bearlike embrace. "I'm sorry it's not more," he said. "Stay well, Sarmed, and be safe. I never want to see you here again."

I took a tremblingly deep breath as I struggled not to cry in front of this man who quite possibly had saved my life. Then I muttered a few inadequate words of thanks before turning and leaving the gym, knowing that I could never return.

THE SMUGGLER

I ran all the way home, tears of frustration blinding my eyes. What had started off as a day of jubilation had suddenly turned into the worst day I had endured so far in Jordan. When I arrived back at my tiny apartment, I frantically rummaged through my clothes where I had hidden my passport, then pulled it out to look at it. I sat staring at that document for some time, as if by willing it to be so I could make it genuine, or at least extend the time left on my fake entry stamps by a few months. But of course it remained just as it had always been: a fake passport for an illegal alien. I felt a crushing sense of loneliness. I may have started to make a few friends here in Amman, but in that moment I realized that any sense of belonging I might have felt in the past few months was entirely misplaced. Nothing could change the fact that I was an outsider, on the run from the place that I considered home and not tolerated by the authorities in this halfway house. In the back of my mind I realized I had harbored a vague desire to stay in Jordan for a long time, to continue working at the company, to continue seeing Shireen; but it was suddenly clear to me what a futile hope that was. The gym

owner's parting words had sounded in my ears like a bell, a wake-up call: *You can't live like this forever, Sarmed. It's madness.*

I looked out of my window over the roofs of Amman, and not for the first time, my thoughts took me back to the house in Al-Mansour where my family was still living. It was around dinnertime. My mother would have hosed down the front yard to cool it after the fierce heat of the afternoon sun, and the air would be thick with the humidity and the aroma of the food my grandmother would be cooking in the kitchen. Ahmed and Marwa would be playing; perhaps Saad would have arrived, bringing my grandparents a gift of watermelon or peaches as he always did. Perhaps my mother would speak proudly of her son who was making a new life for himself: he is successful, she would say; he sends money home.

"He's a good boy," my grandfather would mutter. "*Inshallah,* all is well."

And Saad would sit quietly, silently keeping his own counsel.

It made me feel even lonelier knowing that I could never travel back to the place that I missed so much, to that little house that seemed to me to be an oasis of peace and hospitality in the center of the city I had fled. Inside the walls of my home, I could just be myself—no lies, no pretenses, no need to be constantly on my guard.

Suddenly the irony seemed too horrible to consider. I had run away from home, never to return, yet I missed it with every bone in my body. I ached to be with the people I loved, the people who loved me. And somewhere deep down I felt guilt too. Saad had made it clear to me that I was being helped out of Iraq so that I might help my family out, yet I didn't seem to be any closer to achieving that aim than I was the day I arrived in Jordan. Sure, I sent money home, but freedom was more expensive than that. I rummaged in one of my cupboards for something to eat, but gave up when I found nothing suitable. I wasn't really hungry anyway.

As night fell, I took to my bed; but as had been the case so often

in recent weeks, I barely slept. My eyes, wide open, stared at the blackness of the ceiling as I considered my options. My finances were scant: I had been putting aside a little money every month to fund my eventual escape from Jordan, but the rest had been spent on my accommodations and on sending something home to my family as often as they needed it. Even had the coffers been full, however, I wasn't about to announce my desire to get out of the country to just anyone in Hashemite Square—the con men would have been on me like hyenas, and I would never have been able to tell the genuine offers from the bogus ones. Occasionally I sat up straight in bed, struck by an overwhelming sense of panic, and with these thoughts rushing through my mind, the night passed fitfully.

That morning I hoped more than ever to run in to Shireen on the way into work. I felt that more than anybody else she accepted me for who I was, not what it said on my documents, and I had always found that her presence calmed me, despite her refusal to meet me at any time other than on our morning walks; and if ever I needed soothing, it was now. But she was nowhere to be seen, so I shuffled my way to the office with a renewed nervousness that did nothing for my state of mind. All day I moped around, dark circles under my eyes and a constant frown on my forehead. Bakir noticed it, and he barked out instructions occasionally to keep me alert; but at other times I saw him looking at me thoughtfully, as if wondering what was going through my mind. It unnerved me even more. I was thankful that I had not mentioned the name of the company to the police officer, but that didn't mean I felt safe at work. Suddenly I didn't feel safe anywhere or with anyone.

Except one person.

I had maintained my friendship with Abu Firas, the Iraqi architect whom I had met through working at the company. He had legitimately made his home in Jordan and was always neatly dressed, quietly spoken, and modest. My very first opinion when I had met

him some time previously was that he was a reputable and honest man, not at all a charlatan. He often came to Hashemite Square and drank lemonade in the evenings as the heat of the sun faded, and sometimes we talked. Gradually he learned the general nature of my situation—although as always I had refrained from telling him the whole story—and one day he had quietly said to me, "When the time comes, Sarmed, and if you need any help, I know a few people." Nothing more—no brash claims or demands for money that instantly would have marked him out as a crook. It was no surprise to me that he knew about such things. Maybe he did make a little money arranging for people to smuggle themselves out of Jordan, but my impression was that he kept abreast of such matters because, although he had a good job in Amman, he knew that the Jordanian authorities could deport him on a whim, so he had to know the best ways of getting to the West. I had nodded gratefully and stashed his offer of help away in my mind for the moment when I needed it. Now that moment had arrived. I decided to hunt him out that evening.

Sure enough, he was there, sitting alone at his usual table on the pavement outside his usual café, an ice-cold drink and a small plate of tempting baklava placed neatly in front of him. He seemed perfectly content watching the usual daily hustle and bustle of Hashemite Square unfold before him, and he didn't notice me until I was almost upon him. He smiled as I approached and gestured at me to sit down.

"I haven't seen you in a long while, Sarmed," he complained.

"I've been busy, Abu Firas," I explained, glancing nervously around me. "Work."

"And chasing pretty young Palestinian girls, from what I hear." He winked at me as I felt a blush rising to my cheek.

We sat there in silence for a while. Abu Firas watched me as he took a sip from his drink, clearly waiting for me to say whatever it was I had come to tell him.

"I had some trouble with the police yesterday."

He seemed unsurprised. "Is it all sorted out now?"

"Kind of. But I think the time has come for me to leave."

"I'll be sorry to see you go," he replied as though willfully ignoring the subtext of what I was saying. I felt momentarily confused—perhaps I had misunderstood or misremembered the offer he had made.

"You said a while ago that you might be able to help me."

"It's possible."

"How much will I have to pay you?" I thought I might as well get the question out in the open.

Abu Firas took another sip from his drink. "I am an architect, Sarmed, not a people-smuggler. If I help you, it won't be because I want your money. It's because I understand what you are running from."

My eyes narrowed slightly. This was not quite what I had expected.

"You're suspicious," Abu Firas noticed. "Good. You need to be. The circles in which we move are full of corruption, Sarmed, and you need to be careful. If you are going to make it to England, you will have to take great risks. Plenty of people will give you advice, me included. But at the end of the day, every decision you make must be your own. Do you understand?"

I nodded mutely.

"Good. Do you have your passport with you?"

Fortunately I had thought to bring it, thinking he might ask me that. Abu Firas took it from me, held it surreptitiously between himself and the table, and spent some time flicking through it.

"This is a very good fake. In fact I would say that it was originally a genuine blank passport from Baghdad. The only people who will be able to spot that it is not official will be the Iraqis themselves. But your Jordanian entry stamps have expired."

"I know."

He shook his head regretfully. "That was foolish, Sarmed. It makes things much more difficult."

"What am I going to do?"

Abu Firas thought for a moment. "You need to get to Malaysia."

"Malaysia?" It seemed like a crazy route, halfway across the world and in the wrong direction. "Why?"

"Because you can, Sarmed. Look, the Iraqi passport is the most ignored passport in the world. There are very few places it will get you, but Malaysia is one. As soon as you can, you need to go to the Malaysian Embassy and apply for a single-entry visa. The Malaysians won't care that your entry stamps into Jordan have expired. They should give the visa to you there and then."

I stared at him as if he was mad. "But Abu Firas, this is a fake passport. What if they find out?"

"They won't be looking out for it. Like I say, only the Iraqis will know that this isn't genuine. And in any case, only an idiot would apply for a visa in person on a forged Iraqi passport. They'll never suspect anyone would do such a thing." He flashed me a smile that did nothing for my confidence. "Trust me, Sarmed, this is your only option."

"What will I do when I get to Malaysia?"

"I have contacts in the West who can supply you with a fake United Arab Emirates passport. That, I'm afraid, will cost you money—not for me but for the counterfeiters. UAE passport-holders can travel directly between Malaysia and the UK without visas. It should be enough to get you out of Malaysia."

"Can't I just use the UAE passport to leave Jordan?"

"No," Abu Firas replied sharply. "I can help you fake Jordanian entry and exit stamps on the UAE passport just in case you get questioned in Malaysia, but it would be best if the Jordanians do not see

them. They would just need to tap the details into their system and they would soon establish that the UAE passport is fake. If they do that, you'll be looking at a long prison sentence. It's much more difficult for them to establish the authenticity of your Iraqi passport."

"How will you fake the entry and exit stamps?" I asked him.

"I told you, Sarmed. I'm an architect. I draw things and make designs. Forging a little stamp like that won't be a big problem for me."

I sat there quietly for a moment as I tried to absorb everything I had been told. Abu Firas's plan seemed to me to be fraught with risks. So many things could go wrong, but one concern worried me more than any other. "If I leave Jordan on my Iraqi passport, what will the border guards do when they see my entry stamps have expired?"

Abu Firas sighed. "I don't know, Sarmed. The truth is it will probably be up to the mood of whoever interrogates you."

"But they won't deport me?"

"It's possible."

"Then I can't do this."

Abu Firas's face became serious. "I don't think you have a choice, Sarmed. The longer you leave it, the more difficult things will become for you. I know you haven't told me everything about why you had to leave Iraq, but I sense that things would go very badly for you if you were forced to return. That's why I wouldn't suggest this if I didn't think it was the only way. I know what I'm suggesting is risky, but if you sit around waiting for risk-free ways of leaving the country, you'll be an old man before you get out."

He winked at me, a curiously upbeat gesture given our worrying conversation.

"Or at the very least," he said, "I will be."

· · ·

. . .

After my conversation with Abu Firas I was of two minds. I was glad I had him to advise me—he seemed to know what he was talking about, and that was encouraging. But at the same time, he had been eager to point out the risks I was going to have to take. What he had told me represented progress, but it did nothing to increase my peace of mind.

It all seemed so complicated, and I wondered if there might not be an easier way. I had heard that the British Embassy sometimes issued foreign nationals a study visa so that they could travel to the UK in order to attend university. I had shown my capacity for study—perhaps they would take me on. I arranged an immediate appointment for the visa application, and the fact that they agreed to see me so soon filled me with confidence.

As I was waiting at the Embassy, I fell into conversation with an Iraqi woman who was obviously several months pregnant. She told me that she was a British citizen, because her husband was from the UK, and that she was there to inform the Embassy that she was returning to Iraq to have her baby there.

I was astonished. "Why do you want to do that?" I asked her. "What if you don't get back out again?"

"That's why I'm informing the British Embassy," she told me, her serious face full of concern.

"Aren't you scared? You know what it's like there now. It's not a safe place."

"Of course I'm scared," she said plainly. "But despite everything it's still my country, and I hope that someday I will be able to return for good. In the meantime I want my child to be born on Iraqi soil." She smiled at me. "You're very young. One day, perhaps, you'll understand."

But deep down, I think perhaps I already did.

I was ushered into a stark room in the Embassy by an official carrying a cup of coffee. I remember how strange that seemed, for officials in Iraq carried nothing but a stern face and a glower for whomever they had to deal with. "What can I do for you?" he asked as we both sat down.

I handed him an application form. "I'd like to apply for a study visa," I told him.

"I see." His face was inscrutable. "And how do you propose to pay for your course?"

"I have an uncle in England," I told him. "I'm sure he will fund me for the first year."

"And after that?"

"I'll have to get a job," I told him honestly.

The official shook his head. "No," he told me. "I'm afraid it doesn't work like that. I need to see that you have the funds to pay for your entire course and your living expenses, *before* I issue you a visa."

"But that could be sixty or seventy thousand pounds," I protested.

"Yes," he replied shortly. He looked down at my application again. "You're from Iraq, I see. Why don't you finish your education in Iraq?"

"It's not as simple as that," I told him.

"Have you completed your military service?"

I shook my head.

"Why not?"

"Because I don't want to serve a criminal."

He looked at me with undisguised disapproval. "I suggest you return home and continue your military service," he said as though ignoring my previous statement. "Then you can complete your studies there. We can do nothing for you here."

I couldn't believe what I was hearing—that a foreign official

186 ESCAPE FROM SADDAM

could be so naive. But it was clear from his demeanor that I could do nothing to change his mind, so I made my excuses and left.

Knocked back, I was still reluctant to follow Abu Firas's advice, so I quietly let it be known among a few of my acquaintances that I was looking for someone who could help me leave. Suddenly I was inundated with offers, shady characters pretending to be my closest friend and offering me promises that they could get me anywhere in the world in return for more money than I could pay them—in advance. But without exception, when I probed a little deeper into their plans for me, I found that they were either nebulous or nonexistent; and when I suggested that I would pay them only after I was successfully in England, they melted away, never to be seen again.

So I contacted Abu Firas once more, to tell him that I intended to go ahead with his plan.

He agreed to make arrangements for the UAE passport, and I prepared myself for the first hurdle: a trip to the Malaysian Embassy, false Iraqi passport in hand, to apply for a visa. To my astonishment, and just as Abu Firas had predicted, it was issued without question. Suddenly I began to have a little more faith in my benefactor.

There were other problems, though. Along with my photograph, I had given Abu Firas half the money, the other half to be handed over on delivery of the passport, and this would all but wipe out my savings. Somehow I was going to have to raise the money to pay for my flights to Malaysia and to England, and there seemed to be no way of doing so. My friends couldn't help me out, and asking Abu Firas for a loan seemed to me to be a favor too far. Still, until I had the UAE passport in my hands, it was all just a dream anyway. I had no idea how long getting it would take, so I kept my head down and continued my work at the company, squirreling away as much of my pay as I possibly could.

Days became weeks, and the passport did not arrive. Occasionally I saw Abu Firas and asked him if there was any progress. His re-

sponse was always the same: "These things take time, Sarmed. It will come."

But it didn't come, and I started to wonder if Abu Firas had been stringing me along after all.

The stress of waiting started to become almost unbearable. My nights were increasingly wakeful, and I continued to suffer the mysterious stomach pains that had been plaguing me over the past few months. I did my best to distract myself by redoubling my efforts with Shireen. Our morning strolls were just as frequent and just as cherished. We had fallen into the easy companionship of good friends, but still she refused to meet me at any other time. In my eagerness to be with her, though, I started plotting a wild scheme in my mind.

"Do you ever think about leaving Amman?" I asked her one day as we were walking along together.

"Sometimes," she replied mysteriously. "Why?"

"Oh, I just wondered," I told her, doing my best to hide the smile I felt inside.

As the days passed I asked the same question in roundabout ways. Had she ever thought about living in England? What would she do if she went there? Would she miss her family? I began to persuade myself that her answers contained a happy subtext. She knew I would not stay in Jordan forever. Perhaps I could persuade her to follow her dream and come with me. I fantasized about the idea— about having someone by my side in the grueling times ahead whom I trusted, whom I felt close to. If I could persuade Shireen to come with me, it seemed to me that all my prayers would be answered. But I refrained from asking her because as yet I had nothing to offer.

Some weeks after my initial meeting with Abu Firas, I was quietly going about my business at work when I got a call from the receptionist. "Sarmed, courier for you." I was perplexed. Who would

be sending a package to me here? I went to collect it and suddenly found myself having to catch my breath. It was a small package. Passport size. I thanked the receptionist then swiftly went to find a deserted corner of the office where I could open it in private. With trembling hands I unsealed the packaging, slid the pristine new document out of its envelope, then spent several minutes nervously examining it. My photograph was there, above the false name *Adel Mahmoud Ahmed*—it was an odd juxtaposition, but I was going to have to get used to it.

In every way the passport was perfect.

Enclosed with the passport was a brief handwritten note: "May Allah guide your steps and may you be successful in all you set out to achieve, and *inshallah* you will arrive safely." It was short, sentimental even, but this anonymous message from a faceless well-wisher in a far-off country meant a great deal to me. I stood there, passport and note in hand, and looked out through the window over the busy streets of Amman. I suddenly realized that whenever I had done this sort of thing before, I had felt somehow inferior to everybody else down there. They were okay. They were allowed to be here. In Amman, at least, they were better than me. But today all that changed. With the arrival of the small but powerful document in my hand, I was as good as anyone else because now, like them, I had a future.

My musings were interrupted by Bakir, shouting my name somewhere nearby. I tucked the passport safely into one of my pockets and went back to work.

That afternoon I went straight to the library at the British Council and applied for a membership card in my new name, using my new passport. The card was readily given and certainly not an official document, but I thought it might be helpful should I run into any difficulty. Then I hurried back to Hashemite Square, where I had arranged to meet Abu Firas. He took the passport from me.

"Now you need to buy your tickets," he told me. "Remember you need two—one in your Iraqi name, one in your UAE name. You use the Iraqi one to leave Jordan, and the UAE one to enter Malaysia. When you have them, let me know the date you are leaving and I can forge your exit stamp for you."

I nodded my head. How could I tell him after everything he had done that even now I didn't have the money for the tickets? I had racked my brain trying to come up with a solution. None of my acquaintances were in any sort of financial state to help me, and I couldn't very well go to my family. There was only one thing I could think of, one path open to me that would allow me to go through with my plan. It was a long shot, and it would have to wait until the following day.

I arrived at work early the next morning and made sure that Bakir's tea was on his desk before he had the opportunity to ask for it. He took a sip without uttering a word of thanks, then pretended not to notice me as I stood by his desk, waiting expectantly for him to realize that I wanted to ask him something. "What is it, Sarmed?" he eventually asked wearily, relaxing his corpulent body back in his chair and flicking his thumb from under his armpit as was his habit.

I cleared my throat as I nervously prepared to ask the question I had been practicing all night. "Mr Bakir," I began. "I'm thinking that I might like to do some traveling."

Bakir's face twitched as though he could sense I was about to ask him a question he wouldn't much like.

"I was wondering if the company would advance me the money I need for my airfare."

For a few moments Bakir did not answer. In fact he didn't even look at me, choosing instead to gaze noncommittally across the room. Then he took another sip of his tea before turning to me and finally speaking. "Unless I am mistaken, Sarmed, you do not intend to return to Amman once you have left."

I was too shocked by his insight to reply.

His voice became sharper. "Am I right?"

"No, Mr. Bakir . . ." I started to say, but he interrupted me immediately.

"I'm not stupid, Sarmed. I lose a secretary and my money. What's in it for me?"

That wasn't a question I could answer. I watched him carefully—his indecision was written plainly on his face. Somewhere deep inside he wanted to help me, I think, but in the end his fear of the consequences got the better of him. "I can't authorize this," he said with uncharacteristic quietness.

I nodded in mute acceptance, understanding that as a Jordanian he would not want to be seen giving money away to an Iraqi. I had no idea whom I could turn to now.

Then he continued. "I don't blame you for wanting to go, Sarmed. I've had my eye on you for quite a while now. You're a good lad, but it's been clear from the outset that you wouldn't stay here for long. Why don't you speak to Zaidoon? Maybe he will help you."

It was a good idea. Zaidoon was Mushtaq's deputy and was that rare thing: an Iraqi with an American green card. We got on well. He was a very decent person who was happy to help hardworking, decent Iraqis working for the company, and he always seemed to have time for my incessant questions about life in the West. I went to find him immediately.

"How much do you need?" he asked me.

I plucked a figure out of thin air—more than I would require, probably, and a seemingly huge amount to me; but to Zaidoon it was no doubt a small sum.

He considered it for a few moments. "Very well," he said finally. "The company sometimes makes loans to its employees. I'm sure we

can arrange something. But remember, it's a loan. If you ever find yourself in Amman again, you will be expected to pay it back."

"And if I don't?" I held my breath.

"Then you can send it to us when you settle in the UK." His words spoke of doing things by the book, but his eyes flashed in a friendly way that made it clear that he, at least, would not expect the money back.

I smiled at him. "Thank you," I said.

He nodded in acknowledgment. "Good luck, Sarmed. If I'm honest, it sounds to me like you're going to need it. Now if I were you, I'd get back to Bakir and fetch him another cup of tea. He doesn't pay you to stand around chatting with me."

I bought two tickets to Kuala Lumpur, one in the name on my Iraqi passport, one in the name on my UAE passport. I gave the dates to Abu Firas, and two days later he returned my UAE passport, complete with perfectly forged Jordanian entry and exit stamps. I also bought an expensive suit to make me look like a well-to-do young UAE citizen, not a desperate Iraqi refugee. It was light gray in color, and I complemented it with a pink tie. As I looked at myself in the mirror, I was reminded of my father—it was the kind of suit he used to wear. What would he think if he saw me now? There would be a harsh word, no doubt. He would tell me that what I was doing was ridiculous, that I would never have the skill and the nerve to go through with this dangerous plan. Certainly there would be no hint of encouragement. I removed the suit and stashed it safely away for the day of my journey.

Two days before I was due to depart I went to try to find Shireen. She was walking along the road to work as usual, and I fell in beside her.

"I need to talk to you," I said urgently.

She stopped, surprised I suppose by the tone of my voice. "What is it, Sarmed?"

"I'm leaving."

"What do you mean?"

"Leaving Amman. For good."

"When?" I was pleased to note that she seemed genuinely saddened by the news.

"In two days' time. I have a flight booked to Malaysia, and from there to England. I want you to come with me."

Shireen's eyes widened. "Sarmed," she said. "I don't know what to say . . ."

Silently I urged her to say yes.

". . . but there's just no way I can come with you to England."

Her words were like a knife in my heart. "Why not?" I whispered.

She looked at me with what I suppose was genuine sympathy. "You're a sweet man, Sarmed," she managed eventually, "and a good friend. But not that sort of a friend. Besides, my family would never forgive me if I simply left them."

"But it would be for a better life . . ."

"A better life for you, Sarmed. Not for me. The people I love are here—it's my home."

"I thought you considered yourself a refugee."

"I do, Sarmed. But I've lived here all my life, and home is where your family is. They wouldn't want me to leave them."

"Maybe I could talk to your family," I persisted. "Persuade them . . ."

"No, Sarmed," she said firmly, "because I don't want to leave them either." She lowered her eyelashes in a sorrowful way. "Sarmed, there's something I have to tell you. I've been waiting for the right moment but it has never arrived. I'm engaged to be married."

I was momentarily speechless, before feeling a hot flush of embarrassment creep up my neck. "I'm sorry, Shireen," I said finally. "If I'd known I wouldn't have asked you. Forgive me."

Gently she kissed me on the side of the cheek—a particularly forward gesture for a young Arab girl. "Of course I forgive you, Sarmed."

We stood there in awkward silence, which was finally broken by Shireen. "Is it safe, what you are doing?"

I shrugged, effecting more bravado than I felt. "I'll be okay. I have good people helping me."

"I hope so, Sarmed." And then the words that I desperately didn't want to hear. "I don't suppose I'll see you again, shall I?"

I shook my head.

"Good-bye then," she said quietly but firmly. "*Allah maa'k*. God be with you. I will miss you."

Shireen turned and continued down the street. I watched her until she disappeared from sight.

I returned to the flat, shut the door, and kicked the wall in frustration. My emotions for the rest of that day were more confused than they had ever been. There was sorrow, certainly, tinged with shame at the embarrassment my request had caused. But as time wore on and I was forced to come to terms with what had happened that morning, I realized how improbable it had always been that Shireen would come with me. Not everyone was as displaced as I was. Not everyone felt the need to cross over the fence to a greener field. In a strange way, I stoically told myself, it was a relief. Shireen was the only reason I had left for wanting to stay in Amman. Now she was beyond my reach forever, and as a result I felt a renewed sense of purpose, a desperate drive to continue with the rest of my journey.

When the day arrived, I rose early. My bags had been expectantly packed the night before, so I put on my suit, straightened my

tie, and checked my two sets of documents for the umpteenth time. Then I placed my Iraqi passport in one inside pocket, my UAE passport in the other, picked up my bags, and went to catch the bus that would drive me on the thirty-minute journey to the Amman airport.

It had been more than seven years since I had been at an airport—not since my father had brought me back to Baghdad—and I had forgotten how busy airports could be. Businessmen—some in suits, others in more traditional Arab dress—marched purposefully across the concourse paying little or no attention to the young Iraqi standing alone in the middle with his luggage and wondering where to go. Eventually I located the desk I needed and checked in nervously but without any difficulty. I was in good time for my flight, but I decided nothing was to be gained from going through passport control too early. If they decided to question my documents, I did not want them to have too much time in which to do so, so I remained on the main concourse, pacing up and down, trying to keep out of sight of any officials as my anxiety increased with every minute that passed. At one point I killed some time at an airport café, where I ordered a Coca-Cola and sipped it slowly. If things didn't go as I hoped, I thought to myself, this might be the last time I would taste it for a long while, if not forever.

I had been mentally preparing myself for this moment for weeks; but now that it was upon me, every instinct in my body screamed at me to leave the airport. It was too dangerous. So many things could go wrong, and if they did I would be on the first transport back to Baghdad. Every time that thought struck me, I shuddered, closed my eyes, and tried to put it to the back of my mind.

Eventually, I could put it off no longer. Taking deep breaths to calm my nerves, I approached passport control, where an unsmiling border guard took my Iraqi passport. He had a computer terminal

in front of him and, glancing through my documents, typed some-thing into the system. "What's your father's name?" he asked.

I told him, wondering what that had to do with anything.

He tapped at the keyboard again without looking at me. "Hmm . . ." I heard him grunt.

I tried to keep calm. "What's wrong?" I asked.

"Wait here," the guard said. He left his post and went to talk to another official. I watched them in huddled conversation as they examined my passport and looked back toward me. Eventually he returned to his post. "How did you enter?"

"My entry stamps are there," I told him curtly.

The guard shrugged. "I think you entered illegally," he told me. I remained silent, and as I think back on that awful moment I re-member that everything around me seemed to fade into silence as every ounce of my concentration was directed toward what this man, on whose whim my future lay, was saying to me. "Even if you didn't, you've overstayed. They're cracking down on people like you. It looks like you're in trouble. Come with me." His words made my body feel suddenly crumpled, and it took every effort just to stand up straight.

He led me to a side room that contained nothing but a desk and two chairs. "Sit down," he told me without ceremony. I did as I was told, watching him as he appeared to be wondering what to say next. "We've had our eye on you," he said finally.

My heart stopped. How could that be the case? "What do you mean?" I breathed.

"We've had you under surveillance. You're a smuggler. You've been coming in and out illegally. You're not on the system."

"That's not my fault."

He stared directly into my eyes, waiting for me to say something else, and instantly I understood. He was trying to intimidate me.

What he wanted I don't know—a bribe maybe, or perhaps he was genuinely suspicious of my documents and was trying to break me down. I resolved to make sure he would do neither. "You're mistaken," I told him.

"You should have left the country months ago."

"So let me leave."

He shook his head with a nasty smile. "I'm afraid it doesn't work like that, my friend. If you want to leave, you have to pay a fine. One dinar for every day you have overstayed."

It amounted to a sizable sum. The only money I had I needed in Malaysia to buy my ticket to the UK. There was no way I could hand any of it over to this guy. "I don't have the money," I told him firmly.

The guard shrugged and looked at his watch. "Your flight leaves in fifteen minutes," he said. "I'll be back in ten to see what your decision is." He left me alone in the room.

I sat there, sweating in my suit while I decided what to do—though in truth the decision was made for me. I couldn't give him any money, so I had to stick to my story and pray that the business of dealing with me would be too much of an administrative headache. If he wanted me out of the country, the easiest way was to get me on that plane.

True to his word he returned exactly ten minutes later. "Have you decided?"

"I told you," I said. "I don't have the money. I can't pay you."

He looked me up and down, clearly taking in the fact that I was well dressed. "You realize I have the power to deport you? All I need to do is say the word and you are on a police van back to the Iraqi border." He must have seen the fear flicker across my face when he said that, because he nodded in understanding. "Okay, my friend," he said in a nasty tone of voice. "I'll do you a deal. Pay me half the money and I'll let you go."

But even half the money he wanted would have ruined me, so I stood firm. "I'm sorry," I said. "My papers are genuine, but I simply don't have the money to pay you."

He considered that for a minute before speaking abruptly once more: "Come with me." He led me back to the passport control desk, and as I heard the final call for my flight, I felt the eyes of everyone in the waiting line on me. Another official joined him and started asking me the same questions I had already answered, perhaps trying to spot an inconsistency in my story, perhaps just trying to intimidate me more. Still I stood my ground.

Whether the official who was trying to haggle with me about my fine intended the money to go into his own pocket I can't say, but eventually it became obvious to him that I was in no position to pay it. He started huffing and puffing like a spoiled schoolboy denied some treat, and finally he took a big black stamp, opened my passport, and brought the stamp firmly down onto one of the pages. I looked at it: NO RETURN WITHIN FIVE YEARS. "Get out of here," he muttered under his breath before turning to his next passenger.

I looked at him, amazed, but he had already lost interest in me. So I turned away and sprinted to the gate, where my plane was ready to leave.

CHAPTER 11

THE KISS

As I scrambled onto the plane, I received a host of evil looks from my fellow passengers—the flight had been delayed and it was clear to them that it was on my account. I found my seat and stared blankly out of the window waiting for takeoff, my natural fear of flying overwhelmed by the excruciating need to get off the ground. Not until we were in the air would I feel as if I had put enough space between me and the passport control official who had nearly thwarted all my plans. As the flight attendants walked up and down the aisle, I avoided catching their eyes, my paranoia having convinced me that they seemed to be looking at all the passengers with suspicion, as if searching for someone. Only when Jordan was far behind us did I begin to relax, and then only slightly. My satisfaction at having made it onto the flight was mixed with a sense of anger at the passport official, and trepidation: I may have been out of Jordan, but I was by no means safe.

My trip would take me first to Muscat, the capital of the kingdom of Oman, where we would wait in transit for six hours before changing planes. That didn't worry me too much, as I doubted

officials would check my papers while in transit, but I still felt uncomfortable with the two counterfeit passports in different pockets of my jacket as per Abu Firas's advice. Abu Firas had told me that at some stage, on the flight between Muscat and Kuala Lumpur, I should dump my Iraqi passport: that way I couldn't be deported back to Iraq if my UAE passport was spotted as a fake. But it was too early yet—I might need that document before I got on the flight to Malaysia.

The transit lounge in Muscat was as faceless as such places always are. Bored- and tired-looking passengers sat around, some of them reading, some of them chatting, most of them simply staring into space as they waited for the connecting flight. For me, though, the wait seemed to distill my panic, and I hadn't been there long before the familiar pains in my stomach started to make themselves known again. I winced as I felt the stabbing in my abdomen, not because it was bad—not yet—but because I knew how debilitating it could become if I couldn't get it under control. Relaxation was the key—the pains always seemed to be exacerbated by stressful situations, so I made my way to the airport mosque. Perhaps a short period of prayer and contemplation would help me refocus my mind.

The mosque had a comfortable carpet, so I prostrated myself in prayer and then found a quiet corner away from prying eyes where I tried to sleep. But sleep would not come, and the pains grew increasingly bad. They had never been this intense—terrible, excruciating pangs that bent me double and made walking a near impossibility. I did my best not to let the pain show in my face, but before long I was sweating, my dark skin pale and my eyes screwed up in agony. I needed help, so I went to find a flight attendant.

The woman who took me under her wing was like an angel. She sat me down, put her arm around me, and cared for me as solicitously as if I were her own child. Once she had established what was wrong with me, she called a doctor in central Muscat. It took him

the best part of an hour to get to me, an hour that passed as slowly as a day as the pains grew worse and worse. Once he arrived he led me to a sofa in the far corner of the transit lounge and laid me out flat before starting to ask me questions about the pain. Where was it? Had it happened before? I tried to answer him as best I could, but I immediately found myself distracted not only by my condition but also by the group of airport officials who had crowded around and were looking down at this well-dressed young man who seemed to be attracting so much attention.

After listening to my responses, the doctor shook his head and turned away from me. "I can't diagnose him here," he told the officials. "He needs special care, in the hospital. I have to get him into Muscat."

I remember the officials shaking their heads as one. "He needs a visa," one of them said slightly apologetically. "I'm afraid he can't leave the airport."

The doctor shook his head in disgust at this display of red tape, but there wasn't much he could do about it. He knelt down in front of me. "I'm going to give you a quick fix," he said. "Something to relieve the pain. You'll need to remove your jacket so that I can give you the injection."

I shook my head to indicate that I was not going to remove my suit jacket. Despite the pain I was still acutely aware that I was carrying two fake passports on either side of my suit, and there was no way I wanted strangers to get their hands on them. Instead, the doctor rolled up my sleeve, and before I knew it he was approaching me with an injection.

Almost as soon as the needle punctured my skin, I started to feel drowsy.

"What was that?" I heard myself mumbling.

"A tranquilizer," his voice told me, sounding curiously disjointed from his body.

The doctor's face became blurred, as did the faces of the officials standing around him. I became overwhelmed with the desire to close my eyes and succumb to the blanket of sleep that was billowing over me, but I desperately tried to fight it. I'd had no idea I was going to be tranquilized, and although the drug had had an immediate effect on the pain in my stomach I knew I had to combat sleep. I had already attracted attention to myself, and if I was unconscious there was nothing to stop the crowd of officials around me from removing my jacket and discovering the illicit secret it contained. I forced myself to sit up. There were still people hanging around, so I folded my arms so that if I did fall asleep it would be a bit more difficult for them to remove my jacket.

Gradually the crowd of airport staff started to melt away, leaving just the doctor and the flight attendant beside me. Stubbornly I continued to fight off the urge to sleep, much to the surprise of the doctor. In my wooziness I heard him say, "It's not having the right effect. I need to give him a stronger dose."

"No," I muttered, feeling crushed by the effort of speaking.

"But you need to sleep," he insisted.

I shook my head. "Give it to me right before I get on the plane," I managed to ask. "That way I can fall asleep when we're in the air."

The doctor and the flight attendant looked at each other nervously.

"You don't want to have to carry me on," I muttered.

"Why won't you take my advice?" He sounded a little annoyed now.

"I don't want to fall asleep. Not yet."

The doctor shifted uncomfortably, aware that he couldn't force me to be injected but clearly worried about me nonetheless. "Okay," he agreed finally. "We'll do it your way. I'll stay with you until it's time for you to board; but when I say so, no arguments. Understood?"

I nodded my head and spent the next couple of hours desperately trying to remain awake. Then, just as exhaustion threatened to overcome me, my flight was called. I rolled up my sleeve once more for the doctor, received the injection, and then stumbled, accompanied by the flight attendant, toward the plane. As I boarded, I was practically unaware of anyone else. I didn't know if the plane was crowded or empty, or even if there was anyone sitting next to me. I slumped into my seat and instantly fell into a deep, dreamless sleep.

When I awoke, it was dark outside. Confused by the drugs that had been injected into my veins, I was momentarily surprised to be waking up somewhere other than in my little apartment in Amman. Even when the reality of where I was and what I was doing came rushing back to me, it took a while to shake off the chemically induced drowsiness. Gradually I became aware of someone sitting next to me. She was perhaps a couple of years younger than I and looked to be of Asian origin. She was extremely pretty.

"Am I keeping you awake?" she asked with a smile as I yawned rather rudely next to her.

"I'm sorry," I apologized. "I was very tired."

"You must have been," the girl replied. "You've been asleep for more than three hours."

I looked at my watch. She was right—we were well into the flight. The tranquilizer had done its job well, and I was relieved that the stomach pains had subsided; I even found that I was hungry.

"Have they served any food yet?" I asked my companion.

"Not yet." And as if summoned by our conversation, a flight attendant started rattling a cart of plastic meals down the aisle. I ate mine hungrily while the girl and I fell into easy conversation. She was traveling back to Kuala Lumpur with her family, who were elsewhere on the flight, having been to Saudi Arabia to perform the

Hajj, the Muslim pilgrimage to Mecca. I told her that I was visiting friends in Malaysia.

"Where are you from?"

"The UAE," I lied. She seemed to accept my story without question.

"And what do you do for a living?"

"I'm studying to be a doctor." That at least was half true, and it made me feel good to be able to say it.

She told me her name was Khadija, and she started asking me about my family. In my hand luggage I had a small envelope containing some old photographs that were very precious to me. She would not know that they actually had been taken in Baghdad or Mosul, so I showed them to her, pointing out my mother, Uncle Saad, and my brother and sister. She seemed genuinely interested in them, and I found the process therapeutic. I had not talked to anyone about my family for such a long time that to do so now made me feel closer to them even if I was traveling thousands of miles away from where they were.

After a while the overhead lights dimmed and the hubbub of conversation in the plane ebbed away. We fell silent too, and I suddenly became aware that the girl had rested her head against my shoulder. I could hear her breathing deeply. "Are you okay?" I whispered.

She sat up again, nodded, and smiled. There was a momentary tenseness between us, something unspoken that made me want to break away from her wide-eyed glance, but I couldn't. And then, spontaneously, as though by some prearranged signal, our lips touched and we gently kissed.

We stayed in that embrace for several minutes. When she pulled away, she looked sheepishly at me, her cheeks faintly rosy and her big eyes blinking just a bit too much. Once more she put her head against my shoulder and we sat there in silence, our fingers inter-

locked, while everybody about us fell asleep, lulled by the calming hum of the plane's engines. It was a comfort to me to feel her warmth against my shoulder, and it allowed me to relax and collect my thoughts.

My encounter with Khadija lightened my spirits, but my Iraqi passport still felt like a weight in my jacket and I needed to get rid of it. That way, if I had any trouble entering on my UAE passport, the officials would not find it on me if I was searched, and with no Iraqi passport I could not be deported to Iraq. But hiding a passport on a crowded plane would not be easy, and in any case I wasn't entirely sure that the document wouldn't come in useful at some stage in the future. I needed to do something quickly, however. We would soon be in Malaysia, and I couldn't have the thing on me. I glanced down at the girl, whose head was still on my shoulder. There was no doubt in my mind that she would help me if I asked her to, but it would not be right of me to let her know the truth about what I was doing. What she didn't know couldn't incriminate her.

But what if she could help me unwittingly—safely? An idea started to form in my mind, and with it my justifications for acting on it. Looking back, I have to say that I am not particularly proud of what I did next, but it was the only way I could think of achieving what I needed to do.

Surreptitiously I placed the envelope containing my family photos into my pocket. Then I excused myself and walked up the aisle to the lavatory. Safely locked inside, I took my Iraqi passport out of my jacket, slid it inside the envelope with the photographs, then sealed the envelope before walking back to my seat. Khadija and I started talking again in hushed voices, and I waited for an appropriate moment in the conversation before making my request.

"Do you think you could do me a favor?" I asked.

"Of course," she replied. "What is it?"

"I'm not very familiar with the Malaysian postal service. I want

to send these photos to my uncle in England, as he was asking for some pictures. Would you send them for me?"

For a moment she didn't reply, and I silently cursed myself. As I spoke the words, the plan sounded a lot less probable than it had in my head. But I needn't have worried.

"Sure," she said.

Thanking her, I wrote the address on the front of the envelope and handed it over. She placed it with the rest of her hand luggage, and the matter was not mentioned again. I comforted myself with the thought that, as a Malaysian coming back to her home country, it was unlikely that she would be searched; and that even if my Iraqi passport was found on her person, it would probably cause her only some small inconvenience, whereas for me it could spell deportation and the horrors that awaited me back in Baghdad.

And then we landed. As the wheels touched down on Malaysian soil, the familiar feeling of sick apprehension reintroduced itself in my gut, and I found myself wishing to be anywhere but where I was.

"Are you all right, Adel?" the girl asked me. I nodded. "Well, I guess I should say good-bye. It was nice to meet you." She gave me her phone number and address in the area of Petaling Jaya and then flashed me a coquettish little grin, which I struggled to reciprocate. As the plane came to a halt, she stood up and went to join her family.

In the airport terminal I held back at passport control as I wanted to make sure that my Iraqi passport had made it safely through before I presented my documents. I saw the girl and her family waiting to pass through the control booth, and it was with a sense of relief that I witnessed them being waved through without any difficulty. They were Malaysian, of course, but it didn't seem as if anybody was being questioned in any great detail—not that that did anything to allay the panic I was feeling at what I was about to do. I felt my stomach churning and droplets of sweat dripping

down my back; out of the blue I realized how much more crumpled my appearance was than when I had put on my suit the previous morning. It wasn't long before my turn came.

I stepped confidently up to the booth and fixed the border guard firmly in the eye as I handed him my forged documents. He leafed through the pages of the passport, stopping only briefly to glance at Abu Firas's phony Jordanian entry and exit stamps. As he turned the page to examine my photograph, I silently said a prayer of thanks to my architect friend and his dexterous skill. The border guard stared at my photograph for a moment, and then at me. I saw his eyebrows crinkle into a frown as he looked back at the photograph, and I stopped breathing momentarily as he began to examine the document a little more closely.

"Where have you come from?" he asked politely.

"Jordan."

"How long are you staying, sir?"

"A week, maybe two."

"And where will you go to then?"

"Turkey," I said confidently—it was another country UAE passport-holders didn't need a visa for.

He continued to look through my documents as he appeared to mull over the answers I had given.

"How much money have you got, sir?"

"About a thousand dollars."

"Okay." He continued reading for a moment, then looked me up and down.

Suddenly, he stamped the passport, slammed it shut, and handed it back to me.

"Welcome to Malaysia, Mr. Ahmed," he said with what almost passed as a smile.

. . .

. . .

I couldn't wait to leave the airport, and having collected my luggage I practically ran across the concourse to the exit doors, which slid open with a satisfying hiss. Immediately when I stepped outside I hit a wall of humidity that soaked my skin practically on impact—a very real and tangible reminder of how far from home I was.

I took a taxi into the center of Kuala Lumpur. The driver made a few attempts to coax me into conversation, but I didn't speak his language and in any case my thoughts were too much of a whirl-wind of relief for me to have been able to talk sensibly to anyone. I kept pulling my UAE passport out of my pocket and looking at it: it was such a small thing, yet it had got me so far. Fifty percent of the way. A ticket to freedom.

I found myself a shabby hotel in a backstreet in one of the less salubrious quarters of the city—it was all my meager budget would allow. Dirt cheap, my room was little more than a couple of meters square, with filthy bedding and cockroaches as roommates. Sleep would be difficult, as the constant clatter of Malaysian families washing their dishes in the courtyard of the shabby tenement block opposite rang through the air seemingly twenty-four hours a day. But the squalor didn't bother me in the least. If all went according to plan, I would be there for only a few nights before I managed to book my passage to London. Of far greater concern was the fact that I had to leave my precious passport at the reception desk. I wanted to guard that little document with my life—it *was* my life—and I had tried to argue with the hotel owner, to persuade him to let me carry it with me. He was adamant: the rules were there to be obeyed; and if I wanted a room, the passport would have to be stashed in the open pigeonholes behind his beaten-up desk. Anyone could have

taken it—I knew from my experiences over the past few months how vibrant the market in stolen passports was—and this guy had no incentive to keep it safe. And so, several times a day, I found myself wandering back to the hotel to glance at the pigeonhole and check that my passage to freedom had not been stolen.

The following day, I scoured the local travel agents and, having begged the receptionist to let me have my passport for an hour in return for my room key, bought my ticket to London. That, at least, I could keep with me, and it didn't leave my person while I spent the next few days until my flight wandering the streets, taking in the sights and sounds of Kuala Lumpur. It was such an alien place to me—four thousand miles from home, and a culture that could not have been more different from Baghdad or Amman. I made calls home, speaking once more in my roundabout way so that my family would know that I was safe without learning anything that would incriminate them. When the time came to eat, I spent my money on cheap fast food from Western-style restaurants because the local food was too strange for me to enjoy. And at night I lay on my small, uncomfortable mattress, listening to the scratching of the insects under the bed, waiting for the time when I could board my plane to England.

When the day arrived, I donned my suit once more, reclaimed my passport with an overwhelming sense of relief, and made my way to the airport. Having checked my luggage in, I strode confidently to passport control—my previous success had invigorated me, and I knew nothing was to be gained by a diffident approach—and handed my documents to the officer. As he began to check my papers, I looked around properly for the first time. All around me were armed policemen, thick, bulletproof jackets protecting their torsos and evil-looking weapons slung across their chests. One of them caught me looking at him and returned my gaze with a flat,

emotionless look. There was a certain swagger in his stance, as though he took sinister pride in his position of authority, and I remember wondering at that moment how much different my life would have been had the same sense of pride been instilled in me when I had joined the military. No doubt this man would have nothing other than contempt for a deserter like me, because although the world had branded Saddam a criminal, it would no doubt scorch me too if I was caught escaping his terror in this way. The gun and that flat stare were harsh reminders of how unwelcome I was.

"One moment, sir. Wait here, please." The passport control officer broke me out of my daydream by addressing me. He turned and walked to a side room, leaving me with a line of people behind shaking their heads in disapproval at the unwanted delay. But I was well used to this by now, so I simply held my head up high and did my best to bristle with confidence. A few moments later the officer returned, tapped the keys of his computer, then handed me the passport and nodded me on. I was through.

I waited at the gate, for some reason more nervous than I had been at passport control, and started muttering prayers under my breath. I knew that Malaysia was a hub for people-traffickers trying to smuggle people from the Middle East out, mostly to Australia and Japan but also to Europe. I wouldn't feel safe until I was in the sky. It was with huge relief that I boarded and felt the now-familiar press of gravity as the plane took off. This time there was no pretty girl to distract or help me—just a faceless businessman who spoke not a word to me for the entire flight. He did not notice, as our airline meals were cleared away, that I held back the plastic serrated knife and secreted it up my sleeve; or if he did, he didn't mention it.

I knew that I had to destroy my UAE passport to avoid any chance of deportation once I arrived in London, but in my youthful

naïveté I supposed that it would be better to do this once I was in European airspace in case I was somehow discovered while we were in the jurisdiction of some place less friendly. It was foolish of me to think, of course, that the plane would be forced to land on account of one stray Iraqi soldier, but I wanted to play it as safe as possible. The hours until we were cruising over the West ticked slowly by, but eventually, as we were flying over Germany, I excused myself and made my way to the toilets. Once safely locked inside, I took out my passport and my knife and proceeded to shred that precious document into indistinguishable ribbons. It took an age to slice my way through the laminated paper. When I was finished, I was left with an unrecognizable mass, which I dropped, slightly regretfully, into the toilet bowl and flushed away. Those bits of paper and plastic that had afforded me safe passage so far disappeared in seconds. I then made my way back to my seat and did the only thing that was left for me to do: wait.

Gradually I began to feel the familiar sensation of the plane losing altitude. It bumped and wobbled its way through the cloud cover, and as it did so my hand gripped the arm rest tightly. The sudden turbulence was making me nervous, certainly; but I could not separate the vague sense of panic I was feeling because of the juddering from the increasing apprehension that seemed to saturate every cell in my body now that I was nearing the very end of my journey. In the next hour I would find out if all the advice I had received, from Abu Firas and others, was sound; in the next hour I would know whether or not I was to be sent back to Iraq; in the next hour I would know my fate.

Suddenly the plane burst through the clouds. I looked expectantly through the small window at the scene below. It was a bleak December day, misty and gray, the sort of weather that I remembered with a nostalgic vagueness from my childhood, and that I never would have hoped to see in the arid dryness or torrential rainy

seasons of the Middle East. Fields stretched out like patchwork blankets, their shades of green and brown seeming strange to my Arab eyes. There was the occasional town, gray and sprawling, and long lines of traffic, the car lights on high beam to brighten the way through the foggy atmosphere. It was a bland, chilly, uninviting scene; but I wouldn't have welcomed that sight any more had all the golden palaces and riches of the East been spread out before my eyes. It was breathtaking. Impossible. I couldn't quite believe what I was seeing.

Twenty minutes later we were thundering down the runway. Through the drizzle I could see the sights and sounds of the airport as the loudspeaker crackled into life and made me jump. "Ladies and gentlemen," spoke the voice of the captain that I had heard but not listened to at any point during the flight, "welcome to London."

I felt my eyes fill with tears, and I continued to look resolutely out of the window so that my neighbor could not see that I was crying. I had made it. I had arrived.

As we passed through the gates, there were immigration officials standing by. I held my breath as I walked past them, knowing from hearsay that my life would be made a lot more difficult if I was stopped by one of them. Fortunately they were simply chatting among themselves, so I joined the line at the official booths of Heathrow Terminal Three passport control. I watched with amazement the ease with which my fellow passengers were ushered through—their British passports seemed to give them genuine authority that was unavailable to me.

And then my turn came.

I approached the booth with a sense of expectation—excitement, almost—and a smile that was not reciprocated by the surly uniformed woman who received me; but after the aggression I had experienced in the past week, that was not going to worry me. I

took a deep breath and, with a slight crack in my voice, spoke the words that I had been practicing in my head for days and days, the words that I knew, hoped, would finally mark the beginning of a new life, free from the tyrannies of my homeland.

"I want to claim political asylum," I said.

CHAPTER 12

A KNOCK AT THE DOOR

"**W**here's your passport?"
    The woman stared at me with suspicion.

"I want to claim political asylum."

"*Where . . . is . . . your . . . passport?*" She repeated her question slowly, emphatically, as if talking to a child.

"I don't have one."

She shook her head. "I can't process you without a passport."

I shrugged my shoulders, not knowing quite what to say. We stared at each other in silence until she finally broke the deadlock. "What is your name?"

"Sarmed Mahmoud Alsamari."

"Wait here," she said abruptly, then left her post. A couple of minutes later she arrived back with two immigration officers who eyed me up and down as if I was a criminal before leading me to a nearby interview room. They interviewed me in a waspish, perfunctory manner, and I told them what I had done with my passport. One of them looked straight at me, one eyebrow raised and a superior, authoritative look on his face. "If we decide to, we can recover

your passport, piece it back together again, and deport you. You do realize that, I hope."

His words had a desperate, crushing impact on me. I had just landed in this foreign country—I didn't know what the laws or the rules were, so I had no idea that they probably were saying this merely to make me uncomfortable. The elation I had felt before I claimed asylum was suddenly replaced by a horrible fear: what if everything I had been told was not true? What if I wasn't going to be granted asylum after all? Everything would have been for nothing, and I would be sent back to where I came from, left to fend for myself, to fight a battle I couldn't possibly win. I could think of nothing to say to them, so I remained silent.

They continued to process me. They searched through all my luggage and took photocopies of any documentation or literature I had—my library card from the British Counsel in Amman with my false name on it, and a pile of tourist leaflets from Kuala Lumpur that I had stashed away to prove that I had been in Malaysia. They filled in forms and asked me questions, all the while with not so much as a smile or a welcome. We will tolerate your presence, their behavior seemed to be implying, but don't make the mistake of thinking that you are in any way wanted here. I steeled myself against their attitude. Nobody wants to be made to feel unwelcome, but I knew what the alternative was.

"What are the grounds of your claim for political asylum?" they asked me.

I had thought long and hard about how I would answer this question. I had been warned that if I revealed that I had been in the Iraqi military, they would take a special interest in me. I would be thrown into a holding cell and investigated, to ensure that I had not been responsible for any atrocities or war crimes. The process could take months. And so, although I was bursting to tell them my story—to persuade them that I was not simply the opportunist they

so clearly took me for, to persuade them that I was a political refugee and not an economic migrant—I held back.

"I don't want to live under a tyranny," I told them, rather weakly to my ears. "I don't want to serve a dictator and a criminal."

The officers gave no reaction. They simply wrote my words down.

Just as I was beginning to feel that I might never again see a friendly face, however, they released me into the care of some other officials, who took me for x-rays, medical checks, and blood samples. I was manhandled, prodded, poked, and ordered around, but I was at least treated with a little respect, even an occasional moment of friendliness. I was asked if I had family in the UK, and I told them about my uncle Faisal in Leeds. A call was put through, he confirmed that he would receive me, and I was told to wait.

Eventually, twelve hours after we landed, I was allowed through. The sense of release brought tears to my eyes for a second time that day.

Faisal arranged for a friend of his to pick me up from the airport. I spent that night in the spare room of an apartment somewhere on the outskirts of London, and the following day I was driven to Leeds, to see the man I had been looking forward to meeting for so long.

Faisal was a hero, a veteran of the Iran-Iraq war, and a POW; his name was mentioned with hushed reverence in my grandparents' house back in Al-Mansour. I had not seen him since I was six years old; my grandparents hadn't seen him for twenty years. He had been a good boy, I remembered my grandmother saying. When he was a child, his brothers spent their pocket money on bicycles, whereas he spent his on *hijabs* for his sisters. He was a humble, caring, and religious man. "Faisal," my grandmother would mutter. "He is an angel." And as I traveled up to see him, the words my grandfather had whispered to me when I left Al-Mansour for the final time also

echoed in my head: "May God be with you, and *inshallah* you will reach your uncle Faisal in England."

Inshallah. God willing. As I was driven to the north of England, I reflected on the fact that God had indeed been willing. I had completed my journey, and meeting Uncle Faisal was to be my reward.

To my grandmother, Faisal might have been an angel; to me he was more than that. When we first met, I remember being alarmed by the somewhat horrified look he gave me. I now realize that he must have been shocked by my appearance. Gaunt and exhausted, with skin hanging from my bones, bags under my eyes, and a haunted look on my face, I must have cut a very different figure from that of the well-fed six-year-old he remembered. He asked after his parents and siblings, but I had the impression that he would rather not know the true answer, having seen the state I was in.

"They're fine," I told him. "They send their love."

Faisal took me under his wing. He found me a place to live with two other Iraqis. He showed me around, and he helped me to integrate. Without him, I would have been flailing in the dark.

One day I received a call from Faisal. A letter had arrived at his house, addressed to me. I assumed that it was from Baghdad, secretly sent by my mother or Saad, and as I clung to any small contact I could have with them, I hurried over to read it. When I arrived, however, I was surprised to see something somewhat weightier than what I would have expected from Baghdad. Intrigued, I opened the envelope. As I did so, a sheaf of photographs fell out, along with my Iraqi passport. And with them, in exquisite handwriting on a piece of expensive paper, was a note: "I hope you had a safe journey. Good luck with your new life in the UK. *Inshallah* God will guide you and assist you, and keep you from danger."

I had not told the girl on the plane anything about my plans to travel to England, for fear of incriminating her. I had not told her

that I was illegal. I had not told her that I was making her an unwitting accomplice to my plans. Curiosity must have got the better of her, urging her to open up the package. Either that, or I wasn't as clever as I thought, and she had seen through it all.

In Baghdad or Amman, if you stopped someone in the street to ask for directions or for the time, the chances were good that the conversation would lead on from there. Perhaps you would end up going for coffee; you might even be invited back to your new friend's house, where he would offer to cook food for you. It is the Arabic way: hospitality is prized above almost everything else. And although in Iraq you had to be constantly on your guard for civilians who had the ear of the security forces, constantly aware of the subtext of these impromptu conversations, you nevertheless accepted this friendliness as a way of life.

How different it was in England. The last time I had been here, I was a child, unaware of social subtleties; now I was in the thick of a cultural landscape that could scarcely have been more different from the one I had left. I was lucky, though. At least I spoke the language, and I had a genuine desire to learn everything I could about the country I had set my sights on for so long. For the first six months I was not allowed to work, but the government funded asylum-seekers to study at the local college, so I started working for my English and business studies A-levels—subjects that I thought would help me acclimatize. I also spent a great deal of time simply walking the streets, filling my eyes and ears with the sights and sounds of my new home, looking with wonder at how people were living.

I found English people somewhat colder than their Arabic counterparts—not unfriendly, just not that interested, unwilling to

forge immediate relationships with a young Iraqi refugee who must have looked like any number of other foreigners walking the streets. And so, to start with, I spent most of my time in the Middle Eastern communities. Large portions of my day were spent at the local mosque, praying and socializing with people around whom I felt comfortable and, more important, who felt comfortable around me. Mostly these were young British Muslims of Iraqi, Egyptian, Lebanese, and Syrian origin, simple, genuine, good-hearted people who had no need to ask me why I had fled Iraq or what horrors I had endured. They understood. Day by day they taught me about the way of life in the UK, how I should act, how I should talk, how I should behave. They cared for me more than anyone and became like the family that had been denied me by my escape.

Except, of course, they *weren't* my family. My family was two and a half thousand miles away in a small compound in the shadow of the communications tower in Al-Mansour. My family was still living under the regime that would have me imprisoned, beaten, or even worse if I dared to return to see them. I felt in some strange way as if my soul had been split: half of me reveled in the joy of having made it safely to England in the face of so many dangers and difficulties; half of me ached to see my nearest and dearest again. I could speak to them on the telephone, of course, but that was unsatisfactory to say the least. Calls out of Iraq were limited to ten minutes each, but even when I called Baghdad, we always had to assume that the conversation was being listened to and recorded. On occasion you could even hear the heavy breathing of the silent eavesdropper. We all knew it would have proved deeply unfortunate for my family if they let on that they knew where I was, and so our brief conversations were carried out in a kind of code language that allowed us to establish that we were all safe, but we could never speak the things that we really wanted to say or hear.

As soon as it was allowed by the conditions of my entry into the UK, I started at college. My plan had always been to study medicine, to become a doctor and so give something back to the country that had granted me asylum. But I suppose, in my enthusiasm and naïveté, I had not given proper thought to the realities of such a dream. Any qualifications I had achieved in Iraq were worthless in the UK, and the small exam I had taken when in Jordan was insufficient to get me into a medicine course. Moreover, I would have to pursue more than a decade of study. It would be impossible, not because I wasn't willing, but because I knew now I was here that I had to get myself a job. I would have to wait three years before I could be funded at university; but in any case I had no desire to live off the state, and besides supporting myself I had to be able to send some of my earnings—through convoluted routes—back to my family in Iraq. I hoped that one day I would be able to help them get out. But that would take money—money that I had to earn. Of course it could never be mentioned during my phone calls home, but every time I heard Saad's quiet, calm voice I remembered the words with which he had left me: *the genuine man never forgets his family.*

I did not neglect my studies entirely, however. In February 1996 I enrolled in an English course, then a business studies course, and in my spare time I earned money painting houses. It was humble work, but I relished it. Whenever I grew disconsolate, I thought back to the grim realities of the Iraqi army, or to the danger I had faced working at the heart of the Hussein family's operations in Amman. As time passed, I grew my hair long. I discarded the Western clothes that I had believed to be trendy when I was living in the Middle East—T-shirts with the insignias of heavy metal bands like Metallica and Megadeth. I even took an English pseudonym— Louis—in an attempt to appear more Westernized and so that I could travel undetected back to the Middle East if need be. Later

I changed it to Lewis. Gradually I became more and more inte-
grated. Although it would be a while before I was granted a travel
document that would let me leave the country and return, I even
started to have fun. After several months I found myself a more permanent job as a payroll clerk for a big company, and I moved out of
my shared accommodations into a small one-room apartment. I
spent almost every waking hour working: I had my day job as an accounts clerk, a Saturday job in a department store, and a Sunday job
with a real estate agent. The pace was relentless, but I was determined to make the most of all the opportunities that had been afforded me.

Despite the hard work I was doing, my physical health began to
improve. The stomach pains I had been suffering were diagnosed as
a stress-induced ulcer and I was given treatment, but the fact that
my life was now distinctly less traumatic must have played its part in
the condition clearing up. Even so, I still found myself afflicted by
what I had endured.

Nightly I would awaken from sleep, troubled by dreams of Red
Berets, desert wolves, and flat-eyed immigration officials; I would re-
live my spell in the pit as the sneering *arif* looked on; I would find
myself in the cramped cell on the road from my unit to Baghdad, excrement smeared on the floor and no hope of escape. When I woke
up, my body would be shaking, my bedding damp with sweat, and I
would spend the rest of the night wide awake, waiting for first light,
with sleep just a distant and terrifying memory. Panic would overtake
me, and I would fret about my family back in Al-Mansour. The military police seemed to have forgotten about me and them—but how
long would it be until they remembered or their bribes ran out? Those
lonely nights were filled with a series of horrifying *what ifs*. The doctors diagnosed me with post-traumatic stress disorder: a fancy name
for what amounted to an uncontrollable fear of my own past. I was re-

ferred to a therapist, who spent eight months working with me to try to conquer the PTSD. In the end he judged that it was so severe that I needed medication. I was prescribed maximum doses of an antidepressant and remained on the drug for the next six years.

To try to forget my troubles, I threw myself even more robustly into my work. In the small amounts of spare time that I had left, I started trying to mingle with groups of young English people, and even though I gradually started to feel a greater sense of acceptance on their part, I never quite managed to feel comfortable, never quite managed to shake off the feeling that I was an outsider in a strange world that had started to acknowledge me but to which I would always be an alien.

Until, that is, I met Rachel.

We met in a local bar. It was the sort of chance encounter that you wouldn't expect to lead to anything serious—a glance across the room that led to a relationship that would change both our lives. We fell into an easy, friendly conversation that made us both feel comfortable, and from that night on we spent almost every spare hour we had with each other. I was transfixed by her long, Titian hair and by her modest smile and sparkling eyes that betrayed a vitality and fiery determination that I had never before encountered. She was older than I and had a good job, and I was attracted by her confidence and poise. What she saw in me I can't say, but gradually, as we became closer, I opened up to her.

Since arriving in England, I learned to push my past into a far corner of my mind. My story was different, I knew that, but I wore it like a comfortable suit of clothes and refrained from revealing it to anyone. If people knew what I had endured, perhaps they would treat me differently, and that was not what I wanted. But now, with the stark honesty of two people who were falling in love, we revealed all there was to tell about each other. The look of wide-eyed amazement

mingled with horror and pity that I saw on Rachel's face as I told her everything I had gone through was a sudden, brutal reminder of my own past, and a signal that I would never really be free of it.

"What about your family," she asked me. "Don't you miss them?"

"Of course I do," I told her quietly. "More than anything. But one day, maybe, I'll be able to see them again."

"What can I do to help?"

I smiled gratefully at the offer. "Nothing," I told her. "Not at the moment."

Rachel and I moved in together, and after about six months we started talking about marriage. My uncle Faisal was a very religious man, well respected at the local mosque, and he did not like the idea of the two of us living together as man and wife without the sanctity bestowed on our relationship by a wedding ceremony, so he started to pressure us into getting married. Even if his influence on me had not been so great, however, we would have considered it.

Our wedding day was not huge or lavish—neither of us had the money for that. We had a small civil ceremony, witnessed by a somewhat surprised-looking couple whom Rachel had dragged off the street. Yet, for all its simplicity, the words we spoke could not have been more heartfelt and meaningful. We were devoting our lives to each other, along with all that that entailed. Making the whole event even more potent was the fact that Rachel was of Jewish extraction: her marriage to an Arab seemed to me to symbolize something particularly harmonious.

In the Hollywood movies to which I had become addicted, young couples in love promised the world to each other. They would do anything, they said. They would follow their loved one to hell and back. Little did I know that Rachel would end up doing exactly that for me.

. . .

. . .

Not long after I moved in with Rachel I received a call from Saad. Instantly I could tell from the sound of his voice that what he had to tell me was of great importance, so I restrained my usual effusiveness and listened to what he had to say. *"Habibi,"* he greeted me cautiously with the traditional Arabic term of affection, which served the double purpose of his not having to say my name. "How are you? How is your health?"

"Fine," I replied. "And you?"

"We're *okay.*" He emphasized the word to make it clear that they were very far from being okay but he could say no more.

Soon afterward I received a letter from Saad, sent covertly by way of Jordan because he knew that Iraqi authorities had teams of people reading regular mail. Its contents chilled my blood. The military police had interrogated Saad. The moment I read those words, a sick feeling rose in my stomach. It had been a long time since *Al-Istikhbarat* had questioned Saad, and I had come to believe that they had given up on me.

I could not have been more wrong. Saad was put into a room by himself, where his hands were cuffed behind his back. His eyes were pinned open so that he could not blink, and the light from a large projector was shone onto his face. When he could stand no more, he was taken from the cell and either beaten or interrogated. This was repeated about every four hours for three days, during which time he was given no food or water.

He steadfastly refused to admit that he knew my whereabouts.

When the three days were up, he was released, but it was made quite clear that he, along with the rest of my family, could expect worse than that if they did not comply with the intelligence service's demands.

When I finished reading the letter, I banged the wall in frustration.

I knew I was going to have to remain calm if I was going to be any help to them. I knew anger would get me nowhere. But anger was what I was feeling—anger and an intolerable impotence at being so far away when all this was happening because of me. When Rachel returned home, she could tell from the look on my face that something was wrong, and though she begged me to tell her what had happened, somehow I didn't have the heart. I looked around with distaste at the comfortable apartment we shared: the smart furniture, the carpets, the pictures on the wall, all the trinkets of the affluent West. They seemed ridiculous to me now. How could I surround myself with such comfort while my family was being beaten and threatened on my account? I felt sick to my very soul: despite all my hard work since I had arrived in England, I was no nearer to being able to get them out. I had failed them, and they were paying the price.

From that moment on, my every waking thought was with my family. I would go into fits of panic, unable to sleep and desperate to speak to them. I would spend hours trying to get through on the phone, sometimes successfully, sometimes unsuccessfully. Poor Rachel, when she learned the stark and brutal truth of what was happening in Baghdad, did her best to comfort me, but it was in vain.

Not long after I first heard the terrible news, I received another call from Saad.

"Those people I was telling you about, *Habibi*," he said before I had a chance even to inquire after his health. "They want a bit of money." His voice was abrupt with what I imagined to be a tinge of genuine trauma, and I understood what he was saying—he had to pay another bribe.

"I'll send as much as I can."

"You must, *Habibi*. Otherwise they can't do what they promised. It's too much for me."

I quietly understood what he was saying: the amounts I had been sending home were not enough. Not now.

"I hope you're not enjoying yourself too much," he continued. I didn't know what to say. "You should be thinking of us now. Of your family. Remember what I told you."

Each word he spoke was like a bullet. I knew I had to do something to help, but I didn't know what.

That night I dreamed about my mother. Curiously I did not picture her at home or suffering in the clutches of *Al-Istikhbarat*. Instead I remembered her in England, when I was a child, huddled over the phone with tears in her eyes, speaking to her family in Baghdad. There had been raised voices behind closed doors between her and my father. I had hidden in my room until they died down; and when I next saw my mother, she looked like a broken woman. In my dream she looked at me, her sad eyes seeming to pierce through me, and I awoke trembling and sweating. For a moment I wondered where I was, then was instantly reoriented by the sound of Rachel breathing deeply next to me. I quietly slipped out of bed and moved to another room, where I sat and looked out the window and into the night sky. It was clear, and the crescent moon looked back down at me—the same moon, I remember thinking, that was looking down at my family in Al-Mansour, on the Bedouin desert by the Jordanian border, on the café in Amman where Abu Firas used to sit. I thought of all the people who had helped over the years, who had got me where I was. Safe. Comfortable. Free. I would be repaying their kindness to me poorly if I did not now direct all my energies into helping my family, into granting them the same security that I now enjoyed. What else could I do?

The next day I started making calls. I spoke to my Iraqi friends, and to friends of friends, to ask whether they knew of smugglers based in the UK who would be able to arrange for my mother and siblings to disappear from Baghdad. There were a few vague leads,

rumors of people who could help, but most people said the same thing: it would be difficult and expensive. Everyone wanted to come to England, the routes were full and being watched, and the smugglers had more business than they could handle. Much better, they said, to arrange something from inside Iraq. But how could I do that? The only person I could think of who might be able to help my family was the father of my friend Hakim. He was a Kurd and, unusually, had been appointed to a governmental position because he was loyal to Saddam. Not so loyal, however, that he wasn't prepared to arrange for people to be smuggled through Kurdistan and into Turkey. But as usual there was a price tag. Even if I suggested to my family that they speak to him, I knew they would need more money than they had. They were saving everything I sent them, but the sums involved would be far more substantial.

And so I inquired about loans. I lost count of the number of banks, building societies, and loan sharks I spoke to, but they all gave me the same reply: no. I had no collateral, no equity. To borrow the sums of money I was talking about—tens of thousands of pounds—simply wasn't going to be possible.

I grew more and more demoralized as the doors in front of me shut one by one. Then I received another call.

This time it was from my uncle Musaab, Saad's brother. His voice was breathless, concerned, but he tried to keep it level for the benefit of the third party who we suspected was probably listening in.

"*Habibi,* you know those neighbors of ours, the ones you were trying to write to?"

"Yes," I replied. "I know the ones you mean."

"They're in a bit of trouble."

"What sort of trouble?" I asked the question with a nonchalance that I did not feel.

"They've been taken away. Locked up."

I caught my breath. "Locked up?" I repeated, stunned by this information. "Where?"

There was a pause before Musaab answered. "Where do you think?" he asked me, his voice dripping with meaning.

CHAPTER 13

THE DEVIL, *IBLIS*

In Iraq, they tell the story of a merchant who had a servant. One day the servant went to the marketplace in Baghdad, where he bumped into what looked like an old man. The man turned to look at the servant, who saw that it was in fact Death himself. Death gave him a strange look, and the servant fled back to his master. "Master," he said, "I just saw Death in the marketplace, and he gave me a meaningful look. Please may I borrow your horse so that I may travel to Samarra and avoid what he has in store for me?" The merchant lent the servant his horse, and the servant fled.

Later that day, the merchant went to the marketplace himself, where Death was still waiting. "Why did you scare my servant?" he asked.

"Scare him?" replied Death. "I didn't mean to scare him. I was just surprised to see him in Baghdad. You see, I have an appointment with him in Samarra this evening."

. . .

• • •

Al-Haakimiya. Al-Mukhabarat. The very words encapsulated everything that was evil about life in Iraq. Al-Mukhabarat was Iraq's General Directorate of Intelligence and Al-Haakimiya was its prison; I had been running for fear that I might end up there, to learn firsthand all the horrific secrets its walls contained, but instead my good fortune had been monstrously inverted and my family faced imprisonment.

My sister had been spared. Rumors reached my ear that she had caught the eye of somebody with a certain amount of influence, an official of some kind who had been stalking her, following her in his car when she left the house, and taking an unwanted and unnatural interest in her affairs. By a horrible irony, this unasked-for infatuation had protected her, but that protection was not extended to Saad, to my mother, or to my brother.

It is hard to find the words to describe how I felt when I heard the news. My mind was a maelstrom of powerlessness and indecision. There I was, stuck in the UK, unable to return and make amends. I had no wealth or influence, no strings I could pull or arms I could twist. There was nothing I could do. Worst of all, I had no information, no way of knowing what was being done to my family, or whether they were dead or alive. It was left to my imagination to picture what was happening to them, the desperate kind of state they were in, and my imagination ran riot. Not until much later did I discover what had actually occurred.

Everyone in Baghdad knew about Al-Mukhabarat's prison. Word of its horror was common currency. But few people who had experienced it firsthand ever spoke of it in detail, and even in the time that was to follow, my family was reluctant to describe it. To this day my mother will not speak of her time there, but from conversations with my brother I know this much to be true: The cells

in which my family were placed were tiny—two meters by three—with five or six people in each cell. There were other prisoners, like them, who had done nothing that right-thinking people would consider to be wrong; but there were also plenty of genuine criminals—murderers and thieves—who were not segregated from those accused of lesser crimes. The prison walls were filthy, stained in places with stubborn splashes of dried blood that attracted the always-present flies. The concrete floors were similarly unpleasant, covered with bits of old food, human urine, and clumps of hair; this debris attracted not only the flies but other scavengers, especially cockroaches, which made sinister, shuffling noises at night. The air was ridden with mosquitoes and fleas, and you found lice in your own hair within hours of arriving, so unhygienic were the conditions.

The smell of the cells was matched by the smell of the prisoners: they too reeked of sweat and urine. Their clothes bore visible reminders of the squalor in which they were living: they would sweat in the heat of the day, and the sweat would dry as they continued to perspire. The result was thick, visible marks of salt on their clothes where the sweat had dried. There were prison baths, but they were seldom used, and even when they were used, prisoners came out scarcely any cleaner than when they went in. The paint on the sides of the baths was peeling to reveal rusty old metal, and the sides were covered in a distinct kind of grimy mucus.

Everyone was constantly hungry. The food consisted only of rice or a thin bean stew. In either case it was clear from the taste that the raw ingredients had been putrefying somewhere, because there was always the taste of rot. The only time that taste was ever masked was when salt was added to the food; but when that happened, the salt was added in such gargantuan quantities as to make the food almost inedible. No matter how unpalatable it was, however, the food was always eaten because it was so scarce.

The air was constantly thick with the fumes of cigarette smoke—almost all the prisoners smoked as a way of taking their minds off their desperate conditions—and it was never possible to have any fresh, natural air because most cells were windowless. The windows in the cells that had them were small and high up. As a result, the majority of the prisoners were ill with respiratory diseases—pneumonia and the like. All day and all night there was the sound of sneezing, vomiting, and the bringing up of phlegm. The guards, of course, ignored all cases of ill health other than the most extreme: you had to be unconscious before you were taken off for the rudimentary health care the prison offered.

The guards themselves treated the prisoners worse than animals, never speaking to them other than in terms of insult, always referring to them as "dogs" and "imbeciles." Slaps to the face were commonplace and were among the more lenient treatment that could be expected on a daily basis. Often, and without warning or reason, prisoners were told to sit in a line on the floor, where the guards proceeded to kick them in the face and in the stomach until they were little more than bruised and bloodied messes. On other occasions, they were whipped all over their bodies with short pieces of blue rubber hose about the length of a ruler.

Retaliation, of course, was unthinkable.

It took a number of weeks for them to be released. All the while, I feared the worst. When I finally received a phone call to say they were out, I almost collapsed with relief. I was overwhelmed with the need to find out how they were, and never did the need to speak in our roundabout, coded way seem so difficult.

Gradually, though, I was made aware of the realities of the situation. It had been made clear to them that unless I returned, they would be recalled and could look forward to living in the cramped cells of that stinking prison for the rest of their days—however long that should be—enduring on a daily basis the violent whims of

whichever prison guard felt like beating them up. This mistreatment was not going to stop now that my family had been singled out, so somehow, however we could, we had to raise the money to pay smugglers to get them out of Iraq. They weren't an attractive proposition for a smuggler: three of them traveling together, one of them a middle-aged woman who bore the weight of her difficult years heavily. It would cost tens of thousands of pounds.

Once again I tried to borrow the money but was rejected. Rachel offered to help, but her credit was insufficient, and Faisal was not in a position to help either. I started to go out of my mind thinking of ways to raise the cash, and all the while my mother and brother could be dragged back to prison.

While all this was happening, I was temping in the financial departments of various big companies. All day long I was in charge of transferring huge sums of money from one account to another. The transactions were entirely straightforward, and after a while the amounts involved, which often ran into the millions, became meaningless. Just figures. I finally found myself working in the accounts department of the bookmaker William Hill. Thousands of transactions a day passed through this department, and I fulfilled my duties unenthusiastically, always mindful of what was happening two and a half thousand miles away and constantly distracted by Saad's increasingly frequent phone calls during which he said so little but meant so much. Occasionally the irony struck me that the people around me were spending all their time handling sums of money that would have smuggled a thousand families from under the nose of *Al-Istikhbarat,* but never did it occur to me that I might be able to use any of this money to help my mother, brother, and sister.

Until one day, that is, when I felt the Devil, *Iblis,* tap me on my shoulder.

I was working quietly at my desk, shuffling papers rather unenthusiastically and without fully taking in what I was reading. Suddenly I became aware of a conversation happening at the desk in front of me between two of my colleagues. They were working at the computer, transferring money from customers' betting accounts into the relevant bank accounts. Clearly one of them had his own betting account, and it came up on the screen. "Look," he told his friend, "I've won a tenner."

I watched as his friend glanced at the screen. "Nice one," he said. "Shall we transfer it now?"

The winning employee nodded, tapped his password into the computer, and made the transfer. As he did so, his friend spoke: "Hang on, you've transferred a hundred, not ten."

The employee nodded, and with another tap of the keyboard transferred the money back. "Nice try," his friend noted, and they both laughed.

"What do you think would happen if I'd just left it there?"

"They'd track you down, mate, and fuck you over."

It was as simple as that. Not only had the Devil given me a way to save my family, he had also told me what would happen if I followed the path he showed me.

I hesitated while I weighed the pros and cons of the idea that was forming in my mind. I told nobody what I was planning to do, not even Rachel, who saw that I was increasingly distracted but just put it down to the stress of the news that was coming from Iraq. The choice was a simple one: do nothing and risk my family spending the rest of their lives rotting in Al-Haakimiya, where they would be tortured and maltreated, or illicitly transfer some of William Hill's money to my account to pay for their release. Without question, my employers and the police would catch up with me—I wasn't so naive as to believe that my actions would go undetected—but that probably wouldn't happen until there was an audit of the company,

which would give me several months' grace in which to get my family out. What I was about to do would be entirely premeditated, and I felt sure that the authorities would be severe with me no matter how extenuating my circumstances. But if I was sent to prison, so be it. At least in British prisons you didn't get tortured, brutalized, or killed.

It took me several days to come to my decision, but in reality the decision had already been made for me.

The first thing I needed to do was to open a betting account. That was simple enough: ten minutes in a bright, buzzing Internet café, surrounded by young people happily typing e-mails to loved ones, oblivious of what I was doing. Next, I had to open a number of bank accounts. The amount of money I was planning to steal was considerable, and I imagined that it would be less easy to trace a number of small transactions to different accounts than one big tranfer. The authorities would catch up with me eventually, of course, but I needed to ensure I had enough time to do what I had to do.

The next hurdle was more difficult to overcome. The transfer of money at William Hill was not part of my job, so I did not have access to the passwords that were necessary to affect it. The passwords themselves were guarded quite jealously: all the employees who needed them had their own separate passwords and were unlikely to reveal them to anybody else because they knew that the system would be open to abuse. Moreover, the passwords changed regularly. Once I discovered a password, I would have to move quickly.

I started to fall into casual conversation with the colleague whom I had overheard transferring money in the first place. Over a period of a few days we became as friendly as the stifling office atmosphere would allow. I loitered by his desk, drinking coffee and chatting while he carried on with his work. He was a talkative guy, and we had no difficulty keeping the conversation going. He

showed no signs of realizing the ulterior motive behind my sudden camaraderie, and as we spoke, I was able to glance at his fingers while he was typing. It took a few tries, but eventually I managed to work out his password. I didn't worry that my using it would land him in trouble: why would he use his password to transfer money to my account? In any case, I had no intention of doing anything other than tell the whole truth about my actions when the authorities did finally catch up with me.

I had everything I needed. The following day, I waited for everyone to leave the office at lunchtime, while I stayed behind. I approached a computer terminal and, my heart in my mouth, typed in what I hoped was the correct password.

It worked.

To start, I transferred only a small amount of money—a hundred pounds, I think—just to check that it would work. As soon as I finished, I logged out and walked quickly away from the terminal. No one had been watching, but I couldn't dispel the hot flush of unease that swept across my body at the thought of what I had done. I felt sick and continued to do so for the rest of the day.

Next morning, I checked my bank account. Nothing. The following morning I did the same. Nothing. But on the third day, it was there.

Suddenly I was filled with misgivings. You can't do this, Sarmed, I told myself. It's not right. There has to be another way. That lunchtime I returned to the computer terminal and transferred the money out of my account and back to William Hill.

I didn't sleep that night, my mind awash with conflicting thoughts. It had been so easy to make the transfer; so easy to walk down the route that I knew would lead to huge trouble for me; so easy to decide, after all, not to do it. And maybe that was the right thing. Even if I sent Saad the money he needed, there was no guarantee that my family wouldn't be thrown back into prison. Perhaps

I should simply hope and pray that no harm would come to them, that when their captors realized that I was not going to come back, they would release them unharmed. Deep down, though, I knew that was a vain hope. What went on in the prisons of Baghdad was no secret; indeed Saddam no doubt *wanted* his people to be aware of the evils that awaited them if they transgressed. And as I was growing up I had heard of enough people who had disappeared never to be seen again. The thought of that happening to my family was too much for me to bear. I resolved to go ahead with my plan.

The following day I hacked in to the computer once more—this time, into several accounts. I transferred the very least I knew I could get away with to ensure my family's release from prison and subsequent escape from Iraq. It wasn't a very exact calculation, but it was based on my rough idea of how much I would need: £37,500.

The instant the money hit my accounts, I transferred half of it, through the convoluted routes I had become used to, to Saad. When word came back that he had received it, I rested a little more easily. My relief was to be short-lived, however, as any expectations I had that the transfer of money would effect an immediate release were shown to be optimistic. Two weeks passed, then three, and from Baghdad there was nothing but silence. Saad was trying to make the payment to the necessary people, but it was an excruciatingly slow process. Meanwhile, I felt an increasing sense of paranoia: every time the phone rang, I jumped; every time I saw a policeman, I hid. Since arriving in England, I had forgotten how it felt to be a fugitive, but now that sensation was with me once more.

To keep myself occupied, and mindful of the fact that time was not on our side, I started making inquiries about how I could use the remainder of the money to spirit my mother, brother, and sister out of Iraq. Through acquaintances in the Iraqi community in the

UK, I made contact with people-smugglers to determine the best way to get my family out, and how much it would cost. In Baghdad, Saad did the same. It became apparent, even with the remainder of the William Hill money, that it would be expensive: the smugglers saw our desperation and increased the price accordingly. We soon realized that we still did not have the funds to pay someone to organize the whole thing for us, so I decided that we would have the professionals arrange their transfer to a neighboring Middle East country; the remainder of the journey I would organize myself. Had I known what awaited us, I would never have made that decision.

My mother, brother, and sister had a thick wad of passport photographs taken in differing disguises and then sent to me in England. A Kurdish smuggler met them at home and gave them cloned Iraqi passports with false Kurdish names. It would be most difficult for my brother. He was nearly old enough for military service, so the penalty for leaving the country illegally would be especially severe for him. He had the benefit, though, of looking much younger than his real age, and his passport stated that he was several years younger than he actually was. My mother donned her *hijab* to make herself less recognizable, and within a couple of days of arriving home they said good-bye to Saad and to my grandparents and left with the smuggler in one of the familiar orange and white taxis that swarmed the streets of Baghdad.

The taxi could not simply travel west to the Jordanian border: the Iraqi border guards would quickly have seen that the passports were fake. Instead the route took my mother, brother, and sister north, through my father's hometown of Samarra, past Tikrit, and into Mosul. From there they entered Kurdistan. The Kurds had a separate administration, but this was still officially Iraqi territory, and there was a heavy checkpoint at this stage. Without the help of the Kurdish smuggler, the fake passports would not have got them

through; but he had some of the border guards in his pocket. A few wads of notes from the William Hill money placed into the hands of these corrupt officials soon bought them passage into Kurdistan. From there they continued north into Turkey, before doing an about-face and heading south through Syria and into Jordan. The border guards in those countries had no way of telling that the passports were fake, so they passed through, if not without suspicion, then at least without hindrance.

By now the British government had issued me a document allowing me to travel abroad, and while my family was making their circuitous journey around the Middle East, I had business to attend to. I had had success traveling from Jordan to the UK by way of Malaysia, so I decided that this was the route I would arrange for them. However, they needed false passports, because the fake Iraqi ones they had would be no good. I had nobody like Abu Firas to help me arrange things, so I had to do it all myself.

A friend of mine, a member of the Iraqi community in Leeds at the time, had been smuggled from Jordan to the UK by way of Romania by an Iraqi people-smuggler—an Alsamari called Radwaan—in Romania. That was a difficult route, so it seemed clear that the smuggler in question was skilled and influential. Radwaan and I spoke at length on the phone, not once or twice but many times as we both tried to get the measure of each other. He was persuading himself that I was serious and not simply a time-waster or, even worse, someone trying to set him up. I wanted to be sure that this faceless voice at the end of a telephone line could do what he claimed in return for the many thousands of pounds I was going to have to pay him. Eventually, the rapport between us became more comfortable, and we reached the stage where we could talk plainly about what it was I wanted. I asked him directly if he could provide passports for my family.

"Of course," he replied smoothly.

"What's available? What can you give them that will get them from Jordan and then in and out of Malaysia?"

"It's limited," he told me. "Spanish is your best bet. Or Israeli."

"And are they original passports? Foolproof, I mean."

"Of course they are." He didn't sound offended that I had asked the question. "You can check them out before you buy, if you like. Just go to Germany, and see my brother. He'll show you what you'll be getting for your money—nobody will be able to tell the difference between the passports we supply and the real thing. You won't have any trouble at all."

Something about Radwaan's manner filled me with confidence. He had the quiet, easygoing attitude that had first recommended Abu Firas to me, and he wasn't pushy, didn't try to give me the hard sell. But I had only one shot at this, and he could hear the indecision in my voice. "Go and see my brother," he insisted. "He is the one you'll have to give the money to. Then make your decision."

The brother was living in Mannheim with his Romanian wife and small child. My travel document wasn't officially recognized in Germany, but I decided that I would risk it anyway. Sure enough, I got off the plane and presented my document at passport control, and as soon as the officer saw the words "Great Britain" at the top, I was waved through. The contrast between the power of that slip of paper and the passports I had used in the past was almost shocking. I went to stay at the brother's house and spent hours talking to him, once more getting the measure of the man as I had done with Radwaan. Finally, after several hours of wary and then friendly conversation, he pulled out some sample passports. They were Spanish, and to my eye they looked perfect. The final product, I was assured, would have my family's real names marked inside, along with the photographs that they had sent me. I smiled inwardly: these were as good, if not better, than the fake UAE passport Abu Firas had

arranged for me. But still, they were going to cost thousands of pounds each—money I was still reluctant to pass on to these people, no matter how sweetly they spoke.

"How will you want the money?" I asked him.

"Cash," he said shortly. "In person. Here."

"I can't transfer it from London?"

"No." He shook his head firmly before smiling sympathetically at me. "You are still worried?"

"It's a lot of money for me," I told him honestly. "If this does not work, my family will be stuck. I'm not rich."

"I understand. Perhaps you should go to Bucharest, speak to Radwaan. It's good to know exactly who you are dealing with."

And so I did. From Germany I flew to Romania, again without the necessary visa. When I arrived at passport control, it became clear that my entry into the country would not be as simple as it was in Germany. As a stern official examined my document, though, I heard a voice above the hubbub: "Alsamari! Where is Alsamari?"

I held up my hand, and a rather overweight woman jogged, red-faced, toward us. "You're here to see Radwaan?" she asked.

I nodded, and she spoke a few words out of earshot to the official, who immediately stamped my document and allowed me to board my flight to Bucharest. Clearly Radwaan was a man of more influence than I had expected.

He picked me up at the airport, a jolly man whose friendly demeanor belied a serious, businesslike attitude toward his chosen profession. We went to his house, and he showed me some more sample Spanish passports. "These are the best," he told me. "Original. You can't get better than this. No one will raise an eyebrow at them. And, if you don't like the finished product . . ."

I looked at him expectantly.

"You don't pay for them. It's as simple as that."

Finally I was convinced. I had the recommendation of my

friend in London, I had seen the kind of influence this man had over passport officials, and he wasn't even asking for the money up front. I went to my bag and handed him the thick sheaf of passport photographs my family had sent me. He smiled. "I don't need as many as that," he said before selecting a few of each member of the family and handing the rest back to me. Then he drove me back to the airport.

Once more, as I was passing through passport control, my travel document aroused suspicion. A monster of an official, a huge man with square shoulders and a tiny square head—he looked like Frankenstein's monster—surrounded by three or four much smaller men, spoke to me in broken English with a thick Romanian accent.

"Do you have anything dangerous in your bag, like bombs, or weapons, or gases—anything like that?"

"No."

"Where are you flying to?"

"London."

"You're British. You have British passport."

I handed him my travel document. "Yes," I said confidently.

One of his eyebrows shot up. "This is not a British passport. Open your bags."

Reluctantly I unzipped my hand luggage and gave it to him. It took less than a few seconds for him to pull out the wad of photographs that I was carrying. He looked at them silently; then he looked around at his friends. They all grinned, a nasty expression that made it perfectly clear they knew what was going on. He let me squirm for a few moments without taking his eyes off me before he spoke again.

"Who have you come to see in Romania?" he asked slowly.

"I came to see my friend."

"What is his name?"

"Radwaan."

Immediately I saw the light of recognition in his eyes. "Ah." He smiled. "Radwaan." He turned around to look at his friends. "He's come to see Radwaan!" he told them loudly, and they all started to nod their heads knowingly.

It was clear that they knew who Radwaan was, and what he did. It was equally clear that Radwaan had them in his pockets.

"Okay," he said finally, packing the photographs back into my bag. "Off you go."

As soon as I returned to England, I collected the money I needed and flew back out to Mannheim to deliver it. A week later I went back to Germany to collect the passports. They were immaculate, just as I had been told they would be. All the while, I was illegal in Germany. If I had been caught with these things in my pocket, I would have been locked up; but such thoughts were far from my mind. I can honestly say that I didn't even give the danger of my situation a second thought.

By the time I had all the documents in order, my mother, brother, and sister had arrived safely in Amman. I had no desire to delay things, as I was half expecting the police to knock on my door at any time on account of the William Hill money, but I allowed myself a few days to cobble together any supporting evidence of my family's identity—ID cards, student cards, and the like—before booking my flight to Amman.

But before I did anything else, I had to speak to Rachel.

She knew I was desperate to see my family. How could she not? It had been Rachel who had comforted me in the dark days since my family had been dragged into prison, and Rachel who had put up with my prolonged absences as, unbeknownst to her, I risked my liberty to obtain the Spanish passports. She had lived with my increasing distraction and panic; and at night, when my fears were

increased tenfold, she had soothed me with her quiet, understanding embrace. Now I had to tell her that I was about to do the one thing that I had hoped would never be my lot: return to the Middle East, where I would be illegal, and embark upon a series of events that could result in my family's deportation back to what awaited them in Iraq, and to my own imprisonment.

"I can't pretend it's not dangerous," I told her. "I can't pretend there's not a risk that I won't come back."

Rachel looked into my eyes. Any intuition I had that this would be a tearful moment was instantly dispelled as she stared at me with such immeasurable determination that I was momentarily taken aback. "What?" I asked, afraid for a minute that she was going to try to persuade me to back out of everything.

"I'm not going to let you do this by yourself."

It took a moment before it dawned on me what she was saying, but as it did so I shook my head. "No way . . ." I started to tell her.

But she was adamant. "You don't have to do this by yourself," she insisted. "I'm a British citizen. I can travel wherever I like. You might need help at any stage of your journey, and if so I want to be there."

I continued to object, but she gently put her finger against my lips. "I'm coming with you, Lewis," she told me. "And that's the end of it."

GOING BACK

When Rachel gave me a farewell embrace before my departure to Amman, the plan was this: She would not accompany me to Jordan. Instead I would travel alone, hoping that my inability to get a Jordanian visa would not hamper my entry. After all, I had been waved through in Germany, and I knew there was a possibility that I could just pay a fee if I was stopped at the border. Once in Amman, I would meet with my family and buy them two sets of tickets to Malaysia, one set in their Kurdish names on the fake Iraqi passports that would enable them to leave Amman, and one set in the names printed on their fake Spanish passports that would allow them to enter Kuala Lumpur. I booked myself on the flight to Kuala Lumpur, which was to make a stop in Abu Dhabi. That was where we were to meet Rachel, who had flown from London to Abu Dhabi and also was booked on the flight to Kuala Lumpur. Although she was insistent on coming, I could not tell her the details of my plan because I did not want her to be a party to the risks I was taking. I felt sick lying to her, but it was, I calculated, the only way to keep her safe.

It was complicated and finely tuned, but I figured that I had done it once before, so I could do it again.

Miraculously, I entered Jordan without any difficulty whatsoever. Again, one look at the words "Great Britain" afforded me politeness and expedited my passage in such a way that I would have thought impossible a few years previously. I paid a sum equivalent to ten pounds for my visa and was ushered into the country, all the while mindful of the treatment I had received when I last tried to leave. As I walked into the main arrivals area, it was buzzing with people. I scanned the crowds, trying to spot my family, and for a moment I felt a curious tingle of dread, as I thought they were not there. But then I saw them. They were standing in a far corner of the concourse, huddled closely together and looking around nervously, concern etched on their faces, ignored by all around them and emanating an aura that seemed to beg everyone not to pay them any attention. Never did three people look so uncomfortable and out of place, and only then, I think, did the full impact of what they had been through finally sink in. Having seen them before they saw me, I almost tripped up over myself as I hurried over in their direction, but I gradually slowed down as their faces became more distinct. They looked haggard and drained. The way their clothes hung from their bodies spoke loudly of their malnourishment, and you would have been forgiven for thinking, from the black circles around their eyes, that they had been fighting. They looked as if they hadn't slept in weeks. It cut me to the quick to see them in that state.

And then they saw me. As one, their faces broke into smiles that only seemed to emphasize the pitiful state they were in, but I couldn't help smiling back: it was so wonderful to see them. Silently we hugged, oblivious to the crowds around us, our bodies absorbing the sensation of one another's presence as though we were thirsty and drinking deeply from a cup of cool water. There were smiles and there were tears, and I remember thinking that even if everything

went wrong from now on, it would be worth it just for that first moment of reunion.

The smell of their clothes reminded me of Iraq, and other things too seemed somehow to speak to me of a difference between us, a gulf that had emerged in the time I had been in the West. As we walked away, the three of them stayed close together, their eyes darting around nervously just as they would have done if they knew they were doing something illicit on the streets of Baghdad. I wanted to tell them to look more confident, but then I remembered how I too had felt when I first arrived in Amman, how I had run from shadows and had wanted nothing more than to blend into the background. They spoke to me humbly, almost diffidently, and of matters that seemed to me to be somehow simplistic. Occasionally I caught my brother and sister looking at me with undisguised awe—a flattering yet painful experience. I suppose that in some way it made me feel superior: I had so much to teach them about the life that, *inshallah,* awaited them in the UK. But then I forced myself to remember the realities of what they had undergone in prison and since, and I reminded myself that there was in them both strength and worldliness that comfortable Westerners with their Nintendo machines and expensive Reebok sneakers could never know. So I fell in beside them, listening to the minutiae of their conversation as we left the airport.

How many times I had pictured this meeting in my mind's eye. Now that it had arrived I realized I was unprepared for how beautiful yet horrible an event it would be.

We went straight to my hotel, where I debriefed them about the plan. "As soon as you leave Jordan," I told them, "you are Spanish citizens. You need to be able to hold your head up high and tell people that. Rachel will meet us in Abu Dhabi. Whatever you do, you can't let anyone think that you don't believe your own story."

They nodded diffidently at me, and I secretly wondered whether

they would be up to the task ahead of them. But they had come this far, through Turkey and Syria, so I had to trust them.

Four days remained until our flight to Kuala Lumpur. Ever since I'd known I would be in Amman with my family, I had been looking forward to showing them around, taking them to my old haunts, and I did this. But somehow the place seemed shabbier to my eyes than it had the last time—so far removed from the new me that I felt I was giving my family a guided tour of someone else's life. We saw the company building where I had worked, the gym, and the road where I had lived, but none of them seemed to hold much meaning for me anymore. I pictured myself walking down the street with Shireen, besotted by her, and I couldn't help but smile at my own naïveté. I'd come a long way since then.

My family and I ate together in restaurants I knew—more because I wanted to ensure that they started eating proper food than out of any misplaced sense of nostalgia—but the rest of the time was spent in preparation for our journey. I took my mum and my sister to a hair salon to have their hair straightened and blow-dried in a Western style, and I bought Western clothes for them all, along with electronic gadgets for my brother, such as a personal stereo and state-of-the-art headphones. I knew that presentation would be crucial to our success: they could have the most convincing passports in the world, but if they looked like poor Iraqi refugees, they wouldn't fool anyone.

We waited. We went over the plan. We didn't talk about what would happen if we failed, because it didn't bear thinking about. We waited some more. Then the day for our departure arrived.

I didn't expect any problems leaving Amman, and I was right: we sailed through passport control with hardly a glance and took our seats on the flight to Abu Dhabi, which passed without incident. And, as we had arranged, Rachel was waiting for us there in

the transit lounge. If ever there was a sight for sore eyes, Rachel was it: she embraced my mother as though she was her own and instantly won over my brother and sister. I hugged her too, but we didn't say much. There wasn't much to say: we both knew what she was risking by traveling with us. In the transit lounge we showered, Rachel took my mum to have her hair done again, and we waited some more. I grew increasingly agitated because the more I saw Rachel with my family, the more it became clear to me that you can't just put new clothes on people and expect them to change who they are. Rachel had an aura about her, a confidence that my family lacked. Of course they did: they'd had it beaten out of them.

Then we boarded the flight to Kuala Lumpur.

The Malaysian airport had changed beyond recognition since I had last been there—all marble walls and gleaming floors. It seemed more welcoming somehow. As we disembarked from the plane, I held back a little. I wanted to see my family get safely through passport control. That way if there was any problem, I would be around to help sort it out. From a distance I watched them present their passports. I held my breath. Moments later they were allowed through.

My entry was more complicated. I had hoped to be able to pay for an entry visa at the airport, but it was soon made clear to me that this would not be the case by the team of task-force officers, heavily armed, who arrived to take me away for interrogation. I used my mobile phone to make a desperate call to Rachel.

"They won't let me in," I whispered urgently. "They're saying they want to send me back to London."

"Don't worry, Lewis," Rachel's soothing voice said calmly. "We're through and we're safe. Leave everything to me—I'll deal with it from here."

I clenched my eyes shut. "No," I told her. It wasn't meant to be

like this. I was always going to be on hand, ready to absolve Rachel of any blame should something go wrong. Now it was looking as if she would have to shoulder all the risk.

"I'll be fine, Lewis. Don't worry. We're at the hotel now. We'll just keep our heads down and get on the flight to London in a couple of days. We'll see you then."

She hung up.

Minutes later I was being interrogated again, by unfriendly Malaysians and apologetic airline staff whose responsibility it had been to check my Malaysian visa situation when I had left Amman. I argued with them; I begged them; finally I accepted the inevitable—that I was to be deported to London. And it was only then that they decided they would issue me a three-day transit visa. I felt suddenly as though all my cares had been lifted, and I hurried into a taxi to have a relieved and joyous reunion with my family at our hotel.

Stage one was complete.

Stage two was always going to be more difficult, but the fact that the fake Spanish passports had so easily fooled the official when my family entered Malaysia filled us all with confidence.

We spent the two days before our flight to London visiting around Kuala Lumpur—more to fill the time than out of a genuine desire to go sightseeing. We were all too excited and nervous for that. As we sat down together at mealtimes to eat, I forced my family to practice the few words of Spanish that Rachel and I knew between us, and we repeatedly went over the cover story that I had constructed for them until they could recite it with confidence. My mother had married a Spanish man living in London, which was how they had gained Spanish citizenship. She had brought Ahmed and Marwa to visit Malaysia because it was a Muslim country. They

had long wanted to see Malaysia because they had heard how wonderful and modern it was, but they were looking forward to getting back home.

Every time I heard them repeat the story, I smiled. It sounded convincing; the passports were good; we were going to be okay.

The morning of our departure the tropical rains came like a constant waterfall, purging the streets of crowds and cleansing the grayness of the city. We checked out of the hotel and piled into a taxi, the pouring rain messing my mother's neatly groomed hair as we did so, then traveled the short distance through the torrent to the airport. Once we arrived, Rachel and my family checked in separately, and I waited behind, watching them go through immigration. This was the last hurdle: as soon as I saw them go through, we would have succeeded.

Everything seemed to happen in slow motion. The official looked at Rachel. He looked at my family, each in turn. He examined their passports with agonizing slowness. And then he let them through.

I smiled inwardly; on the outside I did my best not to let any emotion play on my face. I walked confidently toward passport control, knowing that now that my family was through, I should have no difficulty. My papers were scrutinized, and they were scrutinized once more. The official tapped something into his computer, and I started to feel the familiar sense of dread that I remembered from my last illicit journey. Why I was kept waiting there, I don't know, but kept waiting I was. I heard the final call for my flight being announced, and I looked at my watch. Five minutes and still I was being held. Eventually, without any explanation for the delay, my papers were stamped and I literally sprinted toward the gate.

The corridor that took me there twisted and turned, and I attracted a few curious glances as I tore around the corners until finally

I found myself at the seating area at the entrance to the gate. And there I stood still, desperate to catch my breath but unable to do so on account of what I saw. There, before me, were three task-force officers, bulletproof vests on full display and U.S.-style machine guns gripped firmly in their hands. With them was an official-looking British woman in a brown business suit. And by her side, sitting down and looking more dejected than scared, were Rachel, my mother, my brother, and my sister. Apart from them, the area was deserted.

The brown-suited woman approached me. "Can I see your passport, please?"

I handed her my travel document, and she gave it a cursory glance.

"Are these people with you?" Her face and voice were expressionless.

I felt everyone's eyes on me. What could I say? "We're traveling together, yes," I replied quietly.

"Are they your family?"

I nodded. "Yes."

She turned to the task-force officers and gave them a nod. We've got them all, it seemed to say. One of the officers disappeared, and it was obvious that he had gone to tell the airline staff that the flight could now depart.

There was a heavy silence, which the woman broke with her monotonous voice. "Walk with me," she addressed us all. My family looked at me for guidance, but there was little I could do other than nod to indicate that we should do as she said. They stood up and followed us, the armed guards walking behind with their fingers still on the triggers of their guns. As we walked, I suddenly realized that in my pocket I had my family's Kurdish-Iraqi passports, documents that I on no account wanted to be discovered now that we had quite clearly been caught. If there were no Iraqi passports, I reasoned in

my panicked mind, there would be no deportations back to Iraq. They would have to use the Spanish passports, which I knew looked authentic. I stopped and said to the woman, "I need to use the toilet."

She hesitated for a moment, then shrugged and pointed at a door a little farther down the corridor. "Okay," she said. "Toilet's over there."

I hurried through the door. The room was empty, so I shoved one passport into each of three toilets and flushed them away, this time not bothering to shred them as I had done to my own passport several years before. There wasn't time for that, and as a result I watched in horror as the toilets backed up. I couldn't worry about that, though, so I took a couple of moments to regain my composure, then headed back to my family and their armed guard. We walked on in silence.

My mind was churning. Surely there was something I could do, something I could say to get us out of this mess. Eventually I turned once more to the woman and said, "Look, please, I need to talk to you alone for ten minutes."

"All right then." She nodded and took me to one side.

We took a seat together by a large observation window, through which I could see planes taking off as if to taunt me. "What's the matter?" I asked the woman. "Why are we being held?"

She indicated the Spanish passports that she had in her hand. "Do you speak Spanish?" she asked.

I shook my head. "No."

"Then why does your family have Spanish passports?"

"My mum married a Spanish man." I recited the lie as smoothly as I could. "She has citizenship."

The woman acted as if she had not heard what I'd said. "Where did you get these passports from?"

"I told you," I insisted. "They're naturalized Spaniards."

"No they're not," she almost spoke over me. "These passports are counterfeit. They are very, very bad copies. I see them all the time—they're made mostly in Thailand. How much did you pay for them?"

She looked me straight in the eye, and I saw in that moment that I wasn't fooling her. But I couldn't bring myself to answer.

"Did you pay a lot for them?" she insisted.

I nodded.

Her face assumed an expression of something approaching pity. "Well let me just tell you," she continued, "that these things are produced in Thailand for between a hundred and two hundred dollars. They are the worst I've ever seen, and you are unbelievably lucky to have come through immigration with these."

As I listened to her words, my blood ran cold. How could I have been so foolish? Within seconds my plan to rescue my family had been revealed for the ill-conceived scheme that it really was, and I had no idea what would happen to any of us now. The woman stood up, smoothed down her suit. "Come with me," she said abruptly as she walked back to where the others were waiting, a look of expectation on their faces that I had to dash with a single glance and a shake of my head.

We were led to a processing area. Full of desks and computers and phones, it looked more like a call center than anything else, and quite out of place in the environs of the airport. Each desk was covered with piles of passports and other documents, and we were given seats and told to wait. We remained there for a couple of hours, our hearts heavy, the knowledge that we had failed bearing down on us like a crushing load. Overcome by emotion, my mother started shouting at me, and I argued back but only half-heartedly because I knew that what she was saying—this was my fault, I had been too hasty, didn't I know what was at stake here?—was right. Rachel calmed us both down. How she did so I can't think, because she

must have been as sick with nerves as the rest of us. But I thanked God that she was there to exert her calming influence on us all as we fell once more into oppressive silence.

We were searched, our luggage was claimed as evidence, and then we were led around the corner from the processing area. I had noticed a few people being taken that way and the guards who accompanied them returning alone. As the same happened to us, I realized why.

In front of us were two enormous cells, one facing the other. Fronted by thick iron bars, one of the cells contained men, the other women, and between the two cells, sitting down, was a fat but threatening Malaysian guard. Along the back wall of each cell was a series of doors, and in the corner was some sort of receptacle that I assumed was the toilet. Around it was a thick, dirty puddle that encroached into the main area of the cell, contaminated with something I could not quite make out, though the stench of human feces and urine gave me a good idea what it was. The part of the floor that was not wet with water and human excrement was black with dirt and covered with a ghoulish human kaleidoscope of prostrate bodies, perhaps three or four hundred of them in each cell. There was not enough room for them all, so they overlapped each other as they lay there, unmoving. None of them seemed perturbed by the flies that were swarming around the room. Maybe, like horses on a hot day, they were used to them.

I couldn't bear to look at Rachel or my family. Suddenly, from behind, I heard screaming. It was my mother. "*La! La! Bidoun Sijan! No! Not prison!*" she shouted hysterically. I watched helplessly as two guards dragged her toward the prison doors; she collapsed herself onto the floor to make it more difficult for them, then continued her terrible weeping. The faces of my brother and sister were stricken too. To have escaped the horrors of Baghdad prisons and undergone all the dangers they had put themselves through only to

end up in a stinking cell in a strange country: I couldn't imagine what was going through their minds. Wordlessly the women were segregated from the men.

I could think of nothing to do other than try to get a message to somebody, to let people know what was happening to us. The only people I could think of were Rachel's parents: it would devastate them to think of their little girl in such a horrific situation, but they had the right to know, and maybe they could help. I had placed my mobile phone in one of my bags, but these had been checked in. Suddenly, however, I saw them arrive and be placed a few meters away from us. Quickly I moved toward my bag to get the phone; but as I did so, one of the officials saw me, a Sikh man wearing a turban. As I lunged for my bag, he grabbed me by my arms, pulled me away, thrust me against the wall, and lifted me up by my neck. He made as if to punch me with his free arm but clearly thought better of it at the last moment.

"Who do you think you are," he spat at me, "doing all this hero business? You think you're Robin Hood?"

I hardly knew what to say. I had only been there a few minutes and already I had marked myself out in their eyes as a troublemaker. Shocked into silence, I looked him up and down as he held me there against the wall. On his jacket he wore a badge with a grotesquely happy, yellow smiling face and the slogan "Service with a Smile."

Eventually the unsmiling official put me down, but his eyes stayed on me. I didn't try to grab my phone again.

I watched as Rachel, my mum, and my sister were pushed into the cell, somehow retaining a sense of dignity—despite my mother's tears—as they stepped over the carpet of human traffic to find themselves somewhere to sit. Rachel turned and managed to force a smile at me that I could not reciprocate as my brother and I were forced into the main cell.

Silently we picked our way to the back of the cell, receiving

grunts of discontent from a few of the people whose limbs we accidentally nudged against but who otherwise treated us with complete indifference. We examined the three doors at the back of the cell. Scrawled into the dirty paint on each door was a label: "The Turkish Embassy," "The Iranian Embassy," "The Iraqi Embassy." I opened the Iraqi door and looked around the corner. The room was no cleaner or more welcoming, but it was filled with Middle Eastern faces who as one looked up to see who the new arrival was.

"Salam," I nodded at them.

They greeted me in return, so I gestured to my brother and we both walked inside.

The Iraqi Embassy was no more than three meters by three meters. Right away I could tell that its eight or nine occupants were shady characters—no doubt they thought the same of me and my brother—but they were welcoming enough, given the circumstances. We found ourselves an empty area and sat down, shocked into silence with disbelief at what had happened to us. There were single sheets of newspaper on the floor, the only protection between us and the hard, cold concrete. The strip lighting above us was intolerably bright, and the air conditioning was on full blast, no doubt to battle feebly against the disgusting stench, though in reality all it did was make the place uncomfortably cold. No matter how many cells you've been in, you never quite get used to being treated no better—and often worse—than animals; but my brother and I did our best as we settled down and started waiting.

After a few hours, we were given food. Its arrival was announced by the sound of someone shouting outside the main cell, followed by a melee as some of the inmates scrabbled to get their share. My brother and I were hungry, so we stood up to go and claim our food, but one of our fellow Iraqi prisoners told us to wait. "There's always enough to go around," he said, "but it's filthy food. You probably won't want to eat it even when you get it."

He was right. When our turn came, an official handed each of us, through the bars, a small polystyrene box. We opened it up to find a mound of crusty, dried-out rice with a suspicious smell—the remnants, I later found out, of what they had fed the Malaysian staff at a previous meal. Laid on top was a pile of fish bones. There was no meat attached to them, just the skeleton, as if we were being presented not so much with a meal as with an insult. *The fish was enjoyed,* the carton seemed to say, *by important people. The bones are for you.* We also were handed a nylon bag full of lukewarm water to drink.

The agonizingly slow minutes turned into hours, which turned into days. Indeed it was difficult to keep track of time in that terrible place. In the main cell, where people had been languishing for who knows how long, certain individuals had become so ill from the conditions that they were hallucinating, shouting out at shadows, laughing hysterically, or causing violent fights because of an imagined slight. Back in the Iraqi Embassy we fell into conversation with our fellow Middle Eastern prisoners—Syrians, Palestinians, Iranians, a true melting pot of Arab culture—and I was astonished by the lengths to which some of them had gone to get themselves to a place of safety. A couple of them had had huge tattoos drawn on their arms and backs in an attempt to make them seem Westernized. Many of them had been trying to get to Australia, New Zealand, or Japan—Japan in particular, because at that time, I soon learned, a large mafia organization there was dedicated to the dirty business of people-smuggling. These people asked me questions about the UK, awed that I had made it there and astonished that I had risked coming back. To kill the tedium of the passing hours I told them about the geography and history of Britain, drawing crude maps in the dust on the floor and even at one point telling them the story that Rachel had told me about how William of Orange had fought in Ireland. It was a surreal moment, seeing these rapt Middle Eastern

faces being taught British history in a Malaysian jail by one of their number, their faces a picture of concentration like a group of children hearing a fairy tale.

Occasionally I went to the front of the main cell, treading over the human carpet of Bengalis and Sri Lankans, and Rachel did the same in the opposite cell. The first time we did this, she smiled across the corridor that divided us and, as cheerfully as she could, called, "You take me to the nicest places, Lewis!" Then she removed something from her pocket: it was the restaurant menu from the hotel where we had been staying. "Now then," she called, "what shall we have for lunch? Lobster?" And so we carried on, doing our best to crack jokes, to make light of the situation and raise each other's spirits; but we knew it was an almost impossible task.

Neither Rachel nor my brother mentioned it, but we were all aware that the long-term consequences for us all could be very severe indeed. And I felt responsible for everything. I had no idea at this stage what would happen to my family, but I suddenly felt a renewed sense of fraternal responsibility for my younger brother. I remembered how I felt when, not much older than he, I was cast into that Iraqi jail on the road north from Basra; I remembered how I felt when I heard that my mother had been imprisoned in Al-Haakimiya. He would be having the same feelings now, albeit with his brother by his side, and I suddenly felt the urge to give him some words of advice for the difficult times ahead.

"Ahmed," I said, "I need to tell you something."

"What is it, Sarmed?"

I searched for the words. "I don't know what's going to happen, but you need to be strong, for your mother and your sister. Remember, this life is a test of your strength. There will be people you encounter who will try to beat it out of you, but you must never let them. You can't fold and give up. So we're in prison. So what? It's just going to make you stronger. At least we aren't dying. Hold your

head up high, puff out your chest, be strong, and don't let anyone treat you badly."

He looked straight into my eyes. "I know what you're saying, Sarmed," he replied. "And I'll try. I really will."

As the time ground slowly on, we became aware of how the place worked. We couldn't bring ourselves to eat the food, but thankfully in my back pocket I had a little money, which I would dole out to one of the less ferocious guards outside the cell. He would go and buy food at McDonald's in the airport—skimming a little money off the top for himself, of course—and deliver the food back to us. I had to buy enough to hand around something to everybody in the Iraqi Embassy, but it felt good occasionally to have some hot food in our stomachs.

Time passed. Other prisoners arrived; a few left. After about three days, an Oriental-looking man, reasonably well dressed, arrived in the cell. Something about his demeanor suggested to me that he was a bit different from the ragtag collection of unfortunates whom he had joined, so more to pass the time than anything else I went up to talk to him.

"What are you doing here?" I asked him after we had made our introductions.

"I don't know," he said, his face a picture of innocence. "I'm an American citizen and my girlfriend is American. I don't understand why we've been stopped." Even then I don't think I believed him, and I was right—sometime later he let his cover story drop and admitted that, even though he really was an American citizen, he had been trying to smuggle this girl to New Zealand. More important, however, he had managed to sneak his mobile phone into the cell so that he could phone the U.S. Consulate in Kuala Lumpur and alert American officials to his presence. But he didn't know the number and had no way of finding out.

I grabbed my opportunity. "I can help you," I told him. "Let me

borrow your phone, and I can call people in England to find the number of the UK High Commission for me and the U.S. Consulate for you."

By now we had attracted the attention of certain others in the cell, and I became aware of them eyeing the American's phone. No doubt everyone would be wanting to use it, and as he handed it over, I noticed that the battery life was limited. We couldn't let any of the others get their hands on it and use up the precious time that was left. I just had to hope that nobody would be so desperate as to try to wrestle the thing away from me.

I used the phone to find the numbers I needed, and then called the High Commission. I explained to the woman who answered what our situation was, and she promised to see what she could do. "But I doubt we'll be able to do anything for the Iraqis in your group," she told me. "They're out of our jurisdiction."

I had known it was unlikely that they would be able to help my family, but hearing the words spoken so firmly made my heart sink. Still, if I could at least get myself out, perhaps I could do something for them. I was useless just stuck in there.

We waited some more.

Eventually, after we had been four days in that stinking cell, I heard my name being shouted: there was a call for me outside the cell. I was allowed out, with the eyes of all the other prisoners boring into me, and taken to a telephone. Someone from the British High Commission was waiting to speak to me.

"We can't guarantee to influence what the Malaysians are doing," I was told. "We can only try."

"But what about my family?" I asked.

"There's nothing we can do for any of them," the British official stated with what sounded to me like a note of boredom in his voice. "They will have to stay here and wait for the Iraqi representative to come."

"There must be something else we can do," I pleaded.

I knew from my conversations with the Iraqis in the cell that the representative came only once a month. And when he did arrive, all he would do was take names and reprimand the inmates. "Why did you do this?" he would demand of them. "Don't you realize what a reputation you are creating for Iraqis in this country? They're not impressed back home with what you're doing . . ." And then he would disappear; what would happen to my family was anyone's guess.

When the call finished, I put my head in my hands and tried to fight off the feeling of furious frustration that was surging through me. Suddenly I felt a tap on my shoulder. It was the task-force officer who had led me from the cell: he had been standing close by while I had the conversation and clearly understood what was going on. I prepared myself to be told to get back into the cell, but I was surprised when he spoke. "Your family," he asked me softly in faltering English, "did they have any documents other than the passports they were stopped with?"

I looked around nervously, unsure whether this was a trap; but I was in a corner and had no option other than to tell the truth.

"Yes," I admitted. "They had Iraqi passports."

"Where are they now?"

"I shoved them down the toilet," I said.

"Okay," he said. "Listen to me. You *have* to get those passports back; otherwise your family will rot in a Kuala Lumpur prison. Trust me, I've seen it happen before."

"How can I?" I asked desperately.

"Leave it to me," the guard said. "I'll have to take you back to the cell now, but I'll try to call you out later."

He led me back to the cell, where I continued my wait—even more scared this time, and more frustrated at the thought that in getting rid of my family's Iraqi passports I may have ruined any

chance they had of getting out of this place. In any case, the likelihood of the passports still being there was vanishingly small. What was more, my opinion of the Malaysians was at rock bottom, and I didn't expect this guard to be true to his word.

He proved me wrong. A few hours later he let me out again and led me to the toilets down which I had stuffed the passports. When we arrived there, I stepped into the first cubicle and gave thanks first that I had caused the toilets to overflow and so remain unused, and second that nobody had seen fit to fix them for four days. Without hesitation I plunged my arm into the water and felt inside the U-bend. Something was there. Persistently I teased it out and with something between astonishment and relief pulled out a document. It was saturated, of course, and smeared; but the photograph was intact and it was clear what it was: my mother's Iraqi passport. Quickly I retrieved the others, which were in the same condition. I shook what water I could from them, then dried them off underneath the electric hand-dryer on the wall. The task-force officer took the passports from me and placed them in little plastic bags as evidence.

Then I was led back to the cell.

With mixed feelings I sat down again next to my brother. In handing the passports over to the Malaysian guard, I knew what would happen: my family would be deported. My gamble was this: as there was no direct flight back to Iraq, and as they had entered Malaysia from Jordan, I hoped that the Malaysians would deport them back to Amman. At least then they would be on Middle Eastern soil, where they could speak the language and hopefully persuade—or bribe—the Jordanians to let them stay. The alternative was, as the Malaysian guard had made so plain, rotting here in a putrid jail. I couldn't let that happen.

Before long, Rachel and I were released. We were informed that no charges were to be brought against us and that we were free to go back to London.

"I'm staying," I told our captors defiantly. What else could I say? My family was still here, and I couldn't desert them. We took a room at the airport hotel, where we cleaned ourselves up; but every time the water splashed on my skin or my eyes glanced at the soft, fresh bedding, great anger welled up in me. How could I be here while my family was in those squalid, cramped, and stinking conditions? They were people too—surely it was time they were treated as such. I visited them four or five times a day, bringing with me the hotel food that I didn't have the stomach to eat and begging the guards to give it to them.

After a couple of days, I was told they were to be interviewed. I was allowed to act as their interpreter but was forbidden from having any other kind of conversation with them. One by one they were taken in front of Malaysian officials and instructed to make statements. They told the truth: about their imprisonment, about their journey through Kurdistan, Turkey, and Syria, about the fake Spanish passports. And then they were told what would happen to them. They had a choice: either their case would be taken before a Malaysian judge—which would take weeks and would probably result in a further spell of imprisonment, as there was no asylum in Malaysia—or they could pay a fine and be deported back to Jordan. The fine amounted to $750 each. Money they didn't have.

I needed to find $2,250. I was stuck in Malaysia, and all I had was a debit card, a credit card, and the ability to withdraw £200 a day. Immediately I got on the phone to my bank in England and begged them to increase my overdraft and my withdrawal limits. Rachel and I cobbled together all the money we could—it took two days—and in the end we just about managed to put our hands on the amount we needed. We took it back to the cells and handed it over to a sneering official. He sat at his table, handed us a receipt for the money, put on a pair of latex gloves, removed the Iraqi passports from their bags, and stamped them. Then, having placed them in a

plastic bag, he held them out to us at arm's length as though they were diseased. His aloof silence spoke with an eloquence that I'm sure he could not have managed with mere words: *So it's come to this for you people,* he seemed to say. *Your lives have come to this.* There was no sympathy, no indication that he knew what my family was running from or what they were being sent back to, and there was no point trying to educate him. I simply took the passports from him and left him to his delusions.

And so, finally, the time came for my mother, sister, and brother to be deported. Still we weren't allowed any direct contact with them. All Rachel and I could do was wait behind a glass screen at their gate so that we could see them one last time, even if we weren't allowed to talk to them. When they arrived, the sight pierced my heart. My mother, brother, and sister were handcuffed like criminals and led by armed officials to their gate. The Western clothes that they had worn for their journey now looked like a cruel, ragged parody. My mother looked even more bedraggled and beaten down than when she had first arrived. As she passed us, she refused to look me in the eye, and I didn't blame her as she shuffled past. I hung my head, and Rachel put her arm around me. My sister saw us and managed a half smile. "Good-bye, Sarmed," she mouthed. "Good-bye, my brother." She followed her mother.

Finally I saw Ahmed. He was walking slowly, and when he saw me, his tired and worried face struggled into a broad smile. *Don't worry about us,* it seemed to say. *We'll be okay.* And then, just as I had told him to, I saw him hold his head up high and stick his chest out proudly. He nodded at me, I returned the gesture, and he walked on, disappearing from my sight as my mother and sister had just done.

Walking into whatever the future held for them, without me.

CHAPTER 15

THE GENUINE MAN

My family arrived back in Amman, where the Jordanian officials took one look at the state of their passports and said flatly, "You can't enter our country on these documents." No arguments. No bribes. No chances.

They were loaded, under armed guard, onto a bus and taken to the Iraqi border, where they were dumped. The border police were unimpressed with the condition of these pitiful refugees and their messed-up documents, so they threw them straight into a holding cell to await the next military transport back to Baghdad. There they were placed in a police holding cell to await trial. They were there for several days, undergoing the brutal treatment that they surely expected, before going up in front of a judge.

The court hearing in Baghdad was a joke, but what happened wasn't funny. The courthouse looked serious enough from the outside—an imposing building with a set of scales emblazoned on the front next to the Iraqi flag and some of Saddam's words of wisdom on the subject of justice. But there were no courtrooms or juries inside, nothing to ensure that the proper processes were observed;

there was simply a bare office with a judge sitting at a table to mete out whatever justice he saw fit according to his whim. What terror my family was feeling as they waited silently outside to hear their fate, I can only imagine. Perhaps, after spending so much time in prison cells across the world, they were simply looking forward to knowing how they were to be dealt with. You find hidden strength at times like this: that, at least, I had learned.

My brother was called first. The room was sparse: an old desk, a flag, a fan, a picture of the leader, and a radio playing Arabic music. On the desk was a pile of paperwork, and by the judge's side was a secretary, scribbling notes as the proceedings progressed. The judge, in his late fifties, sat there in casual clothes, smoking a cigarette. He didn't look up as my brother walked in. Why would he? This was not a person who had come in front of him; it was just another criminal to be processed.

"What's your name?" the judge asked.

My brother responded quietly.

The judge was handed his charge sheet. He asked no more questions—just glanced at the sheet of paper in the most cursory manner. "Three years' prison," he announced briskly before taking another drag on his cigarette. "If you pay a fine, perhaps I will reduce it." But my brother had no money, so the negotiations could not proceed. He was taken away.

The same treatment was then inflicted on my sister and finally on my mother. The sentences they received were identical.

All three of them were escorted to Abu Ghraib prison.

Rachel and I returned to England the same day my mother, brother, and sister were deported. It felt good to breathe the damp English air and to be treated like a real person once more. But as we returned to Leeds, I felt crushed by the weight of my failure. My

family was back where they started, and I had to shoulder the responsibility. I knew I would have to try again, that I would have to raise money to bribe them out of mistreatment in Abu Ghraib and then pay smugglers to start a second attempt at escape. But money was scarce now, and all avenues seemed closed to me.

My first instinct was to get in touch with the people who had sold me the bogus passports and try to force them to give me the money back. I tried calling, but the number had been changed, of course. What did I have to lose, though? I knew where they lived, so I boarded a flight to Germany to try to track them down. The last time I had sailed through German immigration without any difficulty; this time it was not so easy. The official who looked at my travel document was more on the ball: "We don't recognize this document," he told me. "You can't enter."

I used all the charm I could muster to wheedle my way in. This is a legitimate travel document, I told the German officials. It is recognized everywhere. But they went to check with high-ranking immigration people; they even checked the wording of German immigration legislation. The document wasn't recognized, they repeated. I couldn't enter Germany.

I started to argue with one of the officials. I had been to Germany before, I explained; desperate that I not be forced to leave. I showed documents that proved I had entered the country in the past. The official raised an eyebrow. "So," he said, "not only are you trying to enter illegally, you have already been here illegally . . ." He turned to some of his assistants. "Bring him in," he told them cryptically. "Let him enjoy the hospitality of our lovely motels. I hope you enjoy your stay."

Only when they locked me up did I understand what they were talking about.

I was questioned and searched more thoroughly—and intimately—than I had ever been searched before. I was left in a cell

overnight, and in the morning I was handcuffed and escorted to a military vehicle with a flashing light. The van took me to a plane bound for England and I was ushered, on foot and under armed guard, into the plane. Only when I was sitting in my seat were the handcuffs removed, and with the suspicious eyes of all the passengers on me, I was deported. There was no way I was going to get that money back.

In Baghdad, Saad still had some of the William Hill funds left, and he was determined to use it to get my mother, brother, and sister out of Abu Ghraib. Inside that awful place, there was a religious course where inmates were instructed to memorize huge swaths of the Koran. They were tested and had to speak it out loud, and if successful would be given a full pardon for whatever crime had sent them there, as long as their crimes were not of a horrific or political nature. Unsurprisingly, it was almost impossible for inmates to get themselves into this incredibly popular course.

Saad was unable to use the William Hill money to bribe corrupt officials to release my family, but he *was* able to buy their way in to the course. And so, after suffering the inhuman indignities of that place for longer than anyone deserved, they were set free. But as ever, we did not know how long it would be before someone came for them once more. Their situation hadn't changed: someone still had to try to get them out of the country.

My finances were at rock bottom. So were Rachel's. Aside from what I had sent to Saad, I still had a tiny amount of the William Hill money, but not nearly enough to pay smugglers to get all three of them over to the UK, and I knew now that I couldn't risk trying to arrange things myself. This had to be done by the professionals, as and when I managed to earn the money. My mother, brother, and sister would have to come out one by one. With what was left of the money, and by scrimping and saving, I managed to put together enough for the first attempt, and in April 2001, about three months

after my return from Germany, it was decided that my sister would leave first.

While the secret and illicit arrangements were being made, I could concentrate on nothing else. The sense of apprehension I felt could not have been more intense had I been the one who was making the escape attempt, but I had to try to keep things as normal as possible; otherwise I would have gone mad. I still had my Saturday job at a big department store in Leeds—I needed the money now more than ever, after all—and one Saturday I was going about my business in the store when, across the floor, I saw a face I recognized. It was my former boss from William Hill. He was gazing around the department as though looking for something, or someone, so I put my head down and tried to remain inconspicuous in an attempt to shake off the cloak of paranoia that had suddenly descended on me. Before long, however, I heard a voice behind me that made me start.

"Lewis!"

I slowly turned to confront him, fully prepared for what I thought was about to happen. But when I looked at him, I was surprised. There was a big, friendly smile on his face—he seemed genuinely happy to see me. "When you left," he boomed, "we had to employ an army of number-crunchers to do your work for you!" I smiled awkwardly. We chatted for a few minutes and then he left, clearly unaware of what I had been up to. For myself, I felt a surge of relief: it looked as if I had some more time.

Saad made arrangements for the first leg of my sister's escape from Baghdad. He found another Kurdish smuggler and arranged a price for delivery out of Iraq. Marwa took the same route as last time, through northern Iraq and into Kurdistan and then Turkey. From there, I arranged with somebody in the UK for her to travel in the back of a truck to Dover, where she crossed over using an Austrian refugee's travel document, probably sold to smugglers by the original owner. It was a slow business—probably more painfully

slow for those of us waiting to hear good news than it was for her, distracted as she was by her nerves and her fear. To be deported back to Iraq once was bad enough; she couldn't risk things going wrong again.

She succeeded. The thrill of excitement I felt when I took the call to say she needed me to receive her at UK immigration was more wonderful than I can express. I rushed down there and took her in my arms, holding her for what seemed like hours in an embrace that I didn't want to end. The last time I had seen her had been in the airport in Kuala Lumpur. Then she had the haunted expression of a person who had had all the fight sucked out of her, who was resigned to the fact that she was going to meet an unknown and unwanted fate. Now that she had claimed asylum, however, all that fell from her. I remember thinking what a remarkable effect freedom has on people.

More to the point, we had now established that the route my sister had taken actually worked. All that remained was to raise the money to pay smugglers to get my brother and mother out, because their joy at knowing that my sister was safe was tempered by the constant fear of a knock at the door. But we were nearly there. I could almost taste the success, and in my mind I constantly replayed our imagined, joyous reunion on British soil.

Safe.

It was so close.

Not long after my sister arrived, I was out walking and I bumped into another familiar face: the recruitment consultant who had found me the job at William Hill. Something about the way he looked at me as he approached made me feel uncomfortable, but it would have been rude to turn away when I had so obviously noticed him. Besides, it was probably just my paranoia talking.

"Lewis," he nodded knowingly at me, "how are you doing?"

"Okay," I replied, not wanting to have to explain all my troubles in the street.

"So tell me, what have you been up to?"

I shrugged. "The usual." Something told me that I wanted this conversation to finish as quickly as possible.

"You know, it's a real coincidence," he continued persistently. "Someone came to the office yesterday asking about you."

I fell silent.

"He said he was an investigator."

I smiled nervously. "Don't be silly." I tried to laugh it off. "What would an investigator want with me? It's not like I get up to much worth investigating."

"Maybe not," he said thoughtfully. "But be careful, Lewis," he warned before going on his way. "He looked like he meant business."

I ran all the way back home. I had expected this, of course, but that didn't stop it coming as a shock to learn that someone was on my trail. I couldn't be put away now, not with my family still stuck in Baghdad. In a state of paranoia I shut myself in a room and re-formatted the hard drive of my laptop computer. I don't know what I thought anyone would find there, but it comforted me somewhat to feel as if I was doing something to cover my tracks.

And then everything went quiet. Ostensibly Rachel and I went about our daily lives, but I felt as though a sword was hanging over me by a thread. As often as I could I tried to speak to Saad and, in our roundabout, coded way, give him the message that I so desperately had to impart: time is slipping away. We *have* to get them out, and soon.

One Saturday two or three months later I received a phone call while on duty at the store. It was security.

"Lewis," one of the security guards greeted me amicably, "could you pop down to see us for a minute?"

"Sure," I replied. I assumed I had forgotten to remove a security tag from an item of clothing and someone had complained—it was easily done—so I sauntered down to the security offices. The door was opened by a large female security officer of whom I had always been rather wary but who on this occasion seemed to be almost oversolicitous.

"Come in, Lewis." She smiled at me.

I walked in to find two men in suits. One of them was fairly nondescript; the other was enormous—six foot three with broad shoulders and a thick black and white goatee. Each man stood in one corner of the room. The big man looked at me.

"Are you Lewis Alsamari?" he asked without formality.

I nodded. "Yes."

"Please take a seat." He gestured at a chair in front of him, and I sat down.

"Did you work at a company called William Hill, Lewis?"

As soon as he asked the question, I knew that all the horrible suspicions that had been flitting through my brain in the last thirty seconds were about to be confirmed.

"Yes," I replied.

He nodded calmly. "Lewis Alsamari," he recited. "I'm arresting you on charges of conspiracy to defraud. You do not have to say anything, but it may harm your defense if you do not mention when questioned something which you may later rely on in court. Anything you do say may be given in evidence."

Nobody spoke. I did my best not to let the emotion show on my face as I tried to think clearly. What should I do? Admit everything? That had always been my plan when I had assumed that my family would all be safely in the UK. But I didn't know what they would do to me if I confessed now, and I had to make sure I was around to help my family in what I hoped would be their final attempt to

leave. So should I deny everything? Or should I keep my own counsel and not say anything for the moment?

I chose the latter course of action.

The large man broke the silence. "We're going to take you away now, Lewis," he said firmly but not unkindly. I was led to my locker, which I opened; my wallet and keys were removed and placed into an evidence bag.

"Now then, Lewis," I was told, "we have a choice. I can handcuff you now and lead you out of the store. I don't want to do that, so I'm going to trust you not to run away. But the two of us will be walking very close to you on either side, so no funny business. Understood?"

I nodded, strangely humbled by the faith they had in me. If and when the authorities came knocking for my mother and brother, I knew they would not be afforded the same respect. "Thank you," I said.

Flanked by the two men, I was escorted to the staff entrance of the store, then out into the adjacent shopping arcade. I can't say there were no thoughts of escape in my mind, but I knew how foolish it would be to abuse the trust that had been put in me, so I came quietly. We walked out into the street and toward their car. I was placed in the back while the two Criminal Investigation Department (CID) officers sat in the front.

"Where's your car, Lewis?" I was asked.

I didn't answer for a moment; instead I bowed my head sheepishly. "It's over there." I pointed to a big building on the other side of the road.

The two men looked at each other. "What do you mean, it's over there? That's the police station."

I nodded. I had cheekily been parking there in order to save money. The reasons were too complicated to explain there and then,

and I didn't blame them for sharing a look that indicated their incredulity at my chutzpah. If only they knew the truth, I thought to myself. If only they knew that getting into trouble for parking my car in a West Yorkshire police lot was the least of my worries! They searched my car—a Nissan Sunny worth about £200—thoroughly, then took me to a smaller police station for processing. Not for the first time in my life, I was placed in a cell. To my astonishment, as I was escorted in, the duty officer said, "I'm sorry about the conditions." For a moment I thought it was a sick joke, but one look on his face showed me that he meant it. And if he thought I would find the conditions unpleasant, he could not have been more wrong. There was a bed with a mattress, a steel water fountain, and a moderately clean toilet. Compared to some of the cells in which my family and I had found ourselves, this was positively luxurious.

While I was in the cell, Rachel heard a knock on the door of our house. She was having coffee with a friend and excused herself to go and open the door. It was CID. The officers explained what was going on and asked to search the house. Rachel had no option: she let them in. The officers collected all my documents and my laptop computer and took them away.

Four or five hours later I was removed from the cell and taken to an interview room.

"I'm not going to charge you," the CID officer said. "I'm going to release you on bail. I've taken all your stuff, and you need to come and report to the police station on a regular basis so we know you're still around. But I'm going to interview you now, and you have the right to a lawyer. Do you want one?"

"Yes," I nodded.

A lawyer arrived, and I was placed in his hands. He was pleasant and friendly, and I wanted to trust him, to feel comfortable with his advice, but I found it difficult. After everything I had been through, the truth was that I trusted nobody except Rachel. I certainly didn't

trust any persons in authority, no matter whether they were Iraqi, Malaysian, or English. All sorts of possibilities ran through my head: that this man might be working with the police, that they might be trying to get me to incriminate myself. I didn't realize that that wasn't the way things are done in England. All the trust I might have afforded the lawyer had been sucked out of me, but I did my best to pay attention when he explained that I had the right to remain silent or to say "No comment" to any question but warned that doing so could affect me in the future.

When the interview started, I faced a barrage of questions. I admitted nothing.

I knew I wouldn't fool anyone, but the more I thought about it the more I realized I had to postpone the inevitable for as long as possible. I would be no use to my family in jail. When the interview finished, the CID officer said, "Right, Lewis, I'm going to be investigating this further. I'll be in touch through your lawyers."

And I was allowed to go free. For the time being.

Suddenly, the pressure had doubled. I wasn't afraid of going to prison, but I was terrified of doing so before I could complete the job of getting my family out of Iraq. I knew that it was only a matter of time before I found myself in court; and when that happened, I would not be able to keep up the pretense of my denial anymore. But I simply didn't have the money to pay anybody to smuggle my mother and brother all the way to the UK. There was no way I could risk them being in Baghdad while I was in jail, however. So in conjunction with Saad, I arranged for them to flee.

They departed under cover of night, leaving the little house in Al-Mansour that had been their home for so long. They traveled north to Mosul and remained there for a while, not exactly safe, but unknown to the authorities in that town and farther removed at

least from the risk of being dragged back into Abu Ghraib. I sent them what money I could to subsist. And while the case against me was being established in England, Saad and I carried on, working hard to arrange for them to be sent farther north, into Kurdistan and eventually Turkey. The situation was far from ideal—I wouldn't be able to rest easy until they were by my side—but it was a start.

Finally the day came, as I knew it must, on which I was charged. A trial date was set. My lawyer told me I had two options: to plead not guilty and deny all the charges or to plead guilty and claim mitigating circumstances. I asked what the worst punishment I could expect to receive was if I pleaded guilty. Two years in prison, I was told, and a deportation order. The prison sentence I could endure; the deportation could spell death to me, but it was a risk I was going to have to run: I had never intended to deny what I had done, and denial would have been pointless in any case. The evidence was all there. I had to hope that I would receive more lenient treatment from my judge than my family had received from theirs in Iraq.

I gathered together as much evidence as I could—receipts from the fine I had to pay in Malaysia and the like—to show where the William Hill money had gone. I wanted to show that I had not squandered the £37,000 on revelry but rather had used it to save the people I loved from torture and worse. I made a statement and so did my sister. I dug out records of telephone calls to Iraq and to shady people-smugglers. I even made a plea to William Hill that I would repay the money—I didn't know how I would be able to, but perhaps I would find a way. I amassed all the mitigating evidence I could put my hands on, but in the end I knew it would come down to the sympathy of one man: the judge who was trying my case. He would decide my fate, and as my family was still relying on me, he would also decide the fate of those two faceless refugees so many miles away.

When my trial date was set, it seemed a long way off, but it ar-

rived with inexorable speed. The lawyers for the prosecution and the representative from William Hill avoided my eye as, three years after my return from Malaysia, I took my place in the dock and waited for these men to argue the rights and wrongs of what I had done. When the lawyers for the prosecution made their case, I felt like screaming at them. "What would *you* have done?" I wanted to ask them. "Picture your own mother being beaten for no crime greater than trying to live her life quietly. What would *you* have done?" But I kept quiet and hoped that my story would speak for itself.

The judge was inscrutable as he listened to the case. I spent my time examining his face, looking for any sign of shock or sympathy, but I could see none. He simply listened, impassively, directing the court and asking the occasional question but otherwise showing no emotion whatsoever. Silently I begged him to give me some sign, some indication of how he was going to deal with me, but he was aloof and professional. I would have to wait until the verdict.

When the time came, the court fell silent. "Stand up, Mr. Alsamari," the judge intoned.

I did as I was told. And then he started his summing-up. He recited the charges in such a way as to make them sound premeditated in the extreme: "You stole or adapted to your own use the sums of, in total, £37,000 from your employers by effectively falsifying records by access to what was thought to be a secure system on the computer. You pleaded guilty, but on a basis which is wholly exceptional, and which is set out at length by your learned counsel in mitigation, and I need not repeat it."

I bowed my head as I listened. He did not sound remotely impressed.

"I have no doubt whatsoever," the judge continued solemnly, "that it is a true story by virtue of the documents I have seen, and obviously from my own general knowledge."

There was a pause before he continued. I glanced around the courtroom to see that everyone was looking at him with a rapt expression, hanging on every word he said.

"This offense for you is a tragedy. You have lost your good character, and you are an intelligent and hardworking individual who, apart from this incident, has an exemplary character."

I held my breath.

"It is clearly an offense, involving, as it does, breach of trust, the danger that others would be blamed for what you had done, working in the same department, that justifies a custodial sentence. I am asked to draw back from that and pass upon you a community sentence because, aside from anything else, a custodial sentence, whether suspended or actual, will affect your citizenship application, and in one sense rightly so. I have listened very carefully to the mitigation on the basis of your plea, and given you credit for that plea, and I have read the many documents which have been referred to in court both from your family and from others. This is, in my experience, a unique mitigation. And I say this: that I cannot begin to imagine what it is like to have your family living within a regime which has no contemplation of human rights . . . and where the only way that you have to help the rest of your family escape is to bribe corrupt officials with money which you do not have. The knowledge that you had at that time, together with the depression you were suffering from—as I say, I cannot begin to imagine what that is like, and the dilemma that faces you."

As I heard his words, I slowly began to realize that this man was on my side. For the first time ever, it seemed, a person in a position of real authority understood what we had been through and thought of us as human beings. I wanted to smile, but the smile would not come, pushed away instead by the tears that I felt welling up in my eyes. Tears of relief, and of sorrow too for my mother, who was not there to hear what was being said. Suddenly I became aware

of the fact that many of the eyes in the courtroom were now on me, but it didn't matter. And it didn't stop me weeping.

The judge then announced what was to be done with me: "In the circumstances, the sentence that I propose to pass is the maximum one that I can impose on a suspended basis. It is two years, and it will last for two years. I could, as part of my duties today, make a recommendation for deportation. I do not do so, for obvious reasons. I know my sentence will affect your citizenship application and, as I have said already, it is right that it should. I cannot, in view of the serious nature of this matter, mitigate my judgment any further, but, as I have indicated, I do believe that the interests of justice demand in these particular and unique circumstances that the sentence I impose be suspended.

"Understand this: that if you commit any offense punishable by imprisonment within the next two years this sentence can, in whole or in part, be activated and you will then serve it. Do you understand that?"

Through my tears I replied simply: "Yes."

The judge went on to say that he did not propose to make an order for me to repay the money to William Hill. That matter was for them to pursue in the civil courts. They never did.

I stepped down from the dock, tears still in my eyes. I wasn't pleased with what I had done—all I had ever wanted to do was work hard and make a life for myself and my family by honest means. That opportunity had been taken from me, and I had fully expected to pay the price for it.

As it was, I felt humbled by the leniency that had been shown to me. Leniency that my past had shaped me not to expect.

In the months that followed my trial, the judge's warning rang in my ears: "If you commit any offense punishable by imprisonment

within the next two years this sentence can, in whole or in part, be activated and you will then serve it." I had no doubt that he meant what he said, and I knew I had to walk the line carefully if my mother and my brother were to benefit from my help. The need for caution didn't dampen my enthusiasm to be reunited with them, however; if anything, it strengthened it.

It took a long time to spirit my mother and brother out of Turkey; and in the months and years that followed the trial, they moved about constantly, always attempting to keep one step ahead of any suspicious officials who might try to pay unwanted attention to their bogus Iraqi documents. I knew that, having left Iraq, they were free from torture and brutality, but they couldn't rest easy until they could claim asylum in a place of safety, for the threat of deportation was always hanging over them. To my exasperation, the route that my sister had taken became closed to me when the smuggler who had arranged it disappeared—I don't know where—and so once more it was left to me to find a new way to enable my mother and brother to finish the final leg of their journey.

My newfound trust in the British system inspired me to pursue their claim for asylum through the proper channels. I started liaising with members of Parliament (MPs), telling them our story and seeing if they could persuade the Home Office to grant us the right to family reunion; but despite the fact that the MPs had the ability to exercise their discretion to do so, they refused. As the months of red tape turned to years, I became increasingly frustrated as gradually it became more obvious that my mother and brother would never make it to England if they didn't arrive at the border and claim asylum for themselves.

By now I had saved some money, so reluctantly but with a sense of implacable determination, I launched myself back into the sinister yet sadly familiar scene of people-trafficking. I had long conversations with faceless individuals in far-flung corners of Europe; I

negotiated routes and prices; I directed every instinct I had into deciding whom I could trust and whom I couldn't. I had learned a lot about such things, after all.

In the end, I parted with a great deal of money, handed over to a shadowy individual in another country to arrange everything that needed to be arranged. I wasn't at all sure that I wouldn't find myself in the same situation I had with the fake Spanish passports in Malaysia, but I couldn't wait any longer. None of us could wait any longer. Families are meant to be together, and not one of us could rest easily until they were safely with me on British soil.

Finally, after years of trying, we met with success. My mother—frail but determined—and my brother made the fraught, risky journey. The details of how they finally arrived here are another story, one that I cannot expand upon for a number of reasons; but eventually they were able, just as I had done several years previously, to speak the words I have no doubt they had been practicing ever since they left Al-Mansour: "I want to claim political asylum."

When I heard that they had made it, it was the happiest moment of my life.

Some scenes become etched so firmly in your memory that you know you will never forget them until your dying day. In my head there are a number of such visions: the doctor in the south of Iraq pulling a bullet from my leg; the wild wolves in the Jordanian desert; the sight of my family, bedraggled and hopeless, being deported from the Malaysian holding cell. There were times when I thought these images would never be removed from my mind.

Now, though, I have a new scene to remember, one that somehow puts all those others in their place. It is the memory of seeing my mother on British soil again for the first time. I will never forget it. When she made it over, she went immediately to the house of my sister, who had met and married an Iraqi man and was renting a flat in London, and I went straight there to see her. The difference in

her appearance and her demeanor compared with how she looked when I first saw her at the airport in Kuala Lumpur was astonishing. The anxiety had lifted from her face; she would always bear the scars of so many years of oppression—we all would—but there was a softness around her eyes and an easiness to her smile that I did not recognize. I put my arms around her and held her tightly for fifteen minutes. We had so many things to say to each other, but sometimes words aren't enough. It didn't matter: our silence said it all. Finally she was here, along with my brother, and the happiness I felt at being reunited with them in the place I now called home was indescribable. Although there was always the nagging fear in the back of my mind that she could still be taken away from me if her asylum application was turned down, everything that I had learned had taught me to enjoy the moments of happiness that you have, because you never know how fleeting they might be.

Of course, now that my mother was here there was a new responsibility upon me—the responsibility of making sure that this woman who had been beaten and humiliated was able to live a life, if not of luxury then at least of relative comfort. But that was a happy responsibility, because more than anything I was looking forward to being a family again, of reclaiming those years when that one simple thing that everyone in the West takes for granted was denied me. I wanted to be able to eat with them at the same table; to talk to them without the need for coded language and subterfuge; to share my happiness with my brother and sister; and to be comforted by my mother when times were bad. The night I knew that my mother and my brother were safely in the UK, I slept soundly and without interruption for the first time in years. A new chapter in my life was about to begin, and I felt almost like a new person. Sarmed had undergone everything that had happened; I needed to make sure that Lewis never forgot he was the beneficiary of that.

Above all, I was looking forward to having my mum live with

me. When I told my friends that, they looked at me in amused disbelief. "Are you mad?" they asked. "Why on earth would you want to live with your parents?"

I simply smiled and shrugged my shoulders. "I just want to know what it's like," I replied.

But there was more to it than that. Since I had last lived in the bosom of my family, I had been abused and shot, imprisoned and hunted down. I had lived with the knowledge that my mother, brother, and sister were being tortured on my account. I had put my hard-won liberty at risk, as well as that of others. I had compromised my good name in the adopted country that I loved.

Perhaps that makes me mad, or reckless. It's not for me to judge. But what I know for certain is this: I would do it all again, because if there is one thing that is worth fighting for, it is the liberty of the ones you love.

And because, ever since my uncle Saad had left me alone and frightened that night so many years ago in a small Bedouin village on the Iraqi-Jordanian border, all I had ever really wanted was to have the warmth and security of my family all around me. On that moonlit desert night, he spoke those words that were to shape my actions for so many years: *the genuine man never forgets his family.*

I hope I have not let him down.

I hope that, in that respect at least, it may be said that I am a genuine man.

EPILOGUE

One of my earliest memories is of sitting on my father's lap watching *Doctor Zhivago*. Even as a child, I was transfixed by it: the awesome scenery, the grand themes, the beauty and the magnificence of it all.

"Can I be like that?" I remember asking him. "Can I be an actor like Omar Sharif?"

"Of course you can," he replied indulgently. "Just so long as you don't get up to the naughty things that some actors do."

Life, of course, has a habit of taking you in directions different from those that you had planned. In that respect, I suppose, my life was just the same as anyone else's. In Iraq there was no possibility of training to be an actor. It was an impossible dream, and one soon forgotten.

When I received my lenient sentence from the judge, however, I realized that the time had come to reevaluate my life. In the three years leading up to my trial, I had, in the midst of everything else, trained in the martial art of Thai boxing (also known as Muay Thai), been awarded an L.L.B. Honors law degree by studying part-time—

ironically learning from the law while the state was practicing it on me. My conviction meant that I would never be able to practice law, so I started to cast around for other things to do with my new life. After all I had been through it seemed almost churlish to myself not to reawaken the dreams that I had once had. What is the point of freedom, after all, if you do not use it to the best of your ability?

A friend of mine had taken a small part on a soap opera. When he told me about his part, it fanned the spark of interest that still remained deep inside me, and I determined to do the same thing. The second I arrived on set, it all seemed to click into place. I was fascinated by everything around me—the lights and the cameras and the clipboards, the hubbub, the sense of industry, and the artistic endeavor. Immediately I felt comfortable on the set, as though finally I had found the arena in which I wanted to spend the rest of my life. Rachel and I moved to London, and I enrolled at LAMDA—the London Academy of Music and Dramatic Arts— where I studied hard to learn my new craft. Once I received a LAMDA diploma in acting, I threw myself into building an acting career with the same determination that I had approached everything else in my life. Small parts led to bigger parts, and soon I was working enough to make a living from acting.

On September 11, 2001, I watched the events in New York unfold with the same sense of horror and disbelief as everyone else. People asked me, as an Arab, how I felt about what had happened, but the truth was that my reaction was the same as almost everybody else's: shock and deep sorrow for the human suffering that had been caused. But it is perhaps also true that I watched the events that followed from a more rounded perspective. When the allied armies marched on Baghdad with the intention of toppling Saddam Hussein, I watched the footage on television with mixed feelings. I remembered the last time the West invaded Iraq. I had been a child,

living in Mosul with my father. The airwaves were full of anti-American propaganda: the American army was a murderous, invading army, we were told, and it was the duty of all loyal Iraqis to join up and fight against the Americans.

I had phoned Saad in Baghdad when my father was out. "Is it true what they say about the American army?" I asked.

"No," he replied. "They are not like the Iranians. These people have a little bit more respect for Arab life." During the Iran-Iraq war, if the Iranian air force was unable to approach their military targets, the pilots simply dropped their bombs randomly on small Iraqi villages. If they returned with their munitions, they probably would have been shot by their superiors. The Americans, Saad assured me, had better technology and more sophisticated weapons. They would never be so randomly brutal. But it was unsettling, to say the least, being led into a war with the strongest country in the world.

When the U.S. bombs started falling in 1991, I was in the car with my father, driving through the narrow streets of Mosul to buy provisions from the market. Suddenly, from above, we heard the incessant drone of Stealth bombers. Nearby was a warehouse that stored flour, grain, and other provisions, and this was the pilots' target. When the bombs hit, the impact was so great that it lifted our car into the air. As soon as we hit the ground again, we found ourselves hurtling toward a brick wall; my father spun the steering wheel as fast as he could and avoided a collision by a whisker. Had his reflexes not been so fast, we might have been rather less lucky that day. We jumped out of the car and took cover as best we could as bombs continued to rain down on the store.

And so it went on.

When the second Gulf War started, therefore, I had some idea of what people were going through in Baghdad. My uncle Saad and

his family were still there; friends I had known from childhood were still there. I thanked God that my immediate family had made it to safety, but I nevertheless prayed nightly that Saad's original faith in the accuracy of the Americans' weapons would prove to be justified. The horror with which I watched the increasing civilian death count was excruciating: almost daily I expected to hear the news that Saad and his family were some of the most recent casualties of this war on their country that was not of their making. In the end, they endured the siege of Baghdad unharmed. Tens of thousands of others were less fortunate.

When I saw on television the statue of Saddam being pulled down and smashed, it was a strange moment—almost as if my own past were being shattered before my eyes. Was I glad he was gone? Of course. Nobody who suffered from the brutality of his regime could feel otherwise. Thanks to that man, the country I loved had been raped, and the people I loved had been tortured. When I heard that Uday was dead, crushed by the building in which he was hiding, I remembered that time in 14th Ramadan Street when he filled my friend Hakim and me with such fear, and we hadn't been exposed to even the lightest of his brutalities. It was a monstrous death but strangely and morbidly fitting for this monstrous person.

But stories are rarely black and white, and what so many people failed to understand was that it was possible to celebrate Saddam's removal from power and at the same time be suspicious of Western involvement in Iraq. I had read the history books. I knew that you didn't have to go back so very far to find a time when Saddam and the Ba'ath party were being supported by American money and American arms. What we were seeing was just the inexorable march of politics, the arrival of George Bush Sr.'s "new world order," and, as they had been throughout recent years, the Iraqi people were merely pawns in a bigger game.

Now Saddam is dead, and I am glad he has gone to meet his

maker. When I saw him being hanged, I felt a mixture of emotions: intrigue, excitement, irony, the curious feeling that I was reading the last page of an evil book. Saddam sold his soul to the Devil to get into power; when he tried to claim it back, the Devil got the better of him. But watching those scenes, I never once felt happy, or hopeful, for Iraq. How could I? My country seems to be the prostitute of the world, and every other government or group or society is standing in line to rape it.

In 2006 I appeared in a major movie about the 9/11 attacks. *United 93,* directed by Paul Greengrass, told the story of the hijacked airplane, heading in all likelihood for Washington, that was thought to have been crashed in Pennsylvania by the terrorists in order to prevent the passengers and crew from gaining control of it. My role as one of the terrorists was an emotional one, but one to which I hoped I could bring some degree of empathy and realism. It was an important film, and I felt proud to be a part of it. When the film premiered in New York, however, an event occurred that in a way encapsulated so much about my life. Although the U.S. government had allowed me into the country to act in the movie, I was refused a visa to attend the premiere. At first no reason was given; it later transpired that I was not deemed suitable to be in the the United States because of my conviction in England.

When I learned this, I laughed—you often laugh when you want to cover up more complicated emotions. The U.S. government had allowed me into the country before; now they were refusing. Did the government or other entities have their own agenda, their own reasons for not wanting me there? I don't know. All I do know is that the 2003 invasion of Baghdad had been initiated to bring about the liberation of the Iraqi people. I had done what I had done as a direct result of oppression by the very regime they had gone to war to change. Yet now, somehow, I was the enemy.

The irony is not lost on me. The United States and the UK

broke international law and came uninvited into my country, yet now they choose to apply the full force of their own laws on me when it comes to the question of my British citizenship and a U.S. visitor's visa. President George W. Bush and Prime Minister Tony Blair broke the law and got what they wanted; I broke the law and also got what I wanted—my family out of Iraq. But I stood trial, was humiliated, prosecuted, sentenced, and punished fourfold: I was given a suspended jail sentence, I was denied the opportunity to practice law, I was refused British citizenship, and I was refused a U.S. visa. I don't see Bush and Blair experiencing the same troubles.

But when you start from the premise that the world is not a fair place, you don't get too affected by such injustices. I appealed the U.S. government's decision—I even became something of a cause célèbre. But it was not to be. Back in England I am denied naturalization as a citizen because of my conviction. I can't help feeling that if the British and American political authorities were totally committed to helping the Iraqi people, they would exercise a little more benevolent judgment in my case. I'm not proud of what I did, but I do think it is worthy of a little understanding.

However, in the grand scale of things, such complaints seem trivial. Iraq remains a war zone. I have no doubt that it will be so for many years. As I write this, my uncle Saad lives in fear for his life. He is under daily threat of mortar attacks; his car has been burned; his business has been destroyed. Now he lives at my grandparents' house in Al-Mansour, AK-47s at the ready in case he and his family are attacked. Other Sunni men have been abducted and beheaded by Shia bandits. Saad knows that if he is not careful, he could easily become one of their number.

Elsewhere in Iraq, daily civilian casualties can be measured in the hundreds. But whenever I hear the news of another bombing in a mosque or an unspeakable act of sectarian violence, one fact is brought home to me: despite everything—the violence, the fear,

and the heartbreak—that I have been through, I now have the privilege of living in a country where my safety, and that of my family, are ensured. My immediate family is with me now, and the feeling that that gives me is indescribable. My mother is a new woman now, and to be able to see my brother and sister again is so wonderful that I still can't quite believe they are here.*

There is an old Arabic saying: "Every day of your life is a page of your history." I am able to look to the future with confidence. I am able to write those pages myself rather than have them written for me by uncaring regimes and circumstances that are unasked for but nevertheless have to be endured.

I am one of the lucky ones.

---

*The strain of everything we'd been through led to Rachel and me separating, although she is still a close and valued friend and I will never forget what she did for me and my family. As for my father, I wish I could say that we have reconciled; but at the time of writing this, that has not happened, and I have not spoken to him for several years.

A C K N O W L E D G M E N T S

There are so many people to thank. Barbara Levy, my fabulous literary agent, whose enthusiasm for my story has been unwavering from day one; Doug Young, Deborah Adams, Zoe Hood, Rebecca Jones, Emma Musgrave, Madeline Toy, and all the brilliant team at Transworld, for doing what they do so well; everyone at Crown, especially Julian Pavia and Annsley Rosner, for their hard work on the U.S. edition; and Adam Parfitt, without whose help this book would not have been written. Thanks also to Joanne Adamson, Graham Allen, Tim Bevan, David Bond, Pippa Cross, Nigel Edwards, Eric Fellner, Laurie Fransman, Lex Genn, Nik Goldman, Ana Gonzalez, Paul Greengrass, Kirk Hassig, John Hadity, Theresa Hickey, Tracey Holmes, Dan Hubbard, Nibil Issa, Jan Tun, Christian Johnson, Tim Kent, Richard Lever, Lloyd Levin, Paul Lucas, Terry Newman, Peter Nicholson, Yacine Serir, Raj Sharma, Sean Smith, and Theresa Villers.

To Rachel, for being there. Also to her father.

To all the unknown beacons of light who helped me along my treacherous way.

And finally, to Saad—who was a father to me when I had no father. Thank you for everything.

LEWIS ALSAMARI was born in Iraq and spent a few years of his childhood in the United Kingdom. He is now an actor best known for his role in Paul Greengrass's acclaimed film *United 93,* in which he plays an Al Qaeda hijacker. He now lives in London.

ABOUT THE TYPE

This book was set in Adobe Garamond, a typeface designed by Robert Slimbach in 1989. It is based on Claude Garamond's sixteenth-century type samples found at the Plantin-Moretus Museum in Antwerp, Belgium.